Black Orpheus and the Globalization of Afro-Brazilian Culture

Global Media and Race

Series Editor: Frederick Luis Aldama, The Ohio State University

Global Media and Race is a series focused on scholarly books that examine race and global media culture. Titles focus on constructions of race in media, including digital platforms, webisodes, multilingual media, mobile media, vlogs, and other social media, film, radio, and television. The series considers how race—and intersectional identities generally—is constructed in front of the camera and behind, attending to issues of representation and consumption as well as the making of racialized and antiracist media phenomena from script to production and policy.

Darién J. Davis, *"Black Orpheus" and the Globalization of Afro-Brazilian Culture*
Patricia Saldarriaga and Emy Manini, *Monsters vs. Patriarchy: Toxic Imagination in Global Horror Cinema*
Jossianna Arroyo, *Caribes 2.0: New Media, Globalization, and the Afterlives of Disaster*
Dan Hassler-Forest, *Janelle Monáe's Queer Afrofuturism: Defying Every Label*
Patricia Saldarriaga and Emy Manini, *Infected Empires: Decolonizing Zombies*
Bronwyn Carlson and Jeff Berglund, eds., *Indigenous Peoples Rise Up: The Global Ascendency of Social Media Activism*
Matthew David Goodwin, *The Latinx Files: Race, Migration, and Space Aliens*
Hyesu Park, ed., *Media Culture in Transnational Asia: Convergences and Divergences*
Melissa Castillo Planas, *A Mexican State of Mind: New York City and the New Borderlands of Culture*
Monica Hanna and Rebecca A. Sheehan, eds., *Border Cinema: Reimagining Identity through Aesthetics*

Black Orpheus and the Globalization of Afro-Brazilian Culture

DARIÉN J. DAVIS

Rutgers University Press

New Brunswick, Camden, Newark, New Jersey

London

Rutgers University Press is a department of Rutgers, The State University of New Jersey, one of the leading public research universities in the nation. By publishing worldwide, it furthers the University's mission of dedication to excellence in teaching, scholarship, research, and clinical care.

Library of Congress Cataloging-in-Publication Data
Names: Davis, Darién J., 1964– author
Title: Black Orpheus and the globalization of Afro-Brazilian culture / Darién J. Davis.
Description: New Brunswick : Rutgers University Press, 2025. | Series: Global media and race | Includes bibliographical references and index.
Identifiers: LCCN 2025012672 | ISBN 9781978844148 paperback | ISBN 9781978844155 hardcover | ISBN 9781978844162 eBooks
Subjects: LCSH: Orfeu negro (Motion picture) | Black people in motion pictures | Black people—Brazil | Brazil—In motion pictures |
BISAC: PERFORMING ARTS / Film / History & Criticism | SOCIAL SCIENCE / Black Studies (Global) | LCGFT: Film criticism
Classification: LCC PN1997.O6416 D38 2025
LC record available at https://lccn.loc.gov/2025012672

A British Cataloging-in-Publication record for this book is available from the British Library.

♾ The paper used in this publication meets the requirements of the American National Standard for Information Sciences—Permanence of Paper for Printed Library Materials, ANSI Z39.48-1992.

rutgersuniversitypress.org

For John

Contents

Preface

This work focuses on the global reach of Afro-Brazilians and Afro-Brazilian culture in the mainstream media in the United States and France in the 1960s and 1970s, what many scholars call the long 1960s.[1] It begins with the historical analysis of the 1958 film *Black Orpheus* and traces the ways that Afro-Brazilian cinematic images and music circulated transnationally through the mid-1970s. *Black Orpheus* was an audiovisual experience at a particular historical moment in the middle of the twentieth century. *Black Orpheus*'s visual aesthetics and the soundtrack allowed audiences in multiple countries to experience Brazil vicariously in the rapidly expanding technology of Technicolor. Archival and periodical research and interviews in three languages over a span of eight years have allowed me to reconstruct the making of the film, analyze its impact, and uncover the audiovisual legacies in the United States and France. Of the fifty-eight most important Brazilian watersheds that Joaquim Ferreira dos Santos lists in his work on the year 1958, the release of *Black Orpheus* was the singular cultural signpost that celebrated Black Brazil.[2] I draw on film, music, migration, cultural, and Black studies to provide readers with an understanding of the transnational circulation of cinema and musical productions as artifacts in a post–World War II era beginning in the late 1950s until the mid-1970s. Terms such as 'Black' or 'Afro-Brazil,' like other racial constructions, denote an imagined community, to paraphrase Benedict Anderson, that merits further elaboration.

In "What Is This 'Black' in Black Popular Culture?," Stuart Hall convincingly argues that Black culture is contextual, not a static entity fixed in time or place. Moreover, it is a "contradictory space" and a "site of strategic contestation," distinct from other forms of representation. Hall also warns us against looking for a linear story based on European logos and to look for the truth in "its expressivity, its musicality, its orality, in its rich, deep, and varied attention to speech, in its inflections toward the vernacular and the local, in its rich production of counternarratives, and above all, in its metaphorical use of the musical vocabulary."[3] If we use the traditional European lens, we may miss the fact that style and joy in Black cultural repertoires may not represent or mean something else but rather that they *are* the objectives, the goals themselves. Moreover, music and dance, as we will see, represent more than entertainment but a connection with life and ancestors and a celebration of freedom and survival, which others may see only as Dionysian. Finally, unlike many cultures, Afro-Brazilian culture utilizes and empowers the body, which was often, as Stuart Hall puts it, "the only cultural capital we had" since "we have worked on ourselves as the canvases of representation."[4]

It is easy to understand how *Black Orpheus* constituted a critical signpost in Atlantic world racial representation and celebration of Afro-Brazilian culture in the post–World War II era. It is a mainstream film with a cast understood as majority Black, much like Otto Preminger's Hollywood films *Carmen Jones* (1954) and *Porgy and Bess* (1959) in the United States. While the segregated United States produced race films for African American audiences, Afro-Brazilian and Afro-French communities had no such access to technologies to even contemplate the idea of a Black film market or audience in those countries for much of the twentieth century. In all three countries with predominantly White audiences and filmmakers, different images of Blackness came to represent African descendants of diverse cultural and ethnic backgrounds and skin complexions. In Brazil, terms such as *Negro*, *Crioulo*, *Mulato/a*, *Cabrocha*, and *Mestiço* reflect the diversity among Afro-Brazilians. Most importantly, African and Afro-Brazilian culture has influenced Brazilians of all backgrounds. By the mid-twentieth century, cultural forms such as samba, created by Black Brazilians, became widely accepted as part of Brazil's national culture and consciousness. At the same time, barriers continued to marginalize and limit the participation of Black and Brown Brazilians.

Frantz Fanon called postcolonial bourgeois-driven national consciousness a crude empty shell incapable of "coordinating the crystallization of the people's aspirations."[5] In postcolonial Brazil, the elite attempted to emulate Europe and erase images of Blackness from the major visual symbols of power after independence. As in many other nations in the Americas and Europe, national representation privileged Whiteness, wealth, property ownership, and access to written knowledge. After colonization of the Americas, most Africans and their descendants entered American society as chattel without access to those established privileges. As Brazil pursued modernity, elites also faced a contradiction: they relied on the Black underclass who eventually transformed (creolized) their dominant European traditions. As thinkers from Gilberto Freyre to Gilberto Gil have noted, Brazil created a hybrid Brazilian cultural base that profoundly impacted Brazilians of all racial and cultural backgrounds, particularly in popular culture. In his 1995 book *O Mistério Do Samba*, Hermano Vianna also adds another perspective as he explains how Brazilian musical forms flowed across the Atlantic at the beginning of the twentieth century and how samba developed from a Black cultural expression to a national treasure.[6]

In his work on the Black Atlantic, Paul Gilroy underscores the ambivalence of this pursuit of modernity. Gilroy equates modernity with hybridity and stresses that music became vital to Africans and their descendants as a form of autonomy. This music, later called 'popular' because of its origins, signified Black music, to paraphrase Stuart Hall, despite its hybridity and borrowing from European culture. Within this Afro-Creole history that Hall describes, discussions of authenticity become highly charged and cultural protectionism problematic. Echoing Édouard Glissant, Hall agrees that music and dance became a vital form of communication that allowed the formerly enslaved to emerge from the plantation. Glissant argues that:

> It is nothing new to declare that for us music, gesture, dance are forms of communication, just as important as the gift of speech. This is how we first managed to emerge from the plantation: aesthetic form in our cultures must be shaped from these oral structures. It is not a matter of claiming that writing is of no use to us, and we are aware of the dramatic need for literacy and the circulation of books in our countries. For us, it is a matter of ultimately reconciling the values of the culture of writing and the long-repressed traditions of orality.[7]

To fully understand the global dissemination of popular Black music in general and depictions and recordings of popular Afro-Brazilian music in film and records, one must attend to the impact and the story of Black Brazil in *Black Orpheus* on two levels. First, there is the visible Black Brazil represented by Black bodies and other visible signifiers, including how those bodies move in space and their relationship to music. Second, following the suggestions of Michael Boyce Gillespie, we must study how film or music imparts Afro-Brazilian culture, and determine the value it give to Black subjects. Here, Stuart Hall reminds us that movies can capture embodied subjectivity. Moreover, embodied Black subjectivity can appear in the remotest of places. Films can capture it in a scene for one minute or in a feature-length film. Black performers and actors can also subvert dominant narratives and present value and truths independent of scripts and framings.

In the wake of *Black Orpheus*'s success, Brazilian performers, artists, and musicians began to gain unprecedented access to French and American cultural forums outside of Brazil. Their appearances in various American and European cities helped forge a new postwar idea of Brazil that included Afro-Brazilians, replacing the one-dimensional Hollywood image that audiences associated with performers such as Carmen Miranda. In the 1960s and 1970s, diverse artists such as Vinicius de Moraes, Baden Powell, Haroldo Costa, Carlos Diegues, Carmen Costa, Bola Sete, and others began to promote modern images of Afro-Brazilian culture often in collaboration with French and American producers and interlocutors such as Dizzy Gillespie and Pierre Barouh. In 1968, the military dictatorship forced many artists into exile. While abroad, musicians of African descent continued producing and performing Brazilian-ness in the 1970s, albeit for drastically different audiences. They also celebrated Blackness and the African diaspora in complex ways beyond the images from *Black Orpheus*.[8]

In this era, postwar national powers in the United States and Europe owned the cinematic and musical recording technologies responsible for the transnational circulation of cultural products. *Black Orpheus* became a major transnational cultural product because France, a country with a developed cinematic culture and technologies, also had a global reach. Paraphrasing Arjun Appadurai, the film represented an important signpost in a Brazilian cultural flow or Brazilian 'scape.' Commissioned by producer Sacha Gordine to convert the Vinicius de Moraes's Brazilian play *Orfeu da Conceição* into a film, French director Marcel Camus seized the opportunity. His pacificism and his sense of adventure shaped how he presented Afro-Brazilians and Rio de Janeiro's carnival. His script notes and interviews for the promotion of the film also reveal his fascination with cultural practices with which he was not familiar. At the same time, like many visitors to Brazil before and after him, Camus's experience deepened his relationship with Brazilians. He eventually married the Afro-Brazilian actress Lourdes de Oliveira and helped raise two Franco-Brazilian children. His intention was to promote Afro-Brazilian culture using the opportunities and limitations of the late 1950s.

The Camus family's transnational life constitutes a vital part of the circulation and globalization of Brazilian culture in general and Afro-Brazilian people and cultural products in particular. The transnational production and dissemination of *Black Orpheus* allowed audiences across France and the United States to become acquainted with Afro-Brazilian actors and musicians. They also consumed a 1950s cinematic version of urban Brazil and Afro-Brazilian culture associated with samba, carnival, and the religion Umbanda from Rio de Janeiro.

The movie also opened new transnational opportunities for those performers associated with the film or the musical genres that the film celebrated. In the 1960s, other performers continued taking popular Brazilian culture global in new ways and venues. This work regards those migrating Black performers as a part of the global Brazilian Orphic tradition.

Camus consciously avoided commenting or portraying racism or negative versions of poverty. Black Brazilian joy impressed Camus, and he worked to reproduce that joy, which he considered a gift to humanity, in his films. This joyous but one-dimensional view of Brazil that emphasized the celebration of Afro-Brazilian culture and the perceived harmonious social dynamics was not new. That image began to gain wide circulation at the beginning of the twentieth century and continued in the 1940s and 1950s with the help of European writers such as Stefan Zweig, who published *Brazil: A Land of the Future* (1942), and Blaise Cendrars's *Brésil* (1952). In the shadow of the devastating destruction and ethnic intolerance of World War II and the emerging ethnic tensions in France and the United States, an idealized image of a tropical nation with happy Black people provided an alternative reality. White or near-White Brazilian cultural producers such as Gilberto Freyre also propagated similar views for patriotic reasons.[9]

In my essay "From Oppressive to Benign: A Comparative History of the Construction of Whiteness in Brazil in the Post-Abolition Era," I lay out how post-abolition intellectuals changed the image of Brazil from an oppressive slave society to one that celebrates its Black heritage and the cultural and racial mixing simultaneously. Although many scholars (including this author) have criticized lusotropicalism, Freyre's ideas emerged because of his transnational experiences. In the first few decades of the twentieth century, many Latin American intellectuals imagined communities that were culturally superior to the racially oppressive images of the United States, the global hegemon. *Black Orpheus* portrayed a unique image of Black Latin and Catholic America, distinct from the film images of primarily Black Protestant North America.

Historically, music has played an essential role in the African diaspora. Scholars across the Western hemisphere, including U.S.-based intellectuals such as Amiri Baraka and Eileen Southern, have written about music's intimate relationship to Black survival.[10] Diverse Caribbean diasporic scholars, from Fernando Ortiz to Paul Gilroy, have also produced monumental scholarship on the topic.[11] Brazilian scholars, from Mario de Andrade and José Ramos Tinhorão to Hermano Vianna, have also provided diverse perspectives on Brazil.[12]

Thus, it is clear why music constitutes an essential component of the transnational Brazilscape. Here, we highlight again the fact that *Black Orpheus* is an audiovisual cultural product, and producers capitalized on the popularity of the music by quickly converting the audio into records to be sold globally. Black Brazil circulated in three ways: through film images, through musical scores and records, and through the travel and migration of performers who followed opportunities to perform Brazilian music outside of Brazil.

Black Orpheus placed Blackness at the center of its cinematic construction. This work seeks to shed light on that production process. It also sheds light on films and musical productions referencing Black Brazil after *Black Orpheus*. The cross-border movements and migration of Afro-Brazilian musicians and performers have continued to enrich the Brazilian ethnoscape globally today. However, this work focuses on the significant performers and cultural products in France and the United States in the 1960s and 1970s. They provide us with a window into the global impact of Afro-Brazilian culture in that era and beyond.

Framing Black Brazil and Exoticism Transnationally

Writing about Brazilian culture in English is a transnational act requiring translation from Portuguese and French into English. According to André Lefevere, translation is refraction, "the adaptation of a work of literature to a different audience, to influence how that audience reads the work."[13] Applying this definition to film, archival sources, and interviews, scholars process and understand artifacts and ideas from different cultures through a culturally determined lens. Lefevere's idea of refractions reminds us that this process often occurs through "misunderstandings and misconceptions." He argues that writers and their work are always understood and conceived against a specific culture. Thus, translating refracts knowledge through a given spectrum. In other words, the translator processes the understanding through a unique cultural prism.[14] Cross-cultural producers, creators, and writers may be listening and gaining knowledge through research but may not be able to precisely transfer the complexities of an original meaning within its historical and cultural text. This may be particularly true when discussing issues of identity related to race, ethnicity, gender, sexuality, and nationality.

This work often uses English terms such as 'Afro-Brazilian' and 'Black' interchangeably. Readers in Anglophone North America will understand that choice. However, that linguistic equivalency may be problematic in the Francophone and Lusophone worlds where 'Afro-Brazilian' and 'Black' may carry nuances in different cultural and historical contexts. Moreover, the English term may overlook the complexity and nuance inherent to Brazil's particular historical journey and the country's widespread recognition of various forms of Afro-Brazilian hybridities (Pardo, Cabrocha, Mulato/a, and Sarará, for example). In *Cabeça do Brasileiro*, Alberto Carlos Almeida convincingly demonstrates the subjective construction of race in Brazil and its connection to status. In one survey, researchers showed respondents eight photographs of men ranging from very light complexion with blue eyes and straight hair to dark complexion, Black eyes, and frizzy hair. Researchers then asked the respondents to identify whether they were Black (Negro), White (Branco), or Brown (Pardo). Ninety-six percent of the respondents agreed that the light complexion with blue eyes and straight hair was White, and that the two figures with dark complexion, Black eyes, and frizzy hair were Black. The six figures between those two poles received various responses from White, Brown, and Black.[15] These results demonstrate that as an identity marker, Blackness may be relative nationally and transnationally.

At its basic level, *Black Orpheus* is about a visually Black or Afro-Brazilian community, including people of many complexions, who may go by different names in Portuguese. However, who is Black or Afro-Brazilian in Brazil depends on context and who is doing the identifying as well as self-identification. Here, it is essential to distinguish racial identification from cultural identification. In Brazilian Portuguese, for most people, *Afro-Brasileiro* refers to the cultural heritage rather than the person. In most contexts, Afro-Brazilian popular culture is so ubiquitous that it is simply Brazilian shared by Brazilians of all ethnicities.

I focus on individual Afro-Brazilians who identify as Black, 'Mulato,' or 'Pardo' and whom others describe that way. In my 2000 work on Afro-Brazilians, I show that despite the differences with the United States, Afro-Brazilians (whether Preto or Pardo, the two descriptions used in the Brazilian census) are excluded from economic and social positions in mainstream society.[16] Yet, anti-Black racism continues to affect darker-complected Brazilians most acutely. At the same time, because of the ubiquity of Black cultural influences, many non-Black Brazilians have been instrumental in transporting Afro-Brazilian culture abroad. This may include White Brazilians who grew up living around and absorbing Afro-Brazilian culture or White-presenting Brazilians with Black ancestry such as Sérgio Mendes. This complexity allows us to interrogate who and how Black culture circulates, often hidden in plain sight.

Unpacking this complexity also requires an understanding of the role of exoticism in cross-cultural discourse and when studying Black subjects and culture. Although exoticism has acquired a negative connotation, its role in transnational translation has been powerful. In her article "Performing Exoticism and the Transnational Reception of World Cinema," Daniela Berghahn notes that the term "exotic" was connected to voyages of discovery and Western encounters with "radical cultural difference" in remote corners of the world that elicited "astonishment and wide-eyed wonder."[17] It denotes a perception of foreign cultures and places.

However, exoticism also represents a cultural translation, an attempt to make sense of foreign people. European filmmakers like Camus and his production team are also powerful interlocutors and translators with enormous power to frame the perception of Afro-Brazilians and Afro-Brazilian cultures.

The power relation between the framers and the framed is inherently unequal, but within that inequality, Afro-Brazilians are not entirely without agency. Moreover, the acting, music, and scenes in groups have the capacity to transmit a sense of community beyond the original script. Ironically, Camus's "astonishment and wide-eyed wonder" helped him frame the exotic, the cultural difference in many scenes. However, when the film depicts Afro-Brazilians in typical situations and relations (e.g., romance, jealousy, community), it is also de-exoticizing customs for audiences. The comparisons and references to Greek mythology represent one example. Familiar scenes and symbols often parallel the pioneering anthropologist Levi Strauss's attempts to normalize the "exotic," by showing that so-called savage cultures had equally sophisticated ways of organizing their communities in ways that paralleled Western societies.[18]

By quoting scholars on exoticism, Berghahn demonstrates that viewers often comprehend the exotic. Foreigners may see what they expect to see, for example. As Victor Segalen illustrates, "exoticism is willingly tropical. It conjures up images of coconut trees and torrid skies, not much Arctic exoticism."[19] However, exoticism can also be a tool for learning. It can initiate cross-cultural conversations that rely on translation, debate, and trial and error, especially in the context of transnational reception among different populations. Racialized viewing may be significantly different from those in the White mainstream. As we will see, many African diasporic subjects' responses to the film confirm this.

My Black Orpheus

I experienced the joy and merriment of carnival in the favela, in the streets of the Zona Sul, and in the practice hall of the Mangueira samba school. I also marched with the famous Cordão da Bola Preta in the city center and with the small carnival groups of Ipanema. These experiences gave me a deep understanding of Rio's carnival culture. I also learned a great deal from conversations with adherents of the Afro-Brazilian religions Umbanda and Candomblé. Brazilian pioneers such as Abdias do Nascimento, Léa Garcia, Ruth de Souza, Carlinhos Pandeiro de Ouro, Dom Salvador, and many others provided me with a wealth of information on the Black experience in Brazil in the 1960s.

I left Brazil reluctantly to move to the United States to teach in 1992 during the government of Fernando Collar de Mello. Outside of Brazil, I became interested in connecting to the Brazilian diaspora everywhere I went and in understanding how Brazilian culture circulated outside of Brazil. I later joined a group of scholars interested in charting the Brazilian experience in the United States. Two of my early works ("The Brazilian-Americans: Demography and Identity of An Emerging Latino Minority" and "Before We Called This Place Home: The Precursors of the Brazilian Community in the United States") explore Brazilian cultural experiences abroad. My coedited volume, *Companion to US Latino Literatures*, was the first such volume to include Brazilians in the United States as a part of the Latino community.[20]

In my book *White Face, Black Mask: Africaneity and the Early Social History of Popular Music in Brazil*, I examined important figures who first began to take versions of Afro-Brazilian cultural practices globally in the 1930s and 1940s. I problematize issues of appropriation and authenticity by revealing how White performers from Brazil, including Carmen Miranda, Aurora Miranda, and the Bando da Lua, celebrated Black cultural practices abroad. I ask how performers gained the right to perform cultural practices that may or may not come from their ethnic groups. Miranda and others were celebrating Brazilianness when few opportunities existed for Afro-Brazilians abroad. Following this work, I co-published a series of works on Stefan Zweig with Oliver Marshall and became interested in the outsider's views on Brazil. This research led me to the post–World War II era when new opportunities for diverse Brazilians emerged in the United States and France. The 1950s also expanded opportunities for Afro-Brazilians. In both countries, White and Black interlocutors and collaborators allowed for transnational exchange and collaborations with Afro-Brazilians.

Black Orpheus was a significant signpost of this era. The visibility of Afro-Brazilian actors and actresses in the film and the presence of Brazilian music inspired by Afro-Brazilians helped educate a transnational, transregional generation. Over time, many of these images have become more out of step with the zeitgeists of following generations. Nevertheless, *Black Orpheus* was an undeniable cultural landmark. Several critics believe the film was promoting a one-dimensional vision of Brazil as a carnival country. Critics have also objected to a French director making a Brazilian movie. Others point out that the film seems inauthentic. Still, for many French and American viewers in the post–World War II era, the 1958 Franco-Brazilian film was their first introduction to Brazil and Brazilian culture. Questions of who can produce whose culture remain of central importance to global media studies. For the historian, they must be answered in their proper historical context with attention to the debates, possibilities, and power relations.[21]

In his book *Film Blackness: American Cinema and the Idea of Black Film*, Michael Boyce Gillespie distinguishes Black film from film Blackness. His investigation of film Blackness necessarily requires a "reading practice" that seeks to understand the multi-discursive properties that Blackness signifies in aesthetic, cultural, and political terms. It requires scholars to move beyond speculations of universal Blackness. Indeed, Gillespie calls for a "redrawing of the lines of influence, appreciation, allusion, causality, reference, and exposition." Moreover, Black film cannot "satisfy identitarian fantasies of Black ontology." It must pose questions and understand specificities in context. It is no coincidence, for example, that Gillespie dedicates his first chapter to the 1975 film *Coonskin* by White filmmaker Ralph Bakshi. *Black Orpheus and the Globilization of Afro-Brazilian Culture* attempts to engage and follow a specific reading practice of the *Black Orpheus* audiovisual text and its musical descendants grounded in the zeitgeist of the long 1960s. While I rely on many brilliant film critics, this work is a historical transnational production.[22]

Transnational historical research in multiple languages required a certain amount of patience on my part, including additional studies in French and mastering multiple historiographies and archival procedures. In my quest to uncover the history of *Black Orpheus* and its impact on a generation, I highlight Afro-Brazilian cultural images, including musical forms, religion, secular celebrations, and representations, which were central to the trope of the peaceful tropical country. I bring together studies from history, anthropology, migration studies, and African diasporic studies. At the time of writing, there were no major published studies in English on the transnational history, creation, and legacy of *Black Orpheus* or its influence on the export of Brazilian culture during the Cold War or the 1960s. Indeed, studying the transnational flow of Brazilian culture abroad is a relatively new field. Maxine Margolis wrote the groundbreaking study *The Invisible Minority: Brazilians in New York*. Bernadete Beserra's 2005 book *Brasileiros nos Estados Unidos: Hollywood e outros sonhos* focuses on Brazilian cultural production abroad. Margolis's and Bessera's work provided critical insights into contemporary Brazilian communities outside Brazil and tools to examine the Brazilian migrant community during the Cold War. Anaïs Fléchet has also published multiple works in French on Brazilian culture in France. Fléchet's work on popular Brazilian music in France and her contribution to the commemorative book on *Black Orpheus*, published in 2009, features many historical insights important to my vision. In their 2012 publication *Race in Translation: Culture Wars Around the Postcolonial Atlantic*, Robert Stam and Ella Shohat offer a critical analysis of the relationships among Brazil, France, and the United States. K. E. Goldschmitt's *Bossa Mundo: Brazilian Music in Transnational Media Industries* (2019) provides a lens onto the circulation of Brazilian popular music.[23]

Many literary and film scholars (Robert Stam, Lúcia Nagib, Myrian Sepúlveda dos Santos, Tunico Amâncio, and others) have written about *Black Orpheus* as narrative text. However, few historians have attended to the contextual factors of the 1950s and 1960s that shaped the film's original production, reception, and circulation. Lisa Shaw's 2018 work, *Tropical Travels: Brazilian Popular Performance, Transnational Encounters, and the Construction of Race*, has provided critical insights into the transnational encounters that interest me. Early dialogue with Micol Seigel was helpful, as was her 2009 work *Uneven Encounters: Making Race and Nation in Brazil and the United States.*[24]

My work also engages with broader global studies on Blackness in the media. I also rely on the work of scholars of the Black Atlantic and diaspora studies. Stuart Hall, Paul Gilroy, Abdias do Nascimento, and Livio Sansone have insisted on the centrality of music to the African diaspora experience. Black feminist scholars such as bell hooks and Gwendolyn Audre Foster have also provided critical ideas about gender and global media. I am a better film scholar because of the insights of Manthia Diawara and his work on Black spectatorship. I cite many other scholars who have helped me along the way. These rich sources have helped inform my narrative. I am mindful of Patricia de Santana

Pinho's caution against utilizing the African American racial story as the dominant Black narrative in a world of multiple diasporas. Even as this work seeks to show how the global media curated images of Afro-Brazilians in the 1950s and 1960s, understanding how Afro-Brazilians circulate, collaborate, and engage global media, given their unique opportunities and limitations, will be necessary.[25]

The 1958 film also gave many African descendants their first opportunity to perform on the silver screen, shattering social and racial restrictions. The global success of the film's soundtrack spurred a global interest in the new modern Brazilian sounds that would soon be superseded by a musical form called the bossa nova. Few Black Brazilians could travel to the United States to promote Brazilian popular culture before desegregation. Thus, Carmen Miranda, Aurora Miranda, and other White performers became de facto ambassadors of Brazilian popular culture in the United States. Entertainment opportunities and the easing of racial restrictions allowed Afro-Brazilians like Bola Sete, Baden Powell, and Carmen Costa to travel, migrate, and perform in cities from New York to Paris in the 1960s. In 1968, the military dictatorship forced thousands of Brazilians into exile. Many of them were artists and performers who expanded notions of Brazil and Afro-Brazilian culture in the foreign media. Caetano Veloso and Gilberto Gil were two such exiles. The widespread success of *Black Orpheus* had preceded them, and they would have to contend with the film's legacy and media perceptions of Brazil even as they developed their own images and styles.

Organization and Intent

In the first part of this book, I am primarily interested in analyzing the making of the film. I utilize textual analysis and John O'Connor's historical lens to study the transnational circulation of Afro-Brazilian culture in the 1950s and 1960s. O'Connor saw film primarily as a historical artifact that could be historically understood by attending to three significant issues: story, production, and reception. Given Afro-Brazilians' limited economic and cultural power on the world stage, it will be important to understand how individuals leveraged their agency and their allyship to express themselves and promote their culture even if limited or restrained by cultural norms or practices. Afro-Brazilian women will also have to contend with a dominant male environment.[26]

In his book *Orpheus and Power: The Movimento Negro of Rio de Janeiro and São Paulo Brazil, 1945 to 1988*, Michael G. Hanchard utilizes the figure of *Black Orpheus* as a representative of Black cultural production and Afrocentric celebration. He argues that the myth is a parable for Brazilian politics and the strategies of the Black movement. It captures the problematics of culturalism with its emphasis on "genealogical excavation" in its attempt to capture the past. In this interpretation, Orpheus is self-absorbed, perhaps focusing too much on individualism and preoccupied with trying to go back to the past.[27] In this work, I focus on the parable and treat the metaphor as historical text that constitutes a part of the black archive.

In the second half of this book, I explore the legacies of *Black Orpheus* in the global media in the late 1960s and 1970s. In the first instance, I make direct links with the film and its impact on other cultural productions that were trying to duplicate the film's success or treat popular themes such as carnival and Afro-Brazilian religions. Others utilize Brazilian cultural landscapes, music, and Black bodies in other ways. I also expand the meaning of 'Black Orpheus' beyond the filmic artifact and return to the idea of the Afro-Brazilian performer/ambassador who leaves Brazil and performs and celebrates Brazilian music transnationally.

In chapters 6 and 7 I am primarily interested in exploring how transnational Afro-Brazilian performers advance and express their talents abroad while simultaneously engaging in what Kim Butler and Stéphane Dufoix describe as diasporic dialogues between the homeland and the host countries.[28] After *Black Orpheus*, Afro-Brazilian performers in the United States and France found opportunities to pursue their interests and meet demands for Brazilian performances. Others avoided the expected and desired reproductions in various ways. In this work, I highlight the role of individual Afro-Brazilians who made their transnational contributions through their involvement in the production of *Black Orpheus* and the migrant experience in the 1960s and 1970s. African Americans play an important role in the circulation of Black Brazil. Analysis and descriptions of the roles of individuals from Marpessa Dawn and Dizzy Gillespie in the 1960s to Dionne Warwick and Johnny Mathis in the 1960s and 1970s give us multiple windows into Afro-Brazilian/African American collaboration after the *Black Orpheus* project.

The Chapters

Chapter 1, "Imagining a Brazilian Black Orpheus," tells the story of the film's origin, creation, and production in the late 1950s. I detail the role of White intellectuals such as the Brazilian poet Vinicius de Moraes and French filmmaker Marcel Camus. I highlight their reasons for celebrating Black culture and their connection to Black artists. Chapter 2, "The Black Cast," analyzes the role of the Black actors in the film. Based on interviews and archival documents, I explore the trajectories of the principal actors who represented Black Brazil. I focus on the contributions of Breno Mello, Marpessa Dawn, Léa Garcia, and Lourdes de Oliveira. I conclude by examining the importance of other actors, including the children, who end the film and play important roles at select moments in the plot.

Chapters 3 and 4 turn the attention to the music and the musicians in the film and the transnational reception. Entitled "The Soundtrack," chapter 3 examines the Black voices and their roles on the soundtrack. I provide information on the role of Afro-Brazilians Agostinho dos Santos, the musical voice of Orpheus, and Elizeth Cardoso, who recorded songs on the soundtrack. I also analyze the contributions of White musician-composers such as Antonio Carlos Jobim and Luiz Bonfá. In chapter 4, I shift to the overall reception of the film. "Oblique Gazes: The Transnational Reception of *Black Orpheus*" assesses the film's reception in the late 1950s and the 1960s. It compares the different ways of viewing *Black Orpheus* in Brazil, France, and the United States.

Part II, "*Black Orpheus* Legacies and the Globalization of Afro-Brazilian Culture," includes three separate essays on the circulation of Afro-Brazilian images and music in the United States and France after *Black Orpheus*. In chapter 5, I discuss the film influences and images of Afro-Brazilians in the 1960s. I examine the image of Brazil and Brazilian Blackness in French, American, and Brazilian films after the success of *Black Orpheus*. I also analyze the types of films that American, French, and Brazilian filmmakers produced about Brazil and Black Brazilians and the use of popular Brazilian music in those films. Chapter 6, "Bossa Negra in the United States," examines the impact of *Black Orpheus* on jazz musicians in the United States. It highlights the collaborations between Afro-Brazilians such as Carmen Costa and Bola Sete and African Americans promoting bossa nova.

Chapter 7 examines the career trajectories of Baden Powell and Maria d'Apparecida Marques, two Afro-Brazilians in Paris, representing distinct types of Brazilian Orphic performers promoting Brazilian culture abroad. Both made inroads in Paris in the post–*Black Orpheus* era.

A Note on Conventions

In the process of writing, I have had to make several choices about translations and spelling. I capitalize all racial terms and italicize terms used in Portuguese but not in English (e.g., Black, White, *Mulato, Mestiço*) in all languages. I use single quotes to indicate a special use or to highlight a particular word or phrase. I also use italics to highlight foreign terms (e.g., *cuica, samba de roda*), although I do not italicize terms that are commonly used in English (e.g., zeitgeist, samba). I maintain the original orthography in direct quotes. Many words in Portuguese appear with different spellings in different texts. Proper names (such as Mario/Mário, Antonio/Antônio) may or may not appear with accents. I have maintained the original spellings used by the people in question. Where possible, I change French and Portuguese dates of publications to American standard conventions of month followed by date then year. Brazilians use first names to refer to people in their publications. I use the American convention of using last names except for in direct quotes. There are a few exceptions, especially with artists' stage names. Maria d'Apparecida Marques appears as d'Apparecida and Carlinhos Pandeiro de Oro becomes Carlinhos, for example.

It has taken almost a decade to gather the information, conduct interviews in four countries, write, edit, and complete this work. I have tried to include as many voices as possible in this transnational narrative, but in the end I was not able to include all the Afro-Brazilian actors and musicians from the long 1960s. There is much more to discover in the archives across the globe. I hope that the book inspires more research on the impact of Afro-Brazilians and Afro-Brazilian culture globally.

Black Orpheus and the Globalization of Afro-Brazilian Culture

Introduction

From Stage to Technicolor

Based on the Vinicius de Moraes play *Orfeu da Conceição,* the film by French director Marcel Camus relocated the Greek tragedy of Orpheus to a favela in Rio de Janeiro, then the Brazilian capital. Filmed in the favela, in local buildings, and on the streets in Rio de Janeiro, the movie presented global audiences with an all-Black cast and displayed African cultural influences within a Latin American Catholic tradition of carnival. Camus also employed emerging Brazilian musicians, performers, and composers to give audiences worldwide a window into Brazilian culture. Camus relied on the creative contributions of Brazilians, French, and one American lead actress to construct a version of Black Brazil based on late 1950s Rio de Janeiro. The Portuguese-language film in Technicolor earned the Palme d'Or at Cannes in 1959 and the Academy Award for Best Foreign Film in 1960.[1] *Black Orpheus* has engaged multiple transcultural audiences and debates. The film defies any attempt to establish a single story about its impact and importance.[2]

Many French and American moviegoers in the 1960s and 1970s have opined about the film's impact on their lives. In the United States, musician Dizzy Gillespie wrote about his connections with the Afro-diasporic music tradition through the film.[3] The scholar Henry Louis Gates Jr. explained that when he and his friends watched the film, they thought that "Brazil was the most remarkable of places; a democracy in brown. Brazil, judging from the film, was a mulatto."[4] It also made him want to visit the country since mulatto signified a type of racial tolerance, an embracing of African and European roots, unlike the North American racial model. French singer and actor Pierre Barouh was profoundly moved by the film, and Martinican filmmaker Euzhan Palcy explained how it inspired her to become a filmmaker.[5] Other viewers in Brazil, the United States, and Europe experienced the film with glee.

The film's detractors, including the French filmmaker Jean-Luc Godard, were also prominent.[6] Others have criticized Camus for the film's focus on Black dance and merriment. Brazilian filmmaker Carlos "Cacá" Diegues criticized Camus's film for its foreign gaze, exoticism, and lack of attention to poverty. He believed that the title *Black Orpheus* not only deviated from the poet Vinicius de Moraes's original intent but did not capture the Brazilian way of viewing race. Further removed from the era, President Barak Obama criticized the Dionysian version of Blackness in which Blacks appeared childlike and carefree, "the reverse image of Conrad's dark savages."[7] Other contemporary thinkers, such as Afro-Brazilian filmmakers Zózimo Bulbul and Joel Zito, spoke of the film's limitations yet recognized the historical importance of Black representation.[8]

Black Orpheus was, as a product of its time, a transnational signpost of the zeitgeist of the long 1960s, shaped by dynamics in Brazil, the United States, and France. In Brazil, the democratic election of President Juscelino Kubitschek in 1956 ushered in a new age of optimism that ended in 1968 with the Brazilian military's Institutional Act Number Five. The military dictatorship would endure for twenty-one years. American and French societies also faced social and political challenges. In 1954, the United States Supreme Court issued the landmark *Brown v. Board of Education* decision, which mandated racial integration. At the same time, France's colonial empire began to wane with the loss of Indochina in 1954, followed by Morocco and Tunisia in 1956.

When we return to the flow of Black Brazilian cultural products in the global media in the long 1960s, *Black Orpheus* emerges as one of the era's most important transnational cultural productions about Brazil. It was a critical signpost for two reasons. First, it was one of the first transnational film productions to focus on ordinary Afro-Brazilian everyday life without focusing on racial tensions or postcolonial angst, issues at the forefront of American and French consciousness. Camus's filming and editing styles allowed him to capture historical moments of Afro-Brazilian life and celebration relatively unrehearsed and unencumbered like many documentaries. Second, the production engaged the dialogue about Blackness, representation, and the symbol of Brazil in the post–World War II era. In that context, the film *Black Orpheus* represented a signpost of global Black Brazil.

Carnival and Macumba Mise-en-scène

Black Orpheus utilizes the magical and often chaotic atmosphere of Rio de Janeiro's street carnival to tell two main stories. The first story reinterprets the Greek myth of Orpheus. He is a handsome working-class Black tramway conductor who plays the guitar, sings, and is a superb dancer. He was also well-loved by community members and an avid participant in the community's carnival. Eurydice is an innocent Black woman who arrives from the countryside via ferry and stays with her cousin Serafina, who lives in Babilônia, one of the favelas overlooking the coastal part of Rio de Janeiro. When she arrives in Rio de Janeiro by boat, she is visibly perturbed because someone from her village has been chasing her. As she descends from the boat, a blind man, modelled after Tiresias, a significant blind figure in Greek mythology, stumbles upon her. He attempts to calm her down and adorns her with beautiful yellow flowers, the color associated with Oxum, the goddess of fresh water, love, beauty, and fertility in many of the Afro-Brazilian religions and popular culture. Even though Orpheus apparently has a girlfriend who desperately wants to marry him, he falls deeply in love with Eurydice. However, audiences soon learn that Death, embodied as a man in a gray costume with an image of a skeleton, is pursuing her. In a chaotic moment in the tramway station, Orpheus attempts to turn on the light and accidentally electrocutes her, allowing Death to take her away.

After Eurydice's death, Orpheus is despondent and spends the rest of the movie roaming through the city to bring her back to life. Along the way he receives help from various Afro-Brazilian characters inspired by Greek mythology, including Hermes, his boss. Orpheus eventually enters the underworld to retrieve his beloved after passing the dog Cerberus, named after the Greek multiheaded dog who guards the gates to the underworld. In Umbanda and Candomblé, two Afro-Brazilian religions, worshipers associate the figure of the guardian of cross-roads with the divinity or Orixá Exú, who also serves as a messenger to the other Orixás. The Afro-Brazilian religion Macumba[9] represents the underworld, only in this Afrocentric rendition, audiences experience dancing, drum-beating, and what followers of Umbanda called *pontos*, specific drumming patterns that invite the spirits into the *terreiro*, the worshipping site. Like the Greek counterpart, Orpheus may see Eurydice on one condition: he cannot look back at her as he leaves. As in the Greek myth, Orpheus, the poet-musician, cannot contain his desire to see his beloved, and he turns around and loses her forever. This story ends with Orpheus's tragic death, although the filmmakers use music at the end of the film to underscore the fact that Orpheus's music will live on. This version highlights Brazilian cultural and geographic landscapes during the three most dramatic urban Rio de Janeiro carnival days.

The second story celebrates the diversity of Brazilian popular Black culture, including Macumba. It showcases carnival's merriment, performance, music, and dance. The soundtrack carries audiences through the diversity of Brazilian popular music forms. The audience experiences the city's magnificent urban and natural landscapes while watching inhabitants go about their lives during carnival. Revelers, carnival groups, vendors, favela dwellers, and children connect to the community and carnival through diverse relationships and emotions. The musical score helps set the tone for every scene in the motion picture. From the first scene, the film makes it clear that these two stories are intimately connected. Playing instruments and dancing, a group of Black Brazilians bursts through a static image of the ancient Greek protagonists, disrupting a melancholic tune with a vibrancy emblematic of Brazilian popular culture.

Audiences experience the dissonance between death as a powerful foreboding force and carnival as a beautiful celebration of life. Death also allows for rejuvenation and the perpetuation of love and joy as music passes through the generations. The book's cover image of Orpheus in his golden carnival costume, carrying his deceased beloved Eurydice wrapped in white up the hills with the landscape of Rio de Janeiro, represents that dissonance. It is a Brazilian pietá.

Toward A Historically Contextualized Critique

By dismissing the film outright as exotic or problematic, we miss the opportunity for a nuanced engagement with Black Brazil in the Atlantic context during the social changes of the long 1960s. Moreover, Michael Boyce Gillespie invites us to study intention and production to determine how the film and music impart Afro-Brazilian culture, and the value it gives to Black Brazilian subjects. Archival evidence affirms that Camus wanted to project a Black celebration and create a positive image of Black Brazil. Indeed, *Black Orpheus* promoted the universality of the Black subject precisely by using an all-Black cast for the principal roles and highlighting Blackness in a racist Western world. Moreover, as a visitor who became a lover of Brazil, he was interested in sharing the Brazilian charm he experienced. He used the symbol of carnival, a cultural event that had captivated him, despite the conditions of poverty in the 1950s. At the same time, like many directors of his era, Camus *included* and *depicted* Black subjects without including the Black community in the final decision-making process.

Camus conducted research and asked Black subjects from Umbanda and from the samba schools for permission to film them performing. However, Camus's depiction of incessant rhythmic music and dance clearly represented his 'exotic' perception of carnival, as evidenced by his descriptions of Brazilians "dancing all the time" or "Brazilians dance alone just for the pleasure of dancing." He took no survey of Brazilians or even of the Cariocas, whom he chose to represent Brazil.[10] His production team was also prone to stereotypes and interested in sharing and emphasizing the new and exotic elements that charmed them. The notes on early versions of the unpublished first film script housed at the Cinémathèque française in Paris reveal a production team struggling to create a film that reflected a Black Brazil that European audiences would understand. The notes show a desire to emphasize and translate the 'exotic' nature of the carnival and highlight Black Brazilians as the major protagonists. It also contains language that readers today would find odd. One note uses racialized descriptions such as in the first musical scene, the translators in French use the expression "cri du noir" (a scream from a Black man) when "a scream" would have sufficed, for example, or "La samba de plus en plus violente" (the sound of samba becoming more and more violent).[11] These are editorial notes in the midst of discussions in French in Brazil.

A decade earlier, the French philosopher Jean-Paul Sartre had published his Afrocentric essay "Black Orpheus," in which he celebrated the role of the Black Negritude poets in the Western world.[12] Many observers have pointed out Negritude's essentialist tendencies, but Sartre argued that Negritude's celebration of Blackness was a call for dignity in a "capitalist White world." He praised the poets for their artistry and spirituality as a panacea for the Western world's ills. Camus was following this tradition. In September 1956, Black intellectuals from the Francophone and Anglophone worlds gathered to discuss this subject in Paris for the First Congress of Black Writers.[13] While there is no evidence that Camus knew of the conference, as he prepared his film, discussions of the position of Black artists circulated in places Camus frequented. In the same year as the 1956 congress, Marcel Camus reiterated Sartre's vision. He began preproduction for his film *Black Orpheus*, featuring an all-Black cast, Black voices, and the joy of Black life in Brazil. For him, Brazil could be a social example for the Atlantic world.

Cinema, Music, and the Brazilian Ethnoscape

The transnational consumption of Afro-Brazilian popular culture in the 1960s emerged from the geopolitical and cultural dynamics of the post–World War II era. The development of the film and music recording industries and the proliferation of cinema houses, radio broadcasting, and records would play a more critical role in bringing Afro-Brazilian culture to global audiences after the war. In the aftermath of the film's transnational success, a new musical phenomenon called bossa nova, whose beginnings appear in the movie, would captivate global audiences for the next two decades.[14] Brazilian musicians, singers, and other performers abroad also helped take the music of *Black Orpheus* global. Two critical groups aided these Brazilian transnational performers outside of Brazil: (1) transnational interlocutors, including directors and producers interested in promoting or utilizing Brazilian culture in their works; and (2) talented American and French performers who recorded their own versions of Brazilian musical numbers, who collaborated with Brazilians to help introduce Brazilian popular culture to national consumers.[15]

The circulation of Brazilian performers and cultural products was contingent on demand *and* supply in a mutually codependent and symbiotic relationship that influenced the flow of cultural products, and which bodies would carry them. While foreign consumers may influence the creation of the cultural products exported and consumed transnationally, they do not wholly determine the nature of those products. The triad analysis of diaspora studies (homeland-host land-diasporic group) is helpful here. Brazilian cultural products emerged from within the existing racialized structures of the Brazilian nation-state (homeland), and cultural gatekeepers (interlocutors and producers in the host lands outside of Brazil) influenced who performed and thus what products and bodies audiences consumed.[16]

Beauty, Empathy, Catharsis, and Latin Blackness

The film's reliance on the Black community participation and Black Brazilian performers and actors offered the possibility of capturing a dynamic and complex outlook on the Black community's reality. Camus's decision to create an Aristotelian-type tragedy for the silver screen allowed him to use cinematic devices to induce emotions such as empathy and catharsis through the story in which popular music was central. *Black Orpheus* was also a Technicolor groundbreaker that visually captured views of stunning landscapes and diverse locations in Rio de Janeiro. It was the first international film to focus on the everyday life of ordinary Blacks without highlighting racial tensions, violence, or postcolonial angst, issues at the forefront of American and French consciousness. The film also gave many Black Brazilians their first opportunity to perform on the silver screen, shattering national and racial restrictions that limited the Black presence in national cinema. The film's success eventually led to unprecedented opportunities for Brazilian performers in the 1960s in Atlantic world cities such as New York, London, and Paris.

While *Black Orpheus* celebrated a Black Catholic Latin world, the production of that world resulted from transcultural collaborations between Black and non-Black actors and Brazilian and non-Brazilian producers. This collaboration is symbolic of Black cultural output throughout the Atlantic world. The history and legacy of slavery and disenfranchisement have meant that relatively few Black communities or producers have attained the power or access to capital to produce or promote their own Afro-Atlantic stories or to engage in transnational travel to promote their cultural products in a globalized economy. Black Brazilian transnational circulation mainly relied on foreign collaborators or non-Black Brazilian performers who could travel abroad. Many, like Vanja Orico, understood the importance of African culture to Brazil. As Stuart Hall reminds us, "Black culture is a contradictory space, a site of strategic contestation."[17] The question is not 'Can non-Black subjects help African descendants produce Black culture?' Rather, how does that happen in a globalized world?

Despite their small numbers, Afro-Brazilian performers such as Baden Powell, Maria d'Apparecida, Bola Sete, and Carmen Costa played critical roles in circulating Afro-Brazilian culture after *Black Orpheus*. Many of them were connected to the film or to the musicians involved in the film. Moreover, these early postwar transnational Afro-Brazilian performers would become a part of the tradition of the Black Orpheus, the poet, the musician, and often the griot, ironically a French-derived word commonly used outside of Africa to refer to storytellers and preservers of oral traditions. Their personal trajectories and experiences in Brazil and abroad provide details of the diversity within the global Afro-Brazilian cultural dispersion in the 1960s and 1970s. Afro-diasporic performers and their transnational interlocutors helped create a Brazilian ethnoscape.[18]

The Historical Circulation of Afro-Brazilian Popular Culture Before 1958

According to Joaquim Ferreira dos Santos, 1958 was a year that "never should have stopped." It was the year when Brazil became politically, economically, and culturally visible on the global stage. Of the fifty-eight most important celebratory Brazilian watersheds in 1958 that Ferreira dos Santos lists, the release of *Black Orpheus* was the singular cultural signpost that celebrated Brazilian music and popular Brazilian culture globally.[19]

A handful of Brazilian performers, including the Oito Batutas, and French interlocutors in the global media, such as Michel Simon, promoted Brazilian popular culture in France. Simon had taught French language and culture in Brazil. When he returned to Paris, he broadcasted Brazilian music and culture on his Parisian-based radio show *Watercolors of Brazil*, whose title derived from the 1939 Ary Barroso composition. The show, which received support from the Brazilian embassy in Paris, could be heard in former French colonies such as Senegal. In 1958 and 1959, Simon's program broadcasted the audio version of *Black Orpheus* and played the soundtrack. Cinema, radio, and records facilitated the export and performance of Brazilian music and provided global opportunities for Brazilian actors and producers, sometimes in fetishized formulations, to meet. It also meant that musicians and performers outside of Brazil could also learn and perform Brazilian music without living or visiting Brazil.[20]

American musicians in France and the United States also played an essential role in circulating Brazilian popular music. Sometimes, American-based performers would also travel to France to perform, but music circulated more frequently through the exportation of records and through the cinema. A small group of Brazilian performers had migrated to the United States between the end of World War I and the 1950s. Those performers adapted popular Brazilian culture and themes for consumption by North American audiences. Unfortunately, the North American media often reduced dynamic cultural practices and their multiple signs, codes, and humor, which are understandable to Brazilian audiences, to a few static and essential characteristics, fetishizing Brazil, similarly to their French counterparts. Not surprisingly, while Black performers such as the members of the Oito Batutas band traveled to France to perform, no prominent Brazilian Black musicians had the opportunity to perform in the United States before World War II. Movie actors and performers such as Raul Roulien, Lia Norá, Carmen Miranda, Aurora Miranda, Aloysio de Oliveira, and Ary Barroso were all White or White presenting in Brazil.[21]

American and French attitudes in the first decades of the twentieth century set the frameworks and infrastructures for future generations of performers to engage audiences abroad. While Brazilian popular culture circulated in both countries and across Europe, Nazi Germany's invasion of France in 1940 curtailed the circulation of most popular culture and performers in France during the war. In the United States, the Good Neighbor Policy (1933–1947) provided opportunities to enlist Latin American performers and artists to fight against tyranny in Europe and open South American markets to U.S. cultural products.[22] The policy masked the United States' geopolitical angst caused by the Brazilian government's negotiations with Hitler's Nazi regime. Diplomats in Washington and Rio understood that the two nations needed each other, and thus each engaged in political, economic, and cultural enterprises from which both countries would benefit. Brazilian performers who migrated or traveled to the United States were neither threatening nor disconcerting. Instead, they fit into the idea that South America was a part of the North American sphere of influence. Inspired by the Afro-Brazilian Bahian woman, the image of Carmen Miranda, a White Portuguese Brazilian woman with fruit on her head, moving her body to enchanting tunes, was a prominent example. This "South American Way," the tune from Miranda's Broadway hit appearance, cemented a fun-loving image of Brazil in the American consciousness.[23]

Brazilian musicians often performed in Spanish for Spanish-speaking audiences, creating a pan-Latin experience. This may have also led American audiences to believe that Brazilians spoke Spanish rather than Portuguese. Other performers who followed Miranda adapted to the U.S. gaze as their desire to succeed adjusted to the limitations and expectations of the era.[24] Indeed, Brazilians played an essential role in cementing an American version of "Latinness." The press also reveled in the exoticism, often making fun of the Brazilian-accented English. When Miranda's sister Aurora joined her in the United States in 1941, for example, the *New York Post* and *The New York Telegraph* carried titles that spelled out English words according to Carmen's Brazilian pronunciation: "Hokay, Go Home Keed [*sic*]" and "Miranda beelding Up Leetle Sister [*sic*]." Many of these jokes and images accentuate Brazilians' position as exotic outsiders regardless of racial identification back in Brazil.[25]

The invention of the television, which was quickly becoming a viable forum for the mass distribution of entertainment, would give Miranda new life and an opportunity to adapt her act to a new milieu. Brazilian performers were instrumental in preparing American audiences for the performers of the 1950s, including the *I Love Lucy* show, which starred the Cuban conga player Ricky Ricardo. It is no coincidence that in the third episode of the *I Love Lucy* show on October 22, 1951, Lucy wore the Bahiana outfit replete with fruit on her head.[26] Although the White performers erase the Afro-Latin body in these performances, their influences and connections are apparent to Brazilians and others who understand the Afro-diasporic religions.

An essential aspect of articulating Brazilian-ness in the United States involved the erasure of visual Blackness. In addition, Hollywood relied on Rio de Janeiro's cultural products, icons, and symbols. The *malandro* Zé Carioca from Walt Disney's *The Three Caballeros*, and the Bahiana—which is less Bahian than an adaptation from Rio de Janeiro's carnival—are two such examples. In the 1940s, North Americans learned the samba, heard the *samba-jongo*, and invented a new dance called 'the carioca,' which Ginger Roberts and Fred Astaire performed in *Flying Down to Rio*. The Afro-Brazilian roots would have been apparent to Afro-descendants in Brazil just as most Brazilians understood Miranda's performance as an adaptation or appropriation of Black Brazilian culture, depending on the forum and the performer's intentions. The White Brazilian elite's disdain for Miranda was connected to a general anti-Black attitude and shame over the image she presented of Brazil. Yet, at the same time, White Brazilian performers could pursue opportunities abroad when and where Afro-Brazilians could not.

Transnational Circulation and Afro-Brazilian Agency

So, how did Black Brazilians gain access to global media in the face of foreign migration barriers abroad and challenges at home? First, in the generation after abolition and before World War II, groups like the Oito Batutas persevered through extraordinary resilience. Michael Hanchard called this Black exceptionalism. Afro-Brazilians, like members of the African diaspora elsewhere, have had to demonstrate exceptional abilities to gain access to venues open to White artists. Second, Black Brazilians support non-Black performers who have embraced Black culture as ambassadors. Indeed, many Black Brazilians supported Carmen Miranda and did not view her performances as appropriation, a term that was not necessarily part of the 1930s zeitgeist. Nonetheless, that support emerged when many Afro-Brazilians did not see many Black role models or often could not conceive of Black performers representing them abroad.

Third, Afro-Brazilians and Brazilians in general relied on interlocutors, sponsors, and allies who would help open doors and find opportunities.[27]

Even after World War II, the Brazilian experiences in the European and American media were limited, and few Black Brazilian performers traveled or migrated to Europe or the United States until the 1960s. Indeed, the presence of Afro-Latin Americans outside the region was practically invisible. Thanks to community activists, organic intellectuals, and academics, the Afro-Latin American presence is becoming more visible. Today, actresses such as Ariana DeBose and Zoe Saldaña represent the diverse community. Streaming services also allow Afro-Latin American images and music to circulate globally. In the late 1950s, *Black Orpheus* was an important project that provided a new generation with new possibilities in music and cinema. Although options to perform and produce culture are never unlimited, the economic, political, and cultural power imbalance between 'migrant' and 'native' means that the migrant who performs abroad must necessarily adapt to a new cultural environment. For Brazilian performers, this has often meant performing stereotypes and tropes related to Latin-ness in Europe and the United States.

The late 1950s and 1960s afforded Afro-Brazilian performers such as Baden Powell, Bola Sete, and others the opportunity to experiment and expand the borders that encased Brazilian-ness and Brazilian performance. By the end of the 1960s and early 1970s, non-White Brazilians like Nana Vasconcelos, Gilberto Gil, Caetano Veloso, Maria d'Apparecida, Eliana Pittman, Tânia Maria, and others would expand the Brazilian global performance scape. In effect, they also changed expectations abroad. The idea of Brazilian popular culture had shifted. *Black Orpheus* was a part of that change. The diversity in styles and performances abroad began to reflect the diversity at home, although the trope of the joyous Black or mixed-race nation would remain dominant. Here again, the artistic gatekeepers (interlocutors and producers in the host land) influenced who performed and what products and bodies European audiences consumed.[28]

Brazil's dominant tropes of a joyous Black, *Mestiço*, or *Mulato* nation with few social tensions helped meet the demand for exoticism and difference that was non-threatening. There was also a negative side to the racially harmonious Brazil based on pseudoscience and eugenics that perceived Blackness and racial mixing as degenerate. While a student in the United States at Baylor College and Columbia University in the 1920s, Gilberto Freyre witnessed firsthand negative commentaries about Brazil's racial makeup.[29] Other Brazilian students and visitors often admired many opportunities that the United States offered. Ana Christina S. M. Rocha chronicles the experience of four White Brazilian pioneers (the Bahians Anísio Teixeira and Isaías Alves, the Paulistana Noemy da Silveira Rudolfer, and the Fluminese Lourenço Filho) at Columbia University's Teachers College in the 1920s and 1930s. Compared to Freyre, the Brazilian performers in Hollywood, and other Brazilians who sought support from the Brazilian Foreign Service, Rocha's subjects remind us that the Brazilian travelers to the United States may have shared similar racial backgrounds, but the Brazilian experience in the United States was not homogeneous.

Brazilians moved to France for different reasons before and after the war, but performers often crossed multiple boarders to collaborate on projects regardless of their chosen *host land*, to use the language of diaspora studies. Neither France nor the United States had colonized Brazil and thus would not have to contend with deep historical racial or colonial wounds. International perceptions of Brazil's treatment of Afro-Brazilians and Blackness also played an essential role in the reception of Brazilian culture abroad. Ironically even as late as the 1960s, Afro-Brazilians still represented a small percentage of Brazilians who could travel abroad. An even smaller number officially represented Brazil in official capacities in the diplomatic corps or in official cultural forums.[30] Officials in the Brazilian government also wanted it that way. Yet, the global circulation of Black culture and Black performers and ideas about Black Brazil continued. The postwar development of mass media also played a crucial role in these transnational movements.

Brazilian performers, writers, and musicians may have found France more welcoming in the 1950s and early 1960s. Many found opportunities in the Montmartre neighborhood as artists had done before the war. France had no official racial policies that restricted Brazilians by race as in the United States. Many Brazilian performers and artists found opportunities and spaces to live and perform on the Left Bank among students in cafés, clubs, underground bars, music venues, hotels, and restaurants before and after the war. In the 1920s, many of the modernists had developed close ties with French intellectuals and French cultural institutions. France also received African American intellectuals, artists, and musicians over the same periods, before and after the war. However, there is little evidence of collaborations between the two migrant groups.

By the 1960s there were places in Paris known as Brazilian hangouts where one could listen to Brazilian music and eat Brazilian food. For example, Hôtel du Levant on Rue de la Harpe on the Left Bank was a temporary residence for Brazilians of all races, a feature that stood out to the hotel's staff.[31] The restaurant A Feijoada also became a hangout even though the food was not that good. Brazilians and French creatives frequented the establishment to listen to music and to converse. Discophage, located on the Rue des éçoles, was especially important for Brazilian performances and artists. The duo from the group Les Étoiles recorded their record *Les Étoiles Live* in Portuguese at the establishment in 1979.[32] In addition, Lúcio Costa's Maison du Brésil (Brazil House) in the new City University of Paris, inaugurated on June 24, 1959, became an important space for cultural exchange between Brazil and France. Other symbols of Brazil dotted the Parisian landscape, including Oscar Niemeyer's headquarters of the French Communist Party, inaugurated in 1971.[33]

The 1970s would bring new Brazilian performers to the French capital. Still, there was not a bona fide Brazilian community in Paris. In the meantime, American interlocutors such as Dizzy Gillespie, who had some knowledge of Brazil and access to French market producers, played a critical role in promoting Brazilian music in general and Afro-Brazilian connections. The Americans who followed Gillespie to perform Brazilian-derived cultural products in France included diverse artists such as the jazz musician Lionel Hampton, singers Dionne Warwick and Nina Simone, and the *Black Orpheus* star Marpessa Dawn. In addition, Brazilian migrants who lived in the United States, including Astrud Gilberto and Sergio Mendes, often traveled to Europe to perform Brazilian music, sometimes in English.

Global attention given to Brazil as an influential nation in urban development and soccer helped to augment the visibility of *Black Orpheus* and Black Brazil more globally. The country was building the new capital, Brasilia, which the *Time* magazine cover of February 13, 1956, portrayed as a modern phoenix rising from the interior of the country.[34] Construction began in 1956 and terminated in 1961. Brazil's emergence as a worldwide soccer power highlighted Brazilian male athleticism. The country's conquest of the World Cup in 1958 and the emergence of the Afro-Brazilian Edson Arantes do Nascimento, popularly known as Pelé, garnered Black Brazil attention. Soccer had become a different type of carnival, a celebration now entering living rooms worldwide through television. The *Black Orpheus* project must be seen as part of a broader globalization of Black Brazil and of Brazil in general.

Part I

The Making of *Black Orpheus*

Black Orpheus was a significant signpost in the globalization of Brazilian culture. It centered on Black Brazil and created new audiences interested in consuming, engaging, and reproducing Brazilian culture. In the global capitalist economy, business interests also sought to capitalize on the growing demand for Brazilian culture. Many Brazilian artists seized on the new economic and cultural opportunities to further their careers and promote Brazilian culture outside of Brazil. Each musician and performer embodied the metaphor of Orpheus, performing and recording beautiful melodies and rhythms for global audiences.

1

Imagining a Brazilian Black Orpheus

The classical Orpheus, the legendary musician, poet, and master of the lyre, hailed from ancient Thrace, a region nestled among the Balkan Mountains between the Danube to the north and the Aegean Sea to the south. In one version of the Greek myth, Orpheus symbolizes the eternal lover willing to enter the depths of Hades to resurrect his beloved Eurydice. In another, he was the mournful poet driven to desperation after he lost Eurydice. This tragic story of love told through music and poetry inspired countless composers and performers around the globe. Productions including Monteverdi's 1607 *Orfeo*, Christoph Willibald Gluck's 1762 *Orfeo ed Euridice*, and Jacques Offenbach's 1858 *Orphée aux enfers* represent different versions of the Orphic myth. Gluck even changed the script to give Austrian Empress Maria Theresa a happy ending for her Empire Day celebration. The early operas all envisioned Orpheus and Eurydice as European or White protagonists.[1]

Filmmakers also brought different versions of the Greek myth to the silver screen in the first half of the twentieth century. In 1906, the Danish silent film director Peter Elfelt filmed *Orfeus og Eurydike*, a short three-minute dance scene from Gluck's opera. The French director Jean Cocteau created a black-and-white film trilogy dedicated to the myth, beginning in 1930 with *The Blood of a Poet* (1930). Twenty years later, Cocteau produced *Orpheus* (1950), and nine years later he filmed *The Testament of Orpheus*. Like the European operas, these film productions imagined Orpheus and Eurydice as White European protagonists.

FIGURE 1 Still from *Black Orpheus*: Orpheus and Eurydice in a room in the favela Babilônia. Credit: Lopert Pictures/Photofest. © Lopert Pictures

In 1958, White French film director Marcel Camus broke with that tradition with the release of *Black Orpheus*.

Most French, American, and Brazilian movie audiences in the 1950s and 1960s were unaccustomed to seeing Black protagonists in dramatic mainstream films. Fully fleshed-out Black Brazilian characters were also a rarity in Brazil and abroad. Relying on the play by the White Brazilian playwright and diplomat Vinicius de Moraes, Camus created a cinematic version of a Black working-class Brazilian Orpheus for transnational audiences. Although the film focused on a predominantly Afro-Brazilian working-class favela community in Rio de Janeiro, this representation became a transnational symbol of Black Brazil. Without focusing on racial or class issues, Camus's film captured the Orphic myth through the lives of Black Brazilian characters over three days of carnival. The Black characters celebrate Afro-Brazilian music and popular cultural traditions within a Latin American Catholic cultural context.[2]

By analyzing the film's origin and the producers' intention and praxis in this chapter, we better understand the promises and limits of the *Black Orpheus* project as a symbol of Black Brazil. The film's insistence on Black visibility and representation on the silver screen constitutes one of its greatest strengths. In this regard, the White creators who worked on the project were committed to exploring and celebrating Black culture. They also had their limitations. At the same time, Camus's status as a French director afforded him access to a cinematic industry with a global reach, facilitating the circulation of the film's portrayal of Black Brazil. An examination of the French producers' relationship to Black Brazilian culture, their intention, and praxis in creating that representation in the 1950s reveals the challenges and promises of transnational representation. Camus brought a passion and commitment that created a fantasy focused on joy and celebration of the Black underclass. Camus's French background, the post–World War II cultural relationship between France and Brazil, and his 1950s creative and political praxis shaped an endearing yet reductive vision of a Black Brazilian culture.

The Revision

Camus's cinematic construction of Afro-Brazilian popular culture relied heavily on insights from Vinicius de Moraes's play *Orfeu da Conçeicão* and musical input from Tom Jobim. The story first came to Moraes in 1942 when he visited his brother-in-law Carlos Leão in Niterói, the city across Guanabara Bay from Rio de Janeiro. According to Moraes, while he was reading the story of "Orpheus of Thrace," he heard the *cuica*, the *tamborims*, and the large Brazilian drums in what he called "infernal" rhythmic and hypnotic beatings. He found himself meandering between the ancient Greece of his book and the Afro-Brazilian drumming from one of the hills around him. According to Moraes, he felt the beginning of a "Black carioca tragedy,"[3] and he went on to create a play in verse for an all-Black cast. The Black musician Orpheus would represent a new Brazil in his play *Orfeu da Conceição*. Moraes was well-versed in the patriotic language of Brazilian hybridity, and he also believed that Brazil, the former tropical colony, could represent a new vision of humanity, or as Austrian writer Stefan Zweig called it, "A Land of the Future."[4]

Moraes understood the centrality of the African to Brazilian culture. Still, ironically, it was the White Jewish American socialist Waldo Frank who helped him attain political consciousness in the development of the play. Frank had traveled with Moraes throughout Brazil and visited places where Afro-Brazilians danced, worshipped, and performed music in Rio de Janeiro. Moraes reported that because he traveled with Frank, he developed a greater sense of the importance of the Black influence. This knowledge enabled him to see the parallels between ancient Greek culture and Afro-Brazilian culture. He knew that the favela would be the central scene of his play and that the music would express the human struggle but not necessarily reproduce the popular music of the favela.[5] Furthermore, Moraes decided to write the first act of a play in classical verse, not in Brazilian spoken Portuguese or the popular vernacular. He wrote the second act five years later while stationed in the Brazilian embassy in Los Angeles. On his return to Brazil in 1950, Moraes completed his play just in time to enter and win the top prize in a theater festival competition in São Paulo.[6]

Moraes insisted on an all-Black cast to demonstrate his dedication to Brazil's Black people, who "have already given Brazil so much even under the most precarious living conditions." He wrote: "The work pays homage to the Black Brazilian for what [he] has already given to Brazil, even under the most precarious conditions of existence. But it would be an attempt against this spirit to cast racially mixed actors in the roles. Afro-Brazilians have their own culture and temperament, 'sui generis,' although it is integrated into the Brazilian racial complex."[7]

Moraes's support of the Afro-Brazilian community is undeniable. Yet his comments indicate a cultural distance from and lack of involvement with that Afro-Brazilian community. For example, Moraes saw the culture as less Apollonian and more Dionysian, reflecting his own proclivities as a songwriter and bohemian. There is no indication that he participated in musical or religious activities or consulted Afro-Brazilian religious leaders or informers in Rio for this project. Moraes believed in the national syncretic tradition of melding cultural influences while highlighting the centrality of Black culture in Brazil. As he wrote much later after his collaboration with Afro-Brazilian guitarist Baden Powell, Moraes believed that life "was the art of encounter," and the African was a central character in the encounter that created Brazil.[8]

Like many White bohemians of his generation, Moraes's approximation to Black culture was not through racial or class identity (since he was neither Black nor from the working class) but was connected to his feeling of embracing a new Brazil. He worked with many Afro-Brazilian musicians but probably never encountered Black people in the Brazilian diplomatic corps.[9] Moraes was surely aware of the Francophone Negritude champions, such as Aimé Césaire and Léopold Sédar Senghor, who had made significant contributions to the global conversation about Black culture.[10] In the preface to *Orfeu da Conceição*, Moraes dedicated his work to Black Brazilians "for their organic contribution to the culture of this country" and for what he called "their passionate way of living." Moraes's description of Black Brazilians as passionate was a stereotype that dismissed Black individuality and diversity. However, like many writers, including the Negritude poets who celebrated Africans' gifts of spirituality to the Western world, he thought that Western civilization had overlooked their contributions. Moraes believed that the divine musical creations of the hills of Rio de Janeiro paralleled the heavenly music of Orpheus in ancient Greece.[11]

Moraes worked with many actors associated with the Teatro Experimental do Negro, TEN, or the Black Experimental Theater, in Rio de Janeiro. He also assembled a team of well-regarded progressive White Brazilians to bring his vision to life. Moraes chose famous Brazilians who would bring gravitas and attention to his art and to Black culture in general: Leo Jusi as his director; Oscar Niemeyer as a set designer; Lila de Moraes as costume designer; Tom Jobim, musical composer; choreographer Lina de Luca; and Carlos Scliar as a set painter. All of them would become cultural icons of Brazilian culture in the second half of the twentieth century. Thus, Moraes used a traditional strategy to elevate his Black theme by relying on well-known and emerging talent. He was most interested in presenting Black bodies to his audience, which was primarily White and middle class.

Julia A. Walker notes in *Performance & Modernity: Enacting Change on the Globalizing Stage* that for the era in which he lived, Moraes was pursuing an anti-racist strategy and attempting to disidentify universal themes with Whiteness.[12] Still, his relationship with the Black actors during the rehearsal for the play had its tense moments. At one point, the actors complained that they were not being paid. Moreover, Moraes did not invite Abdias do Nascimento, the director of the Black Experimental Theater (TEN), to help direct his play, for example. Instead, he cast him in the role of Aristeu. Nor did he seek out Afro-Brazilians to work on the set or costumes that the actors representing the Afro-Brazilians from the favela would wear.[13] Instead, he chose Leo Jusi, a talented and well-known personality in Rio's artistic milieu. In 1953, Jusi collaborated with Augusto Boal and Abdias do Nascimento to create a manifesto to incentivize Brazilian theater. Boal, the iconoclast and creator of the Theater of the Oppressed in the 1970s, believed that all theater was political.[14] It was not a common practice in the 1950s to question representation in all aspects of cultural production. Moraes's and Camus's focus on representation on the stage and in front of the camera was already innovative, if not groundbreaking. Nascimento played a critical role in helping to organize the cast for Moraes. However, he would later criticize Moraes for his "elitist bourgeois sensibilities" and his attitude of presenting himself as a legitimate Black culture's proprietor.[15]

In the 1950s and 1960s, Moraes called himself the "Blackest White man in Brazil," a descriptor that smacks of appropriation today. While it is unclear exactly when he began making this statement, Afro-Brazilian contemporary creatives such as Gilberto Gil and Haroldo Costa defended his right to say it because he incorporated Afro-Brazilian themes in his work. Nonetheless, Moraes's metaphorical Blackness obfuscates the fact that he is still White, a constructed racial identity that gave him both power and access unavailable to Black artists of his era.[16] Moraes's credentials as a diplomat also gave him international recognition, having lived and worked in the United States, France, and South America. According to Carlos "Cacá" Diegues, Moraes was an unabashedly patriotic Brazilian at a time when Brazil was "beginning to like itself, to value the original expression of its own art, its own way of living, without disguising its ill."[17] His social milieu and his personal preference to socialize with intellectuals, other creatives, and the French intelligentsia, including filmmakers, allowed him to discuss his work and his desire to make a film based on his play. While serving as embassy secretary in France from 1953 to 1957,

Moraes would meet French film producer Sacha Gordine through dancer and film archivist Mary Meerson, a mutual friend who was also the companion and assistant to Henri Langlois, director of the Cinémathèque française in Paris in 1955. Sacha Gordine would eventually introduce Moraes to Marcel Camus, the future director *of Black Orpheus*.[18]

Filming Black Brazil for the French Screen

Shaped by a history of empire, French global opportunities benefited adventurous French directors in post–World War II Paris, such as Marcel Camus. In the 1950s, Paris saw the emergence of a group of iconoclastic film writers and directors who comprised the Nouvelle Vague, the French New Wave movement. Camus was not as well-known as other New Wave filmmakers such as François Truffaut or Jean-Luc Godard, but he was relatively well connected to the French establishment and to writers and producers in the 1950s. Sacha Gordine was one such producer. Gordine began to produce films, starting with the 1944 *L'aventure est au coin de la rue* (*Adventure is Around the Corner*), directed by Jacques Daniel-Norman.[19] In 1951, he released his adaptation of the opera *Juliette ou la clé des songes* (*Juliette or Key of Dreams*), directed by Marcel Carné and with a screenplay by Jacques Viot. Gordine would later bring Viot and Camus together to work on the film script for *Black Orpheus*.[20]

Afro-Brazilians were absent from these transnational discussions in Paris until the arrival of Haroldo Costa, an actor and performer who was touring Europe with his dance company. Costa's role as an ambassador of Afro-Brazilian popular culture cannot be underestimated, even though he did not participate in the film. Costa performed a reading for Gordine at Moraes's residence in Paris, helping to cement the producers' interest in making a Franco-Brazilian film.[21] An Afro-Brazilian with an enormous stage presence, Costa had been a member of the Black Experimental Theater and would eventually star in Moraes's play. Costa had accumulated experience as an actor and dancer in Brazil and became a critical ambassador of Brazilian folklore and popular culture in Europe, touring and performing from 1954 to 1959 with a company aptly called Brasiliana.[22] At the first European show at L'Etoile in Paris, the company's repertoire included popular musical and dance traditions such as the *coco*, *maracatu*, and *capoeira*. Brasiliana helped open and prepare European audiences for Brazilian Black celebrations in the early 1950s. According to Costa, La Comédie Française and Luis Jouvet's tour of Brazil played an important role in shaping the French appetite for Brazilian popular culture. This also inspired him to create a Brazilian company that would tour Europe.[23]

Once Gordine agreed to transform Moraes's play into a movie, he turned to Jacques Viot to translate and create a script. Viot also helped Gordine to find Marcel Camus. French scholar Anaïs Fléchet reports that Viot and Camus met by chance at a café on the Champs-Élysées, and Camus became enthusiastic about the project. However, it is likely that Camus, Viot, Gordine, and others frequented similar locales. Thus, collaborations among these filmmakers, producers, and actors were not coincidental but part of a field constructed through living and socializing in specific social and cultural contexts. They accumulated and shared opportunities because of what the French sociologist Pierre Bourdieu called cultural capital.[24] Moraes was occasionally a part of these circles and Camus, Viot, and Gordine followed his desire to create a film version of *Black Orpheus*. Camus believed he could make a difference with his art and believed in the power of the Orphic tradition. His working relationship with Viot was personal, cultural, vocational, and generational. Indeed, both men were connected to the surrealist movement and the surrealist poet Guillaume Apollinaire's celebration of Orpheus.[25] They were deeply interested in Orphism.[26]

Viot and Camus had another cultural connection. Like many French intellectuals, the postwar French cultural producers left France and Europe to explore and find inspiration in the African and Asian colonies. Viot had chosen self-exile in Oceania,[27] as he sought a new way of living in the world and cultivating an anti-European way of living. He wrote poems and worked in a gallery. Camus traveled to Indochina, where he shot his first film *Mort en fraude* (*Fugitive in Saigon*). Neither Frenchmen could shed their European education and vision completely, but they would attempt to empathize and understand non-European points of view. Viot's poetry, photographs, and work with Marcel Camus's *Mort en fraude* are examples of that empathetic impulse. The Frenchmen, culturally sensitive to foreign cultures, understood one another.

Camus arrived in Rio clearly understanding that his film was to center Black Brazilians in a way that would celebrate Brazil globally. The cultural magazine *Arts* reported that he had yet to cast his actors.[28] To begin production, he relied on his French cultural capital, French and Brazilian contacts, and Brazilian generosity and neocolonial sensibilities. Camus used the Maison de France in downtown Rio for auditions, for example, and reached out to politicians and the military for logistical support.[29] He also created preconceived drawings of his two protagonists. During the production, Camus appealed to the Brazilian government for equipment, contacted cultural producers, and relied on various personalities and Black establishments, including the samba schools, to create a film centered on the Black experience.[30]

From the outset, Camus intended to follow Moraes's Black casting, although he would introduce non-Black characters to present a realistic vision of Rio de Janeiro. The White grocery store owner and the White pawnshop owner in the film treat Orpheus with great affection, showing the interracial camaraderie across class lines. While representation has been a critical aspect of film production for African descendants for decades, the dialogue between the creative producer and the minoritized group represented is equally important. What role did Afro-Brazilians play in creating the *Black Orpheus* project? How did Moraes and Camus recognize that contribution? Did gender play a role in that representation?

As in the case of Moraes's play, Camus's major crew members were White, for example, albeit from diverse cultural backgrounds and life experiences. One was Catalan and Moraes continued to give his input throughout the filming. The racial dynamics were not remarkable for the 1950s. However, the limited dialogue and the power relationship between those filming and those being filmed resulted in final representations celebrating a specific type of noble Blackness within Black poverty. At the same time, the film captured Black talent, Black joy, and Black freedom through dance and music. Neither the play nor the film approached race or gender critically despite its success in diversifying representations. The production benefited individual Black (and non-White) Brazilian men and women, affording them unprecedented exposure and opportunity on a global level. Still, the story follows typical gendered dynamics regarding casting for the main protagonists. As Laura Mulvey explains, there is often a gendered split between an active male and a passive female, typical of the male fantasy of a female figure. Thus, the women are coded for robust visual and erotic features and as sexual objects to be pursued. However, the film complicates that dichotomy by adding a love triangle and introducing Serafina, Eurydice's cousin who has her own romantic life.[31]

Mainstream theater and cinema audiences now and in the 1950s in France, Brazil, and the United States were predominantly White and middle class. Indeed, Moraes and Camus clearly state their didactic goals for audiences. In an era with few Black producers and few Black plays or films, *Black Orpheus* became the global representative of the Black Brazilian experience rather than one view among many global representations of Black Brazilians. As we will see, particularly in the case of the film, the French producers gained economically with distribution rights and global visibility despite the celebration of Blackness culturally. Indeed, given the lack of contracts and the use of volunteer labor, structurally there was no mechanism to remunerate the thousands of Black participants from various walks of life. Furthermore, Camus almost did not finish the film due to budget constraints. In a 1959 interview with *Time* magazine, Camus reported that he often skipped meals and slept on the beach to save money on hotel bills. He reiterated his financial challenges in an interview on French television.[32]

Although Brazil did not develop formal segregation laws as in the United States, racial prejudice, social restrictions, and Eurocentric biases meant that Afro-Brazilians had few opportunities to appear in the media beyond stereotypical or humorous roles. Incentives for creating and producing Afro-Brazilian productions in cities such as Rio de Janeiro and São Paulo, the centers of national media production, were nonexistent. Even after the passing of the 1951 Afonso Arinos Anti-Discrimination Law, Afro-Brazilian actors had few avenues to access national media forums or production facilities.

As Robert Stam reminds us in *Tropical Multiculturalism*, Black popular culture and Black bodies were present on the silver screen, and Black musicians participated in creating the sound score as early as the silent era of film (1898–1930), but their visual roles were restricted.[33] Black pioneers such as Benjamin de Oliveira (1870–1954) represented Afro-Brazilian characters, although often stereotypical or comedic. In *O Guarani* (1908), Oliveira plays an Indian. The actress Maria Lúcia played a minor role in the film *A Escrava Isaura* (1929), and other Black characters appear in domestic or pejorative roles in films such as *O segredo do Corcunda* (*The Hunchback's Secret*, 1924) and *A filha do advogado* (*The Lawyer's Daughter*, 1926).

The 1930s and 1940s brought new sensibilities and a few new Black actors in front of the camera. Sebastião Bernardes de Souza Prata, better known as Grande Otelo, was one of them. As Robert Stam acknowledges, it is not easy to summarize Grande Otelo's diverse roles in the 1940s and 1950s since he appeared in more than one hundred films, although most were comedic before the 1960s. Otelo was a famous presence in the Brazilian theater having joined the famous Companhia Negra de Revistas (The Black Comedy Revue), founded by the Black poet, performer, and director João Cândido Ferreira, better known as De Chocolat. On film, Grande Otelo quickly became associated with the satirical films known as *chanchadas*. Racial codes severely restricted Black participation of actors and producers, and Grande Otelo spoke candidly about the discrimination he felt. Nonetheless, Afro-Brazilian popular culture emerged in the prewar era through music, art, and many expressions of popular culture and life.[34]

While Moraes provided Camus with a blueprint for an all-Black cast production, as an outsider, Camus fashioned his cinematic vision based on his own life experience and history and his ideas about peace, racial tolerance, and the importance of the Orphic tradition. On the other hand, many critics have argued that Camus approached Brazilian Black culture with an exotic unidimensional foreign gaze reminiscent of the French Negrophilia tradition often associated with the films and presentations of Josephine Baker. Camus was no doubt influenced by that tradition, but the Brazilian popular classes also helped give him an understanding of their lives and the role of carnival. The fact that he walked almost everywhere and slept in odd places allowed him to learn a great deal firsthand from working-class Brazilians. He also spent time in the Babilônia favela, building a set in the location of a hill above what is today the shopping center, Rio Sul.

As a director, Camus attempted to present a more nuanced vision of Black Brazil than many critics allege. Even though Camus's cinematic choices often reinforced the one-dimensional view of Black merriment, his intentions were noble. Documentary footage from the time also illustrates the carnival's frenetic environment and poor Brazilians' willingness to invest in the carnival. With talented Black musicians, actors, and ordinary Afro-Brazilians *in front of the camera*, Camus would make two major contributions to the transnational circulation of Brazilian Blackness in the post–World War II era. First, Camus recreated a cinematic Afro-Brazilian world during three carnival days by filming Black actors, including carnival groups. He created a charming, vibrant, and colorful representation of Black Brazilian joy. Camus's cameras also captured Black geographical spaces and religious and musical practices. He recorded many of these customs on film for a global audience for the first time. At the same time, Camus's production crew was exclusively composed of White Europeans behind the camera, and French producers with whom he worked.

There is no evidence in the archives or in the credits that Afro-Brazilians had any significant input on the script, the cinematography, filming, or editing of the film, for example. Camus often expressed one-dimensional views about Brazilians' love of dancing samba and total immersion in carnival, tropes still propagated by Brazilians and non-Brazilians of all backgrounds. The crew's experience had been limited to Rio de Janeiro, and Rio's carnival became and still represents a symbol of Brazil. Many scholars have treated the history of samba as a Carioca phenomenon. That dance and carnival were important to many Afro-Brazilians is undeniable, but context matters. Who can state this truism, when, and for whom? When it becomes a generalized singular trait of a people without historical context, the discourses and visions become examples of essentialism no matter who is iterating those claims.

Black Representation in Brazilian Cinema in the 1950s Before Black Orpheus

When Camus arrived in Brazil, young Brazilian filmmakers had already begun criticizing Brazil's commercial film industry and its lack of attention to Brazilian social issues although Blackness or Black social problems were not a primary foci. By the 1960s, filmmakers such as Nelson Pereira dos Santos (1928–2018) and Glauber Rocha (1939–1981) headed a movement that would be called *cinema novo* (the New Cinema).[35] Since he was associated with the French Nouvelle Vague or New Wave, Camus knew these debates and issues. However, Camus developed his style that involved adventure, filming nonprofessional actors, and providing social messages within a commercially viable aesthetic. Unlike the avant-garde Brazilian filmmakers, however, his French producers (particularly Sacha Gordine) were connected to global networks in Europe and the United States that would allow his film to gain wider transnational distribution.

Mainstream cinema audiences now and in the 1950s and 1960s in France, Brazil, and the United States are predominantly White. In the United States and Brazil, demographic statistics explain those numbers, whereas in Brazil, economics and social factors largely explain this phenomenon. Afro-Brazilians had made significant contributions to Brazilian films by the late 1940s, but as we have seen, very few Afro-Brazilians played central or complex dramatic roles. That began to change in the early 1950s. Films such as *Sinhá Moça* (*The Plantation Owner's Daughter*, 1953), made before *Black Orpheus*, and *João Negrinho* (1958), which was released the same year, showcased Afro-Brazilian talent for local and national audiences but did not receive widespread global attention in Europe or the United States. Moreover, Afro-Brazilian dramatic roles tended to emerge in roles about slavery, which seemed to be the only genre that featured Black actors.[36]

Based on the nineteenth-century work by Maria Dezonne Pacheco Fernandes, *Sinhá Moça* (directed by Tom Payne and Oswaldo Sampaio) was a dramatic period piece about the abolition of slavery. However, the film centers on the conflict between a White slave-owning father and his White abolitionist daughter. Simultaneously, the film offers complex views and performances by many talented actors, not least of whom was Ruth de Souza, one of the cofounders of the Black Experimental Theater. De Souza's performance is an example of Afro-Brazilian brilliance and beauty amid a story and dialogue that does not revolve around her character. The film also received several important national and international awards, including the honorable mention (the Bronze Bear) at the Berlin Film Festival and the honorable mention (the Silver Lion) at the Venice Film Festival, guaranteeing limited exposure outside of Brazil. *João Negrinho* received no such international attention. Based on a 1948 provincial novel of the same name, the film version was finally completed in 1958 thanks to the Herculean effort by the multiracial community of São João da Boa Vista, a town in the interior of the state of São Paulo. Directed by Osvaldo Censoni, *João Negrinho* treats the period before and after abolition, focusing on the relationship between the White son of a plantation owner and the Black son of an enslaved couple. *João Negrinho* exploits what João Carlos Rodrigues calls a "Black martyr" figure who sacrifices his life and progress for the good of his master in ways that modern audiences would find horrifying.[37]

After the end of World War II, the most important Brazilian film outside of Brazil that featured Black characters before *Black Orpheus* was Lima Barreto's 1953 *O Cangaceiro*. Inspired by North American westerns, Barreto's *O Cangaceiro* presented images of northeastern Brazilian bandits that gained international recognition.[38] *O Cangaceiro* introduced the world to images and music associated with the Brazilian rural northeast, known as the *sertão* through a story based on the *cangaceiro* (or bandit) Lampião (1897–1938). In the film, one of the major bandits, the cangaceiro Galdino, presents as a Black or "almost

Black," to paraphrase Caetano Veloso and Gilberto Gil.[39] Robert Stam argues that the Afro-Brazilian character is anachronistic. Other scholars have described the character as *Cafuso* or *Mulato*, light-skinned but darker than the other characters in the film. The film gained an impressive following and won the Best Adventure Film award at Cannes. It was also popular in the United States thanks to Columbia Pictures buying worldwide distribution rights in the United States, but not before changing the ending and retitling it *The Bandit*.[40]

Lampião was a type of antihero known for violence in the *sertão*, the desolate drylands in the interior of Brazil's northeast. The film portrays the *cangaceiros* as mostly Caboclos or Mestiços, often read as racially ambiguous non-White bandits by coastal viewers and foreigners. Audiences in Brazil and abroad easily associated them with violence, disorder, and savagery, as the 1954 review in *The New York Times* illustrated.[41] It is not surprising that there were not many Black actors in the film, given the racist policies of Vera Cruz film studios, even though Afro-Brazilians were represented among the *cangaceiros*. More broadly, Brazilians associate African diasporic culture with the coast, not the *sertão*, even though Blacks, Mestizos, and other non-Whites make up much of the *sertão*'s population.[42] The Carioca Vanja Orico, or Evangelina Orico, who was born in Copacabana, played the role of the *Cabocla* Maria Clódia in the film. As is the case of many actors who define themselves as White in Brazil, Orico would also play racially ambiguous roles abroad. As a child, Orico lived and studied in Belgium, an experience that gave her international connections and placed her in Europe.[43]

Columbia Pictures released *The Bandit* in the United States the same year that Carmen Miranda, Hollywood's biggest ambassador of global Brazilian popular culture, passed away. The Portuguese-born Carmen Miranda's film performance, beginning in the late 1930s, relied on Afro-Brazilian popular culture inspirations as she performed in drag as the Black Bahian woman from the city of Salvador. It would have been outright appropriation had Miranda not lived in the popular neighborhoods of Rio de Janeiro, where poor Portuguese families intermingled with working-class Afro-Brazilians. Miranda worked with and performed with many Afro-Brazilians in Brazil and became one of the most popular performers in Brazil in the 1930s.[44] Her move to the segregated United States cut off collaborations with those Black Brazilians. However, she managed to appear in programs that often featured numbers by African American performers such as Fayard and Harold Nicholas. Miranda's popularity began to wane in the early 1950s. Her two final films before her death, *Nancy Goes to Rio* (1950) and *Scared Stiff* (1953), featured similar images of Miranda as the Bahian woman, the Bahiana. Camus would have been aware of these images. He would also have been aware or at least heard of Otto Preminger's 1954 film, *Carmen Jones*.

Preminger may have inspired Camus, but there is no indication that the two ever met. Living in France, James Baldwin wrote a scathing review of the film in his polemic essay on *Carmen Jones*. Baldwin decried the one-dimensional portrayals of African Americans and the focus on "the light-skinned mulatta" Dorothy Dandridge as a representation of working-class American Blacks. Nevertheless, the film inspired people throughout the diaspora, including viewers in Brazil such as Maria d'Apparecida, a woman Moraes wanted for the role of Eurydice in *Black Orpheus*.[45] Preminger's interest in working with African Americans and Black culture and talent continued with *Porgy and Bess* in 1959. Both of Preminger's films used Black casting and Black music to appeal to audiences while showcasing Black culture.[46]

The parallels between Camus and Preminger deserve further attention from scholars. They represent important case studies for understanding race and African diasporic representation in film. Both European White directors helped showcase Black talent and Black music. Preminger was an Austrian Jew who migrated to the United States, and Camus served as a World War II prisoner of war in a German camp. During the production of their films, both men also developed romantic relationships with their lead actresses. In the United States, the California Supreme Court only struck down the state's anti-miscegenation laws in 1948, and interracial dating, romance, or marriage remained taboo. Preminger and Dandridge's off-screen romance was secretive and short-lived, given the racial climate of the United States at the time. Interracial marriage was not illegal in France or Brazil. Camus's relationship was certainly not secret and eventually ended in marriage.[47] While it is difficult to use these two cases to make any definitive statement about comparative race relations, of the three countries, the United States was the only one to enforce legal segregation and ban interracial relationships. Very few commercially viable Black filmmakers emerged across the Atlantic countries in the 1950s. Before Camus, Black filmmakers in France were trying to document the Black presence. Jacques Mélo Kane, Mamadou Sarr, and Paulin Soumanou Vieyra's 1955 documentary *Afrique-sur-Seine* focuses on Africans in Paris and included a scene with Marpessa Dawn, who lived in Paris. However, the film did not receive media attention.

Power, Brazilian Performers, and the Global Media

While Brazilian thinkers and foreign commenters wrote of the ubiquitous influence of Africans on Brazilian culture, Black Brazilians were visibly absent from Brazilian politics and from major international cultural forums, particularly film.[48] However, that was beginning to change in radio and popular music production. Although Afro-Brazilian performers such as Grande Otelo garnered national attention in limited stereotypical and comedic roles in the early twentieth century, Brazilian radio and cinema icons remained predominantly White. Similar dynamics were underway in the United States, although prominent actors began to make limited inroads in the 1950s and 1960s. Sidney Poitier, nominated for an Academy Award for *The Defiant Ones* in 1958 and *Lilies of the Field* in 1963, and Dorothy Dandridge, nominated for an Academy Award for *Carmen Jones* in 1954, ensured that African Americans received more visibility in the global media than their Afro-Brazilian counterparts. After all, audiences in France and Brazil consumed these American films, as Maria d'Apparecida and Ruth de Souza attest.[49]

Few Black Brazilian performers migrated or traveled to the United States in the 1950s. Ruth de Souza was one of the pioneers after she received a Rockefeller Foundation scholarship to study and participate in theatrical productions in the United States. De Souza spent time at the Karamu House in Cleveland, Ohio. There, she studied and performed in various plays, after which she explored the country and visited Black universities and cultural centers.[50] When more Afro-Brazilians moved to the United States in the 1960s and 1970s, like their White counterparts before the war, their experiences were not monolithic. Many occupied an ambiguous racial and ethnic space as migrants in the United States, as Brazilians, and as Black subjects, a triple consciousness among citizenship, race, and nationality.

The Preproduction of *Black Orpheus*

The *Black Orpheus* cinema project was a transnational media endeavor that involved actors and musicians from France, Brazil, and the United States. These creatives exercised different levels of power dictated by the specific mode of production in which the director, in collaboration with the writers and editors, played the most critical role in bringing the project to fruition. An analysis of preproduction documents filed with the Brazilian National Cinema Commission reveals the racial and national dichotomy of the production. Except for Vinicius de Moraes, listed as the story creator, the entire preproduction team was either French and White or lived in France. The Conselho Nacional do Cinema in Rio de Janeiro listed the following producers: "Sacha Gordine (producer), Marcel Camus (director), Vinicius de Morais (story) [*sic*], Marcel Camus/Jacques Viot (adaptation), Jean Bourgoin (camera), Amaury Leenhardt (sound)."[51]

Camus received the script in 1956, traveled to Rio in 1957 to experience carnival for the first time, and returned in February 1958 to film on the ground before filming with his cast later that year. He was conscious early on that he would be creating a pioneering film because it would capture the joy of the Brazilian carnival that he experienced and portray something new: Black joy from the perspective of ordinary people. Despite his commitment to the project, his personal observations still revealed an enthrallment with the exotic. Camus was fascinated by the fact that "Black people dance[d] alone" and that it is "total enjoyment at the same time collective and solitary." He also believed that the script was based on a "a marvellous [*sic*] history of love without a doubt the most beautiful of all time," and that Rio during carnival was a dignified scene for such a story.[52]

Camus was smitten by the beauty of the Brazilian capital and the people's energy during carnival. He roamed the city streets with his crew and visited favelas and sacred houses of Umbanda or Macumba, the Afro-Brazilian religion. Ultimately, he would recreate a movie version of a favela called Babilônia for filming in the actual favela called Babilônia, located in the current neighborhood of Leme, between the neighborhoods of Botafogo and Copacabana. For the visual pleasure of audiences outside of Brazil, Camus would deliver a rendition of the largest carnival celebration in the Western world in full Technicolor. The film's intent is evident from the opening lines of the film script: "All of Rio is in the throes of an intense agitation of the day before carnival. On the joyous streets, the people, already excited, dance and sing for no reason."[53] The French script illustrates Camus's commitment to showing the "fever of the last preparations" of carnival and to giving a sense of urgency as time passes rapidly before the last big parade and the period of introspection and sacrifice that Catholics call Lent.[54]

Camus also relied on his French ex-wife Andrée Feix to edit the film, and the Barcelona-born multifaceted artist Isabel Pons took charge of costume design. Pons had moved to Brazil in 1945 and became a Brazilian citizen in 1958. Afro-Brazilian cast members had little input in creating the story, mainly because they were all amateurs with little experience in the film industry. Yet, the cast and the hundreds of extras were central to bringing the story to life. As we will see, Camus played a major role in choosing the Black cast. He took a personal interest in the auditions held at the Maison de France in downtown Rio de Janeiro and traveled the city looking for his ideal protagonists. Camus developed a deep respect for Brazilian popular culture and personally contacted Afro-Brazilian samba schools and musicians he wanted to include in the sound score. Cultural affinity notwithstanding, the unequal and racially structural dynamics of the time benefited Gordine's French production company and rendered Afro-Brazilians invisible as cocreators or coproducers.

The film does not credit Camus's many Brazilian local cultural consultants, nor does it acknowledge the Black struggle that made Camus's Black casting possible. The invisibility of Black Brazilians on the production team (behind the camera) did not necessarily diminish Camus's commitment to Black representation. Camus committed to displaying Black aesthetics through language, music, and dance. He also clearly envisioned who he would cast as his main Black protagonists.[55] They would be beautiful Black performers that the postcolonial Eurocentric world would recognize as such. In addition, Camus would blend scenes of Black Brazilian life with scenes of beauty and magic that would surely be perceived as exotic by many audiences outside of Brazil. For some elite Brazilians, those scenes would be problematic.[56]

On Christmas Eve 1957, before the 1958 carnival season, Camus filmed three carnival nights and in February 1958 he filmed on Rio Branco Avenue in downtown Rio. That year, the samba school Portela carried the top prize for the carnival parade. Camus was enthusiastic about working with the samba schools and capturing their energy on film. The director was also preoccupied with assembling his cast. His publicists published sketched images of the Afro-Brazilian Orpheus and Eurydice in major newspapers in Rio. The sketches projected types of male and female Black beauty based on European ideas. Rather than meeting Black Brazilians first and judging their acting skills, the French producers imagined an ideal Black Brazilian male and female using drawings with defined features that served as models for the production team. The film's promotion attracted the attention of would-be Black actors and actresses, allowing Camus to meet Afro-Brazilians. He worked closely with the Black actors from TEN, many of whom had participated in the stage version of Orpheus.[57]

By September 1958, after Camus had assembled his cast, he began filming scenes.[58] He benefited from the vast cultural and intellectual respect Brazilians had for French culture and society. Rio's small French-speaking community and the Maison de France also helped.[59] Camus also knew that he would have to improvise as he had done in Saigon while filming *Mort en Fraude*. Even though he had a year and a half to study the culture and prepare to film, Camus confessed that it was still difficult. "Filming carnival went very well," he reported, "but waiting seven months to begin shooting was tiring." When the interviewer from *Arts* asked him why it was such a challenge to make the film, he explained that when Gordine was looking for partners and a distributor who would believe in the film. "No one would dare take it."[60] Moreover, Camus highlighted the fact that many producers and distributors harbored their doubts about a film with unknown Black actors set in an underdeveloped country like Brazil.[61]

Collaboration and Brazilian goodwill helped the French producers overcome the challenges. Vinicius de Moraes introduced Camus to Brazilian creatives, musicians, and many Afro-Brazilians. Moraes also collaborated with Viot on the final production. The transnational meetings in Rio were not without tension. Viot and Moraes had their differences as they translated from French to Portuguese and vice versa. Still, Viot had a wealth of experience and worked quickly with Moraes to translate the play into French and help create the Portuguese dialogue. The fact that both were poets helped a great deal.[62] In a publicity packet describing the hill where Orpheus lived, Viot's words set the tone for the script: "This morro is a rocky ridge that descends between two precipices in the heart of Rio. A little old tunnel passed below."[63] Viewed from a contemporary perspective, the descriptions smack of exoticism. Nonetheless, within the Orphic tradition and the political and social context of the Atlantic world in the 1960s, the film was also an elaborate transnational ode of longing and celebration beyond the confines of national borders.[64]

Although viewers continue to praise *Black Orpheus* for employing amateurs and unknown actors, it is important to note that this was only true about the film experience since several Black actors had already worked in the theater, and many wanted to become professionals. Still, Camus hired many other ordinary Brazilians with no theatrical and acting experience.[65] While critics considered many of the black-and-white Nouvelle Vague films avant-garde, too intellectual, and often inaccessible to international audiences, *Black Orpheus* merges myth with Afro-Brazilians' living celebration during carnival in Technicolor for a broader audience.[66]

Translating Brazil

Translators played critical roles in the globalization of *Black Orpheus*. Translation occurred in three phases. First, Moraes and Viot collaborated to adapt the original Portuguese play into the Portuguese and French script, even though the film credits Viot with the original script. Moraes probably translated most of the first dialogue from Portuguese to French. Viot and Camus worked on the French text's adaptation, dialogue, and editing for the producers, most of whom spoke no Portuguese. Camus accepted the challenge of directing the film based on the French script, and the film credits Viot and Camus for the adaptation and dialogue. Second, French and Portuguese could be heard on the set during the filming. Marpessa Dawn was more comfortable in French than Portuguese, even though she learned Portuguese for her role. Others, like Léa Garcia, understood French. The transnational production set was also translingual. Camus also relied on translators and interlocutors from the Maison de France to secure contacts and permissions to film from local authorities. Finally, because the film was entirely in Portuguese, it would eventually have to be subtitled (and dubbed) first in French for the French audience and then in English for audiences in the English-speaking world.[67]

Although almost all the production team members were French, Brazilian assistant director Bartolomeu de Andrade and Brazilian production assistant Silvio Autuori helped the production team navigate the city and Brazilian culture. Camus also met the beloved composer Cartola, who introduced him to other musicians from the samba schools, and Zika, his wife, who cooked for the crew.[68] As noted, Camus also benefited from the support of the Brazilian government, officials from Rio de Janeiro, and countless Brazilians who auditioned for the film, thanks to the publicity in local newspapers.[69]

When *Black Orpheus* received the Palme d'Or in Cannes, none of the Brazilian actors were present. However, Camus and Dawn had returned to France and were able to receive the award in Cannes and celebrate on behalf of the crew. When France won the Academy Award for Best Foreign Language Film the following year, it was clear that the film industry was officially rewarding the producers, the creatives behind the scenes, rather than the Brazilian performers in front of the camera. Audiences in France and the United States had their own view of the matter. Hattie McDaniel had been the lone Black presence on the American stage when she received the Academy Award for Best Supporting Actress in the 1939 movie *Gone with the Wind*. *Black Orpheus* was the first film with a Black cast to ever be recognized in France or the United States. For many this was a Brazilian movie, not a French one. After all, the entire dialogue was in Brazilian Portuguese, not in French. Thus, the Academy of Motion Picture Arts and Sciences awarded the Best Foreign Language Film award to a country that did not speak the language of the film. The Academy had only created the award in 1956, and unlike other awards, the nominations in this category were based on countries that produced films in languages other than English.[70]

Camus's film took Moraes's *Orpheus da Conceição* global through a medium that was becoming widely popular and ubiquitous in North American and European cities. He also packaged Brazil and Blackness for a global audience (assumed to be mostly White) in the late 1950s. He changed the Brazilian title to *Black Orpheus*, explicitly racializing the Orphic myth and adding elements he believed would capture a transnational audience. He relied on interlocutors and promoters in France and the United States after the movie's release. His experience among creatives in France, his travels in the developing world, and his international connections provided him with what Bourdieu has called a habitus that would facilitate the globalization of an image of Brazil and Brazilian Blackness.[71]

2

The Black Cast

Black casting, choosing Black actors and actresses for all the major roles, allowed Marcel Camus to make three significant contributions to the circulation and promotion of Black Brazilian popular culture. First, the film introduced new Black talent through a global cinematic platform in an era of limited Black representation. The main narrative also showcased Afro-Brazilian cultural and aesthetic practices. Second, the film utilized scenes, dialogues, and movement, albeit often at a relentless pace, to highlight Brazilian charm and joy during carnival in Rio de Janeiro. Finally, as a Black empowerment project, *Black Orpheus* served as a springboard and opportunity to promote the careers of many Afro-Brazilians. Many of them would pursue opportunities previously unavailable to Black Brazilians in Brazil. Many actors leveraged their connection to *Black Orpheus* to pursue additional projects. Their trajectories over time are part of the globalization of Afro-Brazilian culture. Indeed, Black and non-Black performers and actors made significant contributions to the global circulation of Black Brazilian images and music.

Directorial Power and Freedom Through Talent and Performance

Camus and the French crew exercised creative power throughout the project. Although the film's vision would evolve, Camus arrived with a general idea of what he wanted to do. His choice of Black casting was a clear top-down political statement. Camus was no White savior, however. He brought his version of Orpheus because Afro-Brazilians, who had been agitating for freedom and power for generations, agreed to work with him, as they had decided to work with Vinicius de Moraes. Indeed, hundreds of Afro-Brazilians gave of their time and talent, while using the opportunity to express their artistry and promote Afro-Brazilian culture. Samba schools would contribute to the aesthetics of the film, but actors and actresses from the Black Experimental Theater played a critical role in helping to portray main and minor characters.

TEN's goals partially coincided with Camus's. Abdias do Nascimento, TEN's director, wanted to place images of Black dignity on the stage and was keen to work with Black and White producers to accomplish that goal.[1] TEN's articulation of Blackness had emerged after World War II and would employ a language of representation that reflected the Brazilian situation. It also served the political ends of the group. As we have seen, other members of TEN, such as Haroldo Costa, were less interested in politics but wanted to display their commitment to celebrating Black culture through folklore, dance, music, and the arts. Costa cofounded the folkloric group Brasiliana and traveled worldwide, showcasing diverse Afro-Brazilian customs from Candomblé religious dances to popular songs and dances such as *capoeira*, *maracatu,* and the *coco*.[2]

Brazilians did not have input or final control over casting or editorial decisions, but the film is an excellent example of diversity within Rio de Janeiro's Afro-Brazilian community. Camus assembled a multigenerational cast with an array of skin tones, for example. Once cast, the Afro-Brazilians demonstrated their talents without exception. Meanwhile, Camus captured scenes of ordinary Brazilians performing in samba schools, marching bands, religious ceremonies, and living on the streets during carnival. Although Camus's curation came from an outside perspective thrilled with carnival, Afro-Brazilians in these scenes manifested a genuine joy and freedom that infused the script with life. This freedom aesthetic is connected to the African diasporic historical connection to music and dance as vehicles of inner freedom while under bondage. It emerges from time to time in many scenes with performers, including children. A survey of the biographies and trajectories of the performers who represented the main protagonists, selected characters and groups, and the child actors help us understand how the cast simultaneously performed within the gendered postwar framework of Camus's script and utilized the film to diffuse Brazilian culture and advance their careers.

The Main Lovers and Black Sensuality

As Euzhan Palcy affirmed, *Black Orpheus* presented Black sensuality in a matter-of-fact manner uncommon for the 1950s.[3] In commercial films in the United States, Brazil, or France, Black sexuality often appears on the silver screen in the form of hypersexual characters or filmmakers do not depict Black sexuality at all. Camus largely avoids sexual stereotypes, which Frantz Fanon tells us disregard the Black man's humanity because they fill White men with anxiety.[4] Donald Bogle and João Carlos Rodrigues delineate the major tropes in the American and Brazilian contexts. However, Rodrigues points out that some of the stereotypes emerge from the Black community.[5]

The romantic scenes between Orpheus and Eurydice show a tenderness between the two protagonists. In one scene filmed on the beach after Eurydice has fainted, Orpheus picks her up (as the leading men of commercial films do) and carries her back to her home, declaring, "You are in my arms now, Eurydice. My arms will protect you now and forever . . . I love you Eurydice." Camus juxtaposes another scene with Orpheus and Eurydice speaking to one another on her bed with a more comedic but equally sensual scene between Eurydice's cousin Serafina and her boyfriend Chico. In several scenes the camera highlights Orpheus's body on the hammock, Eurydice's beauty as she lays in her bed, and Serafina in her underwear as she undresses. *Black Orpheus* also uses images such as Serafina's feet on top of Chico's as she makes suggestive sounds and Eurydice lying on her back in her bed naked (under the sheets) as a bare-chested Orpheus sits on the bed and gazes at her. These scenes are remarkable precisely because they illustrate common heterosexual interactions long depicted and represented by White characters.

Camus challenged the status quo in the depiction of Black sensuality. At the same time, he also relied on his generation's typical gendered casting policies and notions of beauty. For generations, these values have shaped Latin American, European, and American societies. Orpheus represented the athletic, virile male who supposedly had many girlfriends before meeting Eurydice. He is also a versatile and talented dancer. Western audiences would associate these traits with Black men in general and with Latin Blackness in particular. It represented a revision, if not a parallel trope, of the 'Latin lover' that emerged in Hollywood with Rudolph Valentino in 1919.[6] Throughout the film, male and female characters recognize Orpheus's beauty and charm, often reaching out to protect him from Mira's wrath. No one in the film criticizes him for pursuing Eurydice while in a relationship with Mira. Instead, the film narrative encourages the audience to support Orpheus.

Black Orpheus's two major female characters, Eurydice and Mira, emerge as modified versions of the stereotypical Madonna/whore dichotomy first explained by Sigmund Freud at the beginning of the twentieth century and described in the Latin American context as Marianism by Evelyn P. Stevens in the 1970s. This dichotomy represents polar opposites of women within a limited constructed continuum.[7] The film presents Eurydice as an ideal and docile woman who comes from the countryside, yet another geographical trope that projected innocence or ingenuity.[8] On her arrival to the city by boat, the energy and excitement of the city during carnival overwhelms her. She receives directions to her destination from the blind man, reminiscent of the Greek figure

Tiresias, enforcing her image as an ingénue. Men in the port town admire her and give her unwanted attention before she is swept up by someone on the tram and taken to the end of the Babilônia tramline, where she meets Orpheus for the first time. Orpheus, the tram conductor, admires her beauty but calls her "boba" (silly) since she does not know exactly where she is going. Light-skinned Mira, presented as Eurydice's rival, competes for Orpheus's attention. She is on the other side of the Madonna/whore dichotomy. However, rather than introduce audiences to a prostitute, Camus chose to make Mira a loud, often uncontrollable, boisterous woman, a unique representation of the Greek maenads, the female followers of Dionysus, the male god of fertility, wine, pleasure, and madness, depending on the story. She is the on-screen opposite of Eurydice.

Visually, both women represent symbols of Black female beauty, although the film encourages the audience to identify with Eurydice from the beginning. The personal histories of Breno Mello, Marpessa Dawn, and Lourdes de Oliveira and their relationships with Camus and the film help shed light on each one's background and contribution to the global circulation of Afro-Brazil. Their talent and beauty showcased a specific Afro-Brazilian aesthetic that charmed European and North American audiences. At the same time, a closer look at the casting reveals a sexist system and a policing of female bodies. For example, Lourdes de Oliveira revealed that Camus told her that she needed to gain weight for the role, a directive that she promptly ignored. On another occasion, Moraes, who was helping with casting, told a journalist that he had inspected "thousands of Cabrochas" (Mulattas). It also points to a policing of Black women's bodies with an intent to transform them into ideals for the silver screen.[9] We can easily see those experiences today as problematic, although that behavior was ubiquitous in the 1950s and 1960s.

In Search of Orpheus

The French producers searched for a Black Orpheus who could be an example of Black male beauty for the world. The crew published images of this ideal Orpheus and Eurydice in the Brazilian newspaper *O Globo* and disseminated posters throughout the city. Although there were no known examples of colorism in the auditions and in the choosing of the final cast, the published images for the protagonists reveal a proclivity for slightly lighter skin tones and features not necessarily associated with Africans. The auditions drew hundreds of possible candidates, but in the end, one of Camus's team discovered Mello, a soccer player, on the streets of Copacabana.[10] Mello was an ideal choice because he was not a trained actor. His background in soccer would later help in the promotion of the film.[11] In Camus's view, Mello brought a natural, raw feeling to the Orpheus role. He was an excellent dancer and a quick learner with an innocent intensity, making him ideal for the protagonist. Nonetheless,

The New York Times criticized his acting, commenting that he was a better dancer than an actor, but most film reviews praise his authenticity, rawness, and on-screen charm.[12]

The soccer stadium represented the quintessential stage for the modern expression of prowess, masculinity, and accepted male beauty in Latin America and parts of Europe.[13] Mello first came to national attention as a soccer player for the Renner Football Club. In 1954, Renner won the Gaúcho (from the state of Rio Grande do Sul) state soccer championship. Mello's appearance on Renner's winning championship team in 1954 gained him national attention.[14] He went on to play with the Santos Football Club, where he met Edson Arantes do Nascimento, better known as Pelé, before moving to Fluminense, one of the celebrated teams in Rio de Janeiro.[15] In 1958, the year of the film's release, Brazil won the FIFA World Cup, and fans worldwide celebrated Pelé as the first global Black soccer hero. Following in Pelé's footsteps in the realm of cinema, Mello became the first Black Brazilian on screen to gain widespread international attention in an era when most of the leading men were White. Mello successfully captivated audiences precisely because of his good looks and acting skills.

Mello represented Black Brazil transnationally in various forums, although he was not able to travel to France for the Cannes Film Festival in 1959. However, in 1960, organizers in Mexico invited him to participate in the Cinematographic Festival to celebrate the most significant films that won prizes in 1959. Ironically, Mello represented France for *Black Orpheus*.[16] His status as a Black Brazilian cultural icon outside of Brazil cannot be underestimated in the post–World War II era when so few Afro-Brazilians held positions of visibility.[17] *Black Orpheus* had thrust Mello into the limelight at a moment when mainstream opportunities were rare for Black actors in general. Race films in the United States, explicitly produced for African American segregated audiences, provided limited opportunities for Black actors, but no equivalent existed in Brazil. Sidney Poitier and Harry Belafonte were two Black male actors who played romantic roles in Hollywood for national audiences in the late 1950s and 1960s, although these roles were not without controversy. According to Donald Bogle, most of Poitier's roles represented Blacks as respectable and upstanding citizens worthy of White acceptance.[18] Commenting on Belafonte's desexualized character in *Carmen Jones*, James Baldwin highlighted the prevailing White anxiety over Black men's sexuality.[19] In France, Black male actors also faced invisibility or association with hypersexuality. Habib Benglia, the French Black actor born in Algeria, was the sole Black actor to appear in commercial French films before the 1960s. Benglia had considerable talent but his roles in mainstream films, according to Nathalie Coutelet, were reduced to images associated with harems, orgies, polygamy, and sexual liberation. These images were constructed by French filmmakers while the 1934 Laval Decree prohibited Africans from filming images within the French colonies, effectively banning cinematic images of and by colonial Black subjects until 1960.[20]

Black Orpheus presented Mello as a Black Latin sex symbol, a new type of Latin lover who falls in love with the women destined for him. According to Mello, after the success of *Black Orpheus*, French producers went to Brazil and took him away from soccer. They offered him a contract with a monthly salary to participate in four films in two years. The first film, shot in the northeastern state of Bahia, was *Santo Módico*, directed by French filmmaker Robert Mazoyer, the assistant director to Camus on *Black Orpheus*. The other three films were never made or released. Nonetheless, after the success of *Black Orpheus*, Mello became what Michael Hanchard would call an exceptional Afro-Brazilian. In fact, Mello claimed that at this time he never experienced racism. He entered places where Afro-Brazilians were not allowed to go. On one occasion, he took his mother with him. In many respects, like Pelé, Mello temporarily rose above his racialized inferior position because of his fame.

Mello received other invitations to act in films. In *Rata de Puerto* (released in 1963), directed by René Mugica, Mello played the benevolent priest Father Honorio, fighting against Pablo, the town's "rat," played by Wolf Ruvinskis.[21] Mello also appeared in *Os Vencidos* (*The Vanquished Ones*) in 1963. The film tackled taboos surrounding interracial relations and class four years before the groundbreaking international film *Guess Who's Coming to Dinner?* The film focuses on a young White girl who falls in love with a Black fisherman in a small village when such images were not part of Brazilian or American cinema. Mello did not appear in another film until the 1973 *O Negrinho do Pastoreio* (*The Black Man from Pastoreio*) with Grande Otelo. *Black Orpheus* continued to circulate globally, but Mello could no longer support himself from acting.

According to Mello's ex-wife Mana de Xangô, "Mello *was* Orpheus, a charmer and somebody who loved life. He lived with this image of himself for the rest of his life, but he never received the attention he received from Camus's film." Xangô also noted that the lack of attention in his home country often frustrated him and eventually led to bad health, isolation, and a precarious economic situation where he was exhausted and depressed.[22] In her homage to her ex-husband, Xangô penned the poem "Orfeu" in 2007, which criticized him for living in the past and not being able to develop and commit to a relationship with her, his real-life "Eurídice": "I don't want to stay in the past . . ." she writes. "You will feel the sadness/ And the perfume that used to be mine. You will feel the presence of your Eurídice/ Because for me, you will be the great love called Orpheus, eternally.[23] When Mello died in a humble house in the neighborhood called Tristeza (Sadness), neither his family nor his neighbors noticed his absence for some time. "It was his heart," one of his five sons revealed by phone to the Spanish newspaper *El País*. *El País* also underscored the connection between Mello and his tragic on-screen character, as he died abandoned and alone.[24]

Mello had only been recognized in Cannes three years prior to his death. His trajectory from on-screen idol to abandonment is representative of many other stories of Black cultural icons throughout Afro-Latin America. They point to the weak social safety nets and the inability of many Afro-Latin Americans to sustain a decent living, no matter their contributions to society. Structural racism continues to marginalize Afro-Atlantic peoples. Yet, Mello helped introduce scores of foreigners to a charmed Brazil in the 1950s. His character personified what Stefan Zweig called a "Land of the Future"—a country that audiences wished existed, where people celebrated despite poverty, melancholy, and death.[25] Mello's on-screen image and that of the on-screen Eurydice, shaped by the idealized gender roles of the 1950s, contributed to the idea of Brazil.

The Accidental Eurydice: Marpessa Dawn, the African American 'Brazilian'

Marpessa Dawn's role in promoting and representing Black Brazil as a non-Brazilian is remarkable and complex. Her path to securing the role connects to the story of African Americans in France. Vinicius de Moraes wanted to cast the Afro-Brazilian singer Maria d'Apparecida, who was living in Paris in the 1950s, as Eurydice. When Moraes divulged to the magazine *Manchete* that d'Apparecida was going to be Eurydice, producer Sacha Gordine gently admonished him since Camus's team had not begun auditions: "I find it is premature to announce Maria d'Apparecida," he wrote in a letter in May of 1956, "since it is not certain that she will be the person to play Eurydice."[26] When Camus began the auditions in Rio de Janeiro, his crew published a drawing of his female protagonist along with the image of the ideal Orpheus. In the publication, Eurydice has a light brown complexion, ambiguous somatic features not necessarily identifiable with African traits, and long straight hair. These aesthetic choices eliminated Black women with short hair, afros, or other styles.

After many auditions, Camus believed he had found his perfect Eurydice, but she abandoned the project due to pressure from her boyfriend. Camus turned to Gordine, who helped him secure the American-born Marpessa Dawn, a dark Black woman with long hair whom he had met in Paris. Dawn's American background is imperceptible to global audiences. Once in Rio de Janeiro, she immersed herself in the culture and studied Portuguese lines. According to fellow actress Léa Garcia, Dawn liked Brazil. She "got along with everyone on the set, Brazilians and French, although she seemed to spend more time with the French producers since she lived in the hotel."[27] This was, after all, part of her habitus. Like her compatriot Josephine Baker before her, Dawn's connections in Paris allowed her to gain access to global projects like *Black Orpheus*.

Dawn's Journey from the Local to the Global

Born in Redstone, Fayette County, Pennsylvania, in 1934, Marpessa Dawn Menor attended school in the town called Republic, where the African American population was small. Several sources indicate that Dawn's father was Filipino, although she was clearly a part of the African American community in the pre–World War II United States.[28] Dawn eventually moved to New York, where she received attention by winning the Shriners Talent and Beauty contest in 1951.[29] At the time, Blacks were not allowed to compete in the Miss America beauty competition, so the Shriners, a Black fraternity organization, sponsored Black beauty pageants. They aimed to help African American women earn money for college and raise funds for a host of other charities.[30]

According to *The New York Times*, as a teenager, Dawn moved to England, where she began to take minor acting roles in the theater before moving to France, where she worked as a governess to earn money. She also danced and sang in nightclubs.[31] Dawn appeared briefly in the classic twenty-one-minute 1955 film *Afrique sur Seine* by the Senegalese filmmakers Mamadou Sarr and Paulin Soumanou Vieyra. In the French film *La fille Élisa* (Roger Richebé, 1957),[32] Dawn plays the Black female supporting character, 'The Negresse.' These minor roles in local productions allowed Dawn to showcase her talent and meet directors, actors, and producers in the Parisian film and theater industries.

Garcia's observations underscore Dawn's French connections and the saliency of linguistic connections over race, although she was reportedly the only Black person who came with the French crew. Brazil and Brazilian culture were still new to her, and she spent most of her time off set rehearsing her lines and practicing Portuguese. Photographs from the set show a relaxed and confident actress. Like many North American Black performers who found freedom and opportunities outside the United States, Dawn quickly became used to transnational travel and new cross-cultural encounters and languages. She had met British, French, and African filmmakers. The success of *Black Orpheus* also gave her a new role as a promoter of Afro-Brazilian culture in Europe. Many observers outside Brazil believed that she was Brazilian.

Breno Mello did not travel to Cannes for the award ceremony in 1959, but given that France had become Dawn's adopted country, she would play an essential role in promoting the film in Europe, especially in Cannes.[33] Her promotion involved talking about Brazil and performing limited dance and musical productions, even though she had not done either in the film. However, Dawn did participate in the major samba dance scene during carnival rehearsals in the film. In Cannes, Dawn performed an interpretative dance to "Manhã de carnival," the film's theme song, with an image of the Bay of Guanabara in the background. She was also interviewed about her relationship with Brazil and her role in the film, and she often lent her celebrity status to causes in France. Her determination, music, and dance skills and connection with Brazilians helped her promote Brazilian music in the French capital.

Dawn made personal appearances at various venues to promote *Black Orpheus*. In 1960, she appeared in person at Curzon in London.[34] As late as the 1970s, she appeared with Brazilian actress Lourdes de Oliveira (now Camus's wife), who played Mira in the film, to promote Brazilian culture in France. She also recorded Brazilian music. Throughout the 1960s and 1970s, Dawn participated in several smaller productions with no connection to Brazil, although audiences continued to associate her with *Black Orpheus*. Other cinema appearances included her roles as an exotic native girl in *The Women Eater* and in the 1961 film *Le trésor des hommes bleus*. Dawn also continued to appear on French television. In 1964, she performed Djalma Ferreira's composition "Recado bossa nova" ("Bossa nova message") on the French television program *Ce soir à la Grande Séverine*, for example.[35]

Like Mello, Dawn's talent and beauty as a lead Afro-Brazilian character had thrust her into the limelight and opened new opportunities. Europe presented more opportunities for her to perform and advance her career than Mello. However, most of the characters she played abroad were exotic or foreign women. She also enjoyed some musical success singing and recording Brazilian music in Portuguese as well as French songs. *Black Orpheus* had taken Dawn global, and this new visibility also brought her attention from the Anglophone world. In London, Dawn starred in the Richard Rogers musical about an American woman who lives in Paris. Journalists across the globe tended to describe her in exotic terms and often misidentified her. One newspaper compared her to Diahann Carroll, lightening her complexion. *The New Yorker* called her a "light-colored Puerto Rican who lived in Philly and Rio."[36] By the 1970s, Dawn's opportunities began to diminish, as did her association with Brazil.[37] There is no evidence that Dawn ever returned to Brazil or cultivated relationships with her Brazilian costars. Two of them, Léa Garcia and Lourdes de Oliveira, developed international and national connections of their own.

The Supporting Brazilian Actresses

Afro-Brazilian actresses Léa Garcia and Lourdes de Oliveira were central to the globalization of Brazilian popular culture. Both women arrived in Paris in January 1960 to promote their second film with Marcel Camus. He shot *Os Bandeirantes* (*The Pioneers*) in the Amazon with a French and Brazilian crew and gave them parts in the film along with Maria Alice, one of the children who appeared in *Black Orpheus*. This second transnational collaboration, which starred two European leads, did not receive the global recognition of its predecessor. Nor did it focus on Black Brazil. Still, Garcia and Oliveira attracted the attention of French television in front of the Eiffel Tower.

Posters of Garcia and Oliveira, along with images of Marpessa Dawn and Breno Mello, had graced the pages of several major newspapers, magazines, and cinema marquees for several months in late 1959. Garcia and Oliveira taped a television interview in front of the Eiffel Tower. They danced the *samba* barefoot in front of a monument, promoting an image of Brazilian merriment based on the rhythm that *Black Orpheus* highlighted. This symbol of Black Brazil was on display in front of France's most recognizable symbol.[38] Garcia and Oliveira were part of a small but growing group of Afro-Brazilian performers abroad. Garcia would eventually return to Brazil, while Oliveira, who married Camus, remained in France for the rest of her life. Throughout the 1960s and 1970s, Oliveira would give interviews to the French press and appeared on French television to promote Brazilian culture. Oliveira's connection to the *Black Orpheus* project provides us with additional information on the gendered dynamics of filmmaking in the 1950s.

Lourdes de Oliveira-Camus

Oliveira was not a professional film actress, but she was not unfamiliar with the world of performers. Her father, Darcy de Oliveira, a White Brazilian composer and *pandeiro* player, was originally from Porto Alegre, Rio Grande do Sul.[39] Her mother, Dona Odila Riberio, was an Afro-Brazilian *Carioca* woman from humble origins. Blogger Sando Buys's description of family documents and Jean-Christophe Camus's magnificent graphic novel *Negrinha* provide several insights into the family dynamics and the racism his grandmother faced, though Oliveira, born in 1938, recalled that she enjoyed "a happy childhood without any great surprises."[40]

In *Black Orpheus*, Oliveira's character, Mira, represents Eurydice's adversary. Audiences see her from the onset as an obstacle to the destined union between the two main lovers. She is a talented, light-skinned Black woman with a vital role in the carnival parade. In a hysterical fit of jealousy, after she finds out about Orpheus and Eurydice, Mira ultimately throws a stone at his head, killing him instantly.

From her apartment in the fifteenth arrondissement in Paris at the beginning of the twentieth-first century, Oliveira recalled her first audition in 1956 with her "angel," as she called her late husband: "I said hello to him, and he looked at me. He asked if I had already worked in cinema. I responded, 'Non.' [He then told me]: You are good. You have the profile. Your face corresponds to the criteria, but you are a little skinny. You must eat more and then come back and see me. He wrote a list of foods that I should eat to put on weight. That made me smile."[41]

Despite their romantic ties, Camus's comments about Oliveira gaining weight and his suggestions of foods to eat are indicative of the gendered and often sexist relationship between male directors and female actresses. At the same time, it is important to recognize that many film characters call for specific profiles, and Camus wanted Mira to look a certain way. In any event, as Oliviera reported, she did not gain a pound. She asserted her agency and found a way to secure the role.[42]

Oliveira also recorded Brazilian music in France. The record *Os Maracatú—Ritmos do Brasil* (*Brazilian Rhythms*) was released in 1973. By the time she finished working on her third film with Camus, *Otália da Bahia*, she had become a bridge between French and Brazilian culture. She appeared on French television to promote the film and to serve as a translator for Mira Fonseca, the young Brazilian actress who plays the lead role in the film.

In 1971, Oliveira visited the publicly funded College of General and Professional Education (Cégep) with Marpessa Dawn to celebrate the fortieth anniversary of the center with a tribute to *Black Orpheus* and Rio de Janeiro. At the event, Oliveira told the audience that the film had exported the city's image worldwide and that the "silted shadows of the beaches of Ipanema and Copacabana have been recorded for eternity."[43] On another occasion to commemorate the centenary of Marcel Camus's birth, she thanked the village where he was born during a ceremony dedicating a square to her husband: "Thank you to the mayor, to Madame Deputy, and to all the wonderful inhabitants of Les Chappes for this beautiful day! Kind regards to all of you from the Camus family."[44] The square was a signpost that cemented her husband's legacy, who had brought people together from across the globe. When talking about Camus's legacy, Oliveira insisted on the critical importance of *Black Orpheus* for Brazil, promoting the legacy of her husband, who "loved Brazil."[45] Indeed, Oliveira-Camus's presence in France with her children allowed her to play a continued role in the circulation of Brazilian culture for decades and as a contact for Brazilian in France. Léa Garcia was also one such Brazilian.

Léa Garcia as Serafina

Léa Garcia expressed her gratitude to Camus when she learned of his death in 1982. "As a filmmaker, Marcel Camus was my father," Léa Garcia intimated in her interview with the daily newspaper *O Globo*. She repeated this in an interview in August 2010.[46] Garcia had played Mira in Moraes's play, but Camus cast her as Serafina, Eurydice's urbane cousin and protector.[47] Garcia found out about the film production through the Black Experimental Theater and was keen for the opportunity to appear in the film. She went personally to the

Maison de France in downtown Rio to try out for the role of Eurydice, although she was cast as Serafina.[48]

Camus was a "good director," she remembered, although life was not easy. Garcia married Abdias do Nascimento, and they had two children together. When they separated, she was the primary parent responsible for raising her children while also taking care of her grandmother. Still, as roles began to appear, directors sought out Garcia. After her two films with Camus, she began to appear in other movies and in telenovelas on Brazilian television for a predominantly national audience. In many respects, Brazilian telenovelas provided actors and actresses with more opportunities and better pay than Brazilian cinema, leading Mauro Alencar to describe Brazilian telenovelas as "the Brazilian Hollywood."[49] This Brazilian Hollywood also suffered from many of the racist ills of its American counterpart. Joel Zito, one of the few contemporary Afro-Brazilian directors in Brazil, exposed the racism and exclusion in his book and documentary *Denying Brazil*.[50] Many of the telenovelas also attained the global reach of some Hollywood films. Garcia appeared as the enslaved woman Rosa in three episodes of TV Globo's 1976 telenovela *A escrava Isaura* (*The Slave Girl Isaura*). The telenovela attained global success and was broadcast in more than eighty countries according to IMDb.[51] Not until 2004, however, did she appear in another majority-Black film focusing on the Afro-Brazilian experience. She performed in Joel Zito's *Filhas do Vento* alongside Ruth de Souza and Taís Araújo.

Garcia's Trajectory

Born in 1933, Garcia emerged as a Black icon in her own right by the late 1960s. Indeed, she was the only main actor from the *Black Orpheus* project to develop a long and illustrious career in Brazilian cinema and television. Garcia was not politically active when she first started acting, but she soon became a champion of Black rights in the theater, cinema, and TV. She was also unequivocal about the importance of *Black Orpheus* to her film career and to Afro-Brazilians. According to Garcia, Camus had given many Black actors and performers opportunities not available to them in the Brazilian film industry. He was sincere and generous in his approach and continued to support Black artists well into the 1980s. Camus showed that it was racism and not lack of talent that kept many Black artists out of national spaces.[52]

Like many young Brazilian women of her generation, Garcia recalls that American films captivated her. When she saw American actresses such as Esther Williams and Lena Horne on the screen, she remembered imagining with her friends Dulce and Regina that she could one day be an actress like one of them. Unlike Lourdes de Oliveira, who had emigrated to France and eventually retreated from an active career in acting, Garcia's performance in Camus's two films, *Black Orpheus* and *Os Bandeirantes*, garnered her national attention in

Brazil. Today, Brazilians regard her and Ruth de Souza as two of Brazilian cinema's most influential Black female pioneers. According to João Carlos Rodrigues, Garcia is one of the few Black actors to successfully hone their craft and play diverse roles over an extended career.[53]

Garcia had also participated in Nascimento's theatrical productions in the 1950s and 1960s, including his Brazilian adaptations of *Emperor Jones*, *Todos os Filhos de Deus tem Asas* (*All of God's Children Have Wings*), and *Onde Está Marcada a Cruz* (*Where the Cross Is Made*). All the plays were written by Eugene O'Neill, with whom Nascimento had developed a relationship through correspondence. She also received accolades for her performance in Lúcio Costa's *O Filho Pródigo* (*The Prodigal Son*) and Abdias do Nascimentos' *Sortilégio* (*Black Mystery*). According to Garcia, her early international exposure and experience in *Black Orpheus* earned her attention from Brazilian and international filmmakers. She forged a relationship with Cacá Diegues on his films *Ganga Zumba* and *O Maior Amor do Mundo* (*The Greatest Love in the World*) and with Sylvio Back on *Cruz e Sousa, Poeta do Desterro* (*Cruz e Sousa: Poet of Exile*). Garcia's films helped her to become one of the first Black actresses to break into Brazilian Hollywood at a time when the military dictatorship censured television programs. Despite the pressure on the predominantly White writers for the telenovela *A escrava Isaura*, Garcia was able to play a multidimensional enslaved woman. Her character Rosa utilized all the tools at her disposal to assert herself in a cruel world, including vengeance, deception, and seduction.[54] In 1981, Garcia appeared in the telenovela *Marina*. According to fellow actor Milton Gonçalves, Garcia was able to play any character and shape a dignified Black image for Brazilian audiences.[55]

Léa Garcia also used her relatively privileged place in Brazilian film and television history to support other Black actors and actresses. At the same time, she did not shy away from roles that touched on and criticized racism. While working on the set of *Marina*, Garcia asked the writers to rewrite the text to demonstrate more racial sensitivity, for example. Unhappy with the dialogue, Garcia organized a meeting at the Instituto de Pesquisa da Cultura Negra (The Institute for Research on Black Culture or IPCN) in Lapa, the historic downtown neighborhood in Rio, to discuss the text. The meeting resulted in a list of suggested revisions from the point of view of African descendants. Acts such as these have endeared Garcia to the younger Afro-Brazilians struggling to find a place in contemporary Brazil.[56]

Other Afro-Brazilian Actors on the Silver Screen

For Camus, it would have been impossible to celebrate Black popular culture without filming carnival and elements from Afro-Brazilian religious customs. To do this, he relied on various Brazilian personalities, including the musician

Agenor de Oliveira, popularly known as Cartola, and his wife Dona Zica. Cartola appears briefly in the film with Dona Zica when Orpheus and Mira go to the Civil Registry for a marriage license. They appear nicely dressed together outside the Registry shyly trying to steal a kiss when Mira and Orpheus enter. Both of them had one line. Zica's character asks, "Give me a kiss," and Cartola's character answers, "People are coming." The presence of Cartola, one of the early masters of Brazilian samba, and his wife Zica had special meaning for the Afro-Brazilian community. Cartola was also able to help with the production of the samba school scenes and the costumes, while Zica cooked for the technical crew. Cartola went on to play a role in Diegues's *Ganga Zumba*, one of the most important films of Black Brazil, in 1963. In 1956, close to the time Camus would meet Cartola, the journalist Sérgio Porto discovered the musician working as a bricklayer and brought him to the public's attention. This led to his career's resurrection, partnerships with middle-class musicians in the Zona Sul, and economic stability. He and his wife Zica also opened their restaurant, Zicarola on Rua da Carioca, in the center of the city. *Black Orpheus* did not change his career, but Cartola's participation was another emblematic phenomenon that honored Black Brazil.[57]

The participation of the Escola de Capela, Salgueiro, Portela, and Mangueira resulted in the samba schools also providing critical live footage. *Black Orpheus* was not a documentary, but it preserved historical footage of Rio's street carnival music, dance, and art before the celebration changed and eventually moved to the Sambódromo Marquês de Sapucaí in 1984. For the staged scenes, Camus often gave the performers flexible directions to perform in unison or to move in one direction or the other, but the samba schools played and performed their music as if they were in the actual carnival parade.[58] In addition, the film includes scenes of the Afro-Brazilian religion Umbanda as a device to take Orpheus from the world of the living to the underworld to retrieve his beloved. This choice was also innovative for the time. Henri-Georges Clouzot, who was married to the Brazilian actress Véra Gibson Amado, was perhaps the first French film director to attempt to film scenes of African religions in the early 1950s. Clouzot had begun to film a documentary in Paris but was denied approval from the Brazilian government because of the subject's sensitivity. Instead, he published his *Le Cheval des Dieux*, which contained various photographs, in 1951.[59] Six years later, Camus was able to consult with Umbanda practitioners. In *Black Orpheus*, he utilized the figure of an Afro-Brazilian oracle as an example of what he had experienced. The director recreated scenes of a ceremony that he had witnessed and included music that often leads to possession (or 'mounting') of humans by the spirits to help him tell the story of Orpheus's descent into the underworld. Camus utilizes an unknown woman, seemingly in a trance, to convey the idea of the underworld.[60]

Mello was not the only athlete in the movie. Camus cast Afro-Brazilian two-time triple jump Olympic champion Adhemar da Silva from São Paulo to represent the figure of death. Silva won the gold medal in 1952 and 1956. He is dressed in a dark spandex-like costume with white markings and wears a mask of the same color. Throughout the film, da Silva jumps over walls, runs through various scenes, and slips into crowds seemingly unnoticed before leading Eurydice to her downfall in the tramway station.[61] Alexandro Constantino (Hermes) and Waldemar de Souza (Chico) were two other Afro-Brazilian personalities in *Black Orpheus.* Constantino played the older tram driver who helped Eurydice make her way to her cousin Serafina's house. In contrast, de Souza played Serafina's navy boyfriend visiting her in Rio during carnival. Chico and Serafina's love and romance in the story are light, comedic, and carefree, providing a fun and uncomplicated relationship between two Black lovers living a dignified life around joyous neighbors despite the poverty that surrounded them. They also counterbalance the deep and complicated love between the main protagonists.

Black children also play a critical role in the film. Throughout the favela, children interact with adults but also command scenes on their own. In an early scene, Orpheus plays soccer with boys near the tram station. Children are also present throughout the carnival scenes and in the favela. Three of them, Zeca (Aurino Cassiano), Benedito (Jorge dos Santos), and a young girl (Maria Alice), animate the film with a sense of charm and wonderment as fans of Orpheus and the Orphic tradition.[62] Orpheus's music especially enamors the children. They are also the heirs of Brazilian poetry and music who will carry on the traditions for future generations. When the children discover that Orpheus has died, Benedito takes the guitar and begins to play as they all dance as the sun rises. This tragedy, a myth that does not belabor poverty, violence, or death in the Brazilian shantytown, ultimately celebrates life and rebirth. At the same time, the film often presents the boys in dirty or torn clothes. At the movie's end, Maria Alice appears well-dressed in a beautiful white dress and white sandals—the epitome of innocence and a new beginning. In one scene in the middle of the film, just before Orpheus meets Eurydice, the two boys appear barefoot in the conspicuously dilapidated shack. These images reinforced a sense of innocence and a romanticized view of the favela, resonating with earlier European observers such as Stefan Zweig when he wrote from Brazil that he and his wife liked Brazil because life was like in the times of his parents and grandparents and that "people are so extremely nice and even clean in their great poverty." He also remarked that "the poor people are so nice here as you cannot imagine."[63]

Most of the child actors play small parts in future films, but they also garnered attention because of their experience in *Black Orpheus*. Aurino Cassiano went on to play roles in *My Destiny in Your Hands* (1963) and *Vai que é mole*

(*Go, Its Easy*, 1960). Jorge dos Santos also secured roles in *The Golden Mouth* (1963) and *O Santo Módico* (*Holy Modicum*, 1964). Maria Alice will also appear in multiple roles.

Conclusion

Black Orpheus's interpretation of Moraes's vision consciously centered on Black Latin subjects, Black beauty, and the Black music of carnival. In her insightful comparison of Camus's *Black Orpheus* to Cacá Diegues's *Orfeu*, Myrian Sepúlveda dos Santos points to the cultural and aesthetic reasons why Camus's film resonated with global audiences in the 1950s and 1960s and why Diegues's film did not receive comparable reviews abroad in the late 1990s. Dos Santos criticizes Camus's foreign gaze but also underscores how Camus appealed to the mass audiences' sensory perceptions through a Technicolor lens that gives viewers an omniscient and detached yet emotional experience through the music. While Sepúlveda documents "most" Brazilians' criticism of Camus's film, she does not necessarily focus on the impact, exposure, opportunities, and experiences offered to Black actors and actresses. Moreover, Camus's representation was not necessarily less problematic than many Brazilian films of the era. As we have seen, the film also rearticulated popular perceptions about Brazilian culture, including indirect references to racial democracy, an idea that there was no racial discrimination in Brazil, for a new generation of foreign audiences. The film is also less politically engaged and does not encourage viewers to question issues such as Blackness and poverty.

While many film historians and critics have treated *Black Orpheus* as a literary product, the film is also a historical signpost of the Black Atlantic and of global Brazil during the 1960s. Charles Perrone explains how the lasting appeal is wrapped into the shots of the magnificent Brazilian landscape and the vibrant and pleasurable depictions of popular culture.[64] Perrone also concurred that the movie and the soundtrack have been forceful vehicles for propagating ideas about Brazil and that many scholars began studying Brazil after seeing the film.[65] The film and Brazilian music inspired collaborations and transnational links between Brazilian and French creative artists, such as the musicians Pierre Barouh and Georges Moustaki and the actress Brigitte Bardot.[66]

The movie also showcased talented Brazilian actors and actresses who embody pleasing gendered roles for mainstream audiences of the time. Thanks to Brazilian extras and performers, the film captured Brazilian culture in all its splendor. Walter Benjamin saw the possibilities of a cinematic experience to create a new aesthetic experience distinct from traditional notions of art.[67] The understanding of the iconic relationship between film and the organization of human behavior must necessarily grapple with Blackness on the screen. The diverse Black cast represented a new aesthetic and political experience, especially given the dominant anti-Black aesthetics of the Atlantic world. The romantic love story that takes place during the carnival created a magical possibility in an age of racial tensions. The all-Black cast was revolutionary for Brazil, France, and the United States. *Black Orpheus* was also responsible for advancing the careers of many of its actors. The film inspired many others and provided an entry into Brazilian culture through the global media.[68]

3

The Soundtrack

Brazilian music played an essential part in the globalization of *Black Orpheus*. The technical advancements of the film and music industries allowed for art reproduction in what Walter Benjamin dubbed "the Age of Mechanical Reproduction."[1] Thanks to the ability to reproduce film reels, audiences could experience a film version of Black Brazil in select movie houses across the globe. The reproduction of parts or the entire soundtrack in the form of singles or albums allowed listeners to re-experience Brazilian sounds and voices in general and Black Brazil in particular. White Brazilian musicians such as Tom Jobim, Antônio Maria, and Luiz Bonfá helped Afro-Brazilian singer Agostinho dos Santos frame his performance in the film. Anonymous Afro-Brazilian instrumentalists, and the Capella, Salgueiro, Portela, and Mangueira samba schools (overlayed by studio recordings) reproduced the carnival ambiance and infused the work with emotions.

The global dissemination of the soundtrack also anticipated João Gilberto's groundbreaking 1959 bossa nova album *Chega de saudade*. The music of *Black Orpheus* anticipates and provides an early sample of bossa nova, which Gilberto insisted was a form of samba. Agostinho dos Santos and Elizeth Cardoso provided the voices for the recorded soundtrack on the album. Musicians across the globe would cover their songs in multiple languages. The records also immortalized a diverse array of Afro-Brazilian popular forms performed by Black Brazilian carnival and popular community groups for a global audience. It would have been impossible for entire community groups to travel and reproduce those sounds transnationally in live performances the way that individual and small groups could. According to Vinicius de Moraes's

FIGURE 2 Photo of Agostinho dos Santos, singing at a radio studio in São Paulo. Santos is Orpheus's singing voice in *Black Orpheus*. Credit: Public domain / Arquivo Nacional Collection

daughter Suzana de Moraes, Black rhythms are the base of all Brazilian popular musical forms.[2] The soundtrack juxtaposed the rich percussive exuberance of very popular Brazilian rhythms from the *marchinha* (marching band tunes) to different types of samba, such as the *samba de roda* (street or circle samba), the *samba enredo* (themed samba that narrates a story), the slower *samba-canção,* and sounds that many consider precursors to the bossa nova.

Black Orpheus celebrated Black Brazil and preserved many Afro-Brazilian popular musical traditions of the 1950s, including the *frevo*, the *batuque*, and the sounds of the Afro-Brazilian religion Umbanda on film. The film's music and the official soundtrack wove together merriment and melancholy, poetry and the vibrancy of the samba percussion.[3] The dissonance between the more percussive elements and the slow lyricism of the *samba-canção* set the stage for the development of the bossa nova. More importantly, the film score and the recording took Afro-Brazil global through reproducible global technologies. When *Black Orpheus* received the Palme d'Or at Cannes, Philips, the French record label, had already begun producing an LP record of the music on the soundtrack. Soon after the film's release in French cinema on June 12, 1959, the music became widespread, and many French adaptions quickly emerged. The same dynamics occurred in the United States. After the film's appearance in December 1959, Epic Records released records in early 1960.[4]

Ultimately, the film celebrates a multicultural and polychromatic Black Brazil, although it uses the Carioca urban coastal landscape as its main geographical symbol. It simultaneously records Afro-Brazilian and national music forms in a dynamic manner with broad transnational appeal. By presenting diverse music styles, aesthetics, and sensibilities with racial and class overtones, the movie captures the genius of Brazilian music of the time. The film was not explicitly didactic. Indeed, no one on the project was interested in making an overtly political movie, but the choice of actors and singers and the aesthetic choices clarified the political intent. As Haroldo Costa explains in an interview in early 2023, identity and politics may be necessary, but presenting Black aesthetics in art and music is what allows the artist to align with the Black population.[5] Even critics of the film, such as Caetano Veloso, lavished praise on the movie's soundtrack.[6]

Black cultural producers lacked power in the film and recording industries of the 1950s and 1960s. Indeed, as we have seen no Afro-Brazilians or Afro-French producers or editors worked on the movie or the soundtrack. Still, Marcel Camus and Moraes relied on influential Afro-Brazilian performers such as Agostinho dos Santos and Elizeth Cardoso[7] to create what they deemed as authentic Afro-Brazilian aesthetics and 'feel.' The mixture of talents and styles helped music go global in the 1960s when multinational music and entertainment companies searched for new opportunities to promote it. The stories of the musicians help us understand the global appeal of *Black Orpheus* in the post–World War II era.

Musical Antecedents and Precursors

Music played a central role in the construction of an image of Black Brazil abroad well before the production of *Black Orpheus*. Yet even before the 1950s, foreign and Brazilian musicians played critical roles in circulating popular Brazilian culture for French audiences since the nineteenth century. In France, for example, Jacques Offenbach's 1866 music for the opéra bouffe *La vie parisienne* included a number called "The Brazilian" or "Le Brésilien." Inspired by the composition "Le Brésilien" from an earlier stage play, Offenbach and the librettists Henri and Ludovic Halévy drew from French and European conventions and aesthetics for light comedy and did not incorporate Brazilian musical traditions. However, they presented French audiences with a humorous critique of the ostentatious Brazilian elite who traveled to Paris, creating a lasting image that has continued to this day.[8] While cultural intermingling and syncretism have been de facto influences on the creation of Brazilian society since the arrival of Europeans and Africans who intermingled with Amerindians in the fifteenth century, ideas of Brazil as a hybrid nation free of racial prejudice only emerged as a patriotic trope after the end of slavery and the emergence of the United States as a hegemonic power.[9]

Black Brazilian musicians such as the men in the Oito Batutas, including the pioneer Alfredo da Rocha Vianna Filho (better known as Pixinguinha), made important marks on Parisian audiences when they traveled there in 1922. They were the visible exceptions. The band performed in various venues for approximately six months before returning to Brazil.[10] Their trip to Paris also positively impacted the band members' careers. After the war, non-Black Brazilians such as Heitor Villa-Lobos helped meet the demand for Brazilian music in France. Although a classical musician, Villa-Lobos shared his knowledge and love for popular Brazilian music with his French contacts when he lived in Paris. Villa-Lobos, who did not identify as Afro-Brazilian, went to Paris in the 1920s and returned after the war. He performed with Elsie Houston, a woman of African descent who performed various folkloric customs including African and Amerindian music and dances for Parisian audiences. She often gave ethnographic explanations of her work.[11] In 1952, Villa-Lobos made the Hotel Bedford his Parisian home.[12]

Meanwhile, after she moved to the United States, Carmen Miranda emerged as the most popular Brazilian global symbol after she donned a camp version of Afro-Bahian woman. Miranda's role as a promotor of Brazilian popular music from 1929 to 1939 earned her the title of the 'Queen of Popular Music.' She embodied Brazilian popular music and became a de facto promotor of popular Black rhythms and forms, such as the *batucada* and the samba, both within and outside her adopted country. Miranda's commitment to Brazilian popular music at a time when many of the middle and upper classes shunned Black music is well documented. So are the restrictions against Black artists. At the same time, the Brazilian elite criticized her for promoting what they called 'Black music.'[13] The Brazilian positive reaction to the Oito Batutas reception in Paris make them an exception.[14]

Miranda's *Bahiana* became one of Brazil's most recognized global images, largely due to the series of commercial films produced by Hollywood. Conscious of the power dynamics inherent to her own appropriation, Miranda never sang or performed her music in a straightforward manner. By the time of her death in 1955, the Brazilian performers representing Brazilians abroad had already become more diverse, with performers including Sílvio Caldas, Elizeth Cardoso, and D'Alva de Oliveira, who performed in Argentina and Portugal. None of them would attain the global impact of Miranda, however. Nor did any of them move abroad.

The music of Lima Barreto's 1953 *O Cangaceiro* earned a transnational following in the early 1950s. Musical director Gabriel Migliori created a soundtrack that aimed to highlight a version of the culture of the northeast drylands.[15] The somber and often haunting music of the *cangaço* often sounds like a lament. The *O Cangaceiro* soundtrack featured choral music and the accordion, explaining why folk and country singers outside Brazil gravitated to the music. It is not surprising that there were no Black-presenting performers in the film, given the racist policies of Vera Cruz film studios, even though there were Afro-Brazilian *cangaceiros*. As mentioned, Brazilians associate African diasporic culture with the coast, even though Blacks, mestizos, and other non-Whites make up part of the population of the sertão's population.[16] Barreto's film won the Best Adventure Film award at Cannes and special mention for its soundtrack.[17] Barreto filmed *O Cangaceiro* in black and white, and the music undergirded that aesthetic choice. Five years later, *Black Orpheus*'s presentation in Technicolor presented a drastically different experience of Brazil.

Imagining Black Brazil in the *Black Orpheus* Soundtrack

The musical vision for *Black Orpheus* emerged in Brazil during and after filming. Camus relied on Moraes and Jobim to create the major compositions on the soundtrack and the record of the soundtrack. He also hired other musicians and performers. He often consulted Moraes and Jobim, but the collaboration among the three men was not without its tensions. Jobim, whom Camus named musical director, remained suspicious of the Frenchman's ability to shape a Brazilian sound score. While Jobim questioned Camus's legitimacy based on national identity, there is no evidence that Jobim questioned his role as a White composer helping to construct a Black music project. That type of consciousness and questioning would emerge in the late twentieth century. Jobim was also worried about copyright issues and that the Frenchmen would buy the rights and "take it to France."[18]

In a letter to Moraes, who had taken a new position in Uruguay, Jobim complained that Camus was difficult to please and did not understand Brazilian culture or music. Language contributed to the tensions, as Camus's Portuguese was not fluent, and Jobim's French was not fluent either.[19] In the same letter, Jobim reported that Camus requested that he change the words of the song "A Felicidade." Jobim reported to Moraes that he had "some very tough negotiations with Camus." They had "some God-awful telephone conversations in French. Imagine! He objected to everything." Jobim was also bothered by the fact that even though he was responsible for the soundtrack, Camus had hired the Afro-Brazilian crooner Elizeth Cardoso to record on the official soundtrack in the studio without consulting him. Cardoso had not participated in the film like her male counterpart, Agostinho dos Santos.[20]

Camus also commissioned Luiz Bonfá and Antônio Maria, neither of whom identified as Afro-Brazilian, to record "Manhã de carnaval" ("The Morning of Carnival"). This famous song would eventually become the film's theme song.[21] While Jobim's language suggests a suspicion about ownership of cultural property, Camus was no cultural predator. He often articulated generalizations about Afro-Brazilians' inherent musicality and Brazil's Dionysian character in contexts that would have been problematic for an outsider. He also expressed his amazement at the nonstop energy of carnival and the fact that Brazilians danced alone. However, he also captured and preserved performances from Black Brazil by visiting samba schools, favelas, and *terreiros*, the centers of Macumba in the city. Camus also understood the Brazilian Orphic tradition symbolized by the poet-musician and his guitar. In an interview for French television, he underscored his desire to capture what he had experienced, the spontaneous production of Afro-Brazilian joy in the streets during carnival.[22]

Camus curated the compositions of Brazilian composers and edited the scenes with popular Brazilian musicians. According to assistant producer Silvio Autuori, Vinicius de Moraes gave Camus the complete liberty to make any changes he wanted. Autuori remembered that Camus interviewed and rehearsed with a group of dancers for one of the carnival scenes. After choosing the group, he asked the dancers to create a choreography that would allow all the dancers to perform the same steps as they moved down the street. In this way, Afro-Brazilians maintained agency over their bodies and artistic expression, but Camus directed and edited the overall film narrative. Scenes of the samba schools and marching bands illustrate that the film benefited from this legitimacy. The movie captures the uniquely Brazilian sounds of the pandeiro, the *cuica*, the Macumba drumbeats, and other sounds of the city. The dancers used historical knowledge and cues from the samba parades in an era when carnival parades were becoming more organized and regimented since their founding in the 1920s.

Alison Raphael's research in the 1990s captures magnificently the transformation of carnival. Many of her interviews reference the exclusion of Afro-Brazilians from the public carnival parades at the beginning of the twentieth century in Rio. When Afro-Brazilians began to form groups, they did so with joy, dancing and singing often in the rain and with scrappy costumes despite the hardships and police surveillance. One of Raphael's informants reminisced that "[P]eople just put on their straw hats and their sandals and did whatever they wanted." The informant lamented about changes that the samba school rules introduced in the 1950s: "We played, we had fun. I don't think they have as much fun now as we used to have."[23] Raphael attributes some of the changes to outside influences and Rio de Janeiro's increasing reliance on tourism. In this sense, the image in *Black Orpheus* attracted foreigners to the city, as works such as Mark J. Curran's *Adventures of a "Gringo" Researcher in Rio in the 1960s* demonstrate.[24]

Black Brazil, Music, and the Film Narrative

In the opening scene of *Black Orpheus*, the audience hears the soft melancholy guitar notes of Tom Jobim's "A Felicidade," played by the White guitarist Roberto Menescal, who would play bossa nova in the 1962 show in Carnegie Hall.[25] The main chord plays in the background, and the classic static Greek images of Orpheus and Eurydice in black and white appear on the screen. After thirty seconds, a Dionysian joyous Brazilian percussion beat abruptly interrupts the tune for about a minute, as Black men in colorful clothing and headwear burst through the Greek image playing Brazilian instruments, including *pandeiros* (Brazilian tambourine-like percussive instrument), the *agogô* (Yoruba-derived double bell), the *reco* (a Brazilian wooden scrapper), and the *cuica* (a friction drum with an extensive range). Even in the first few minutes of the film, the melancholy tune returns, but the second time it is accompanied by the voice of the Afro-Brazilian crooner Agostinho dos Santos (as Orpheus) humming and eventually singing the lyrics in Portuguese for "A Felicidade":

> Sadness has no end
> but happiness has.
> Happiness is like a feather
> carried by wind in the air.
> It flies so gently,
> but only for a short time.
> It needs the never-ending wind.

Happiness of the poor seems like
the great carnival illusion.
People work all year long
for a dream moment,
when they can fulfill their fantasy
to become a king, a pirate, or a gardener,
and everything ends on Ash Wednesday.[26]

The song not only warns listeners of the ephemeral nature of happiness within a Latin Catholic culture in a country of economic inequalities, it also specifically comments on the fleeting nature of the joy experienced by poor people over three days of carnival. Poor people work hard all day to participate in a celebration that temporarily allows them to become someone else. However, the audience does not see the poor people of Babilônia toiling. We only see the celebration. Thus, the song also warns that what we will witness is an illusion. It also anticipated the tragedy that will unfold. Yet, as the song ends, the percussion music returns in the background of the dialogue, reminding us of the possibility of celebration in the face of social challenge.

The percussive music will continue for much of the film's opening as the camera takes us through the city and introduces the audience to various characters. We first meet Eurydice as she arrives in the city by boat as musicians play various percussion instruments.[27] After experiencing various percussion and wind instruments combined with sounds of the city, the film introduces the audience to a tune of one of Rio's marching bands. As Eurydice crosses the plaza in front of the recently completed Ministry of Education and Culture (designed by the famous France-based Swiss architect Le Corbusier with several Brazilians), the film pans in on the marching band playing a *frevo*, a style originally from the state of Pernambuco, as they march down Rio Branco Avenue, one of the main streets in downtown Rio. According to Carlos Sandroni, the film crew recorded the band by chance during the 1958 carnival celebrations.[28]

The movie will take us through several musical forms by the film's end, including the *samba-canção*, the *frevo*, improvisational singing, the sound of musical instruments like the *cuica*, and the sacred music of Macumba. The recurring tune "A Felicidade" represents what Charles Perrone calls the "only true Bossa Nova, with restrained vocal and characteristic execution of altered guitar chords."[29] The film weaves the different music styles throughout the narrative, often documenting live performances. This documentation allows the original music and performance to emerge unencumbered. For this reason, Johanne Villeneuve describes the film as a combination of fiction and ethnography.[30]

Camus highlights the central narrative tension through the music. The melodic musical style that would later be called bossa nova contrasts with the more percussive samba. As Anaïs Fléchet affirms, the soundtrack is impressive in its diversity since the film provides spectators with a complete panorama of popular music of the 1950s, most of it inspired and performed by Afro-Brazilians. At the same time, the film contributes to the early globalization of bossa nova tunes.[31]

In addition to relying on a racially diverse group of composers and performers, the film includes choral singers in the studio and hundreds of musicians from the samba schools. As previously mentioned, the beloved Cartola (Agenor de Oliveira), a musical institution in Brazil, also helped Camus and appeared briefly in the film with his partner Zica (Euzébia Silva do Nascimento). The presence of these historical figures and the various samples of Brazilian popular music make the soundtrack a valuable source for cultural practices of the post-war era. Rio's elite had resented the promotion of samba and Afro-Brazilian music as Brazilian symbols since the time of Carmen Miranda, as the Orson Welles 1940s documentary *It's All True* demonstrates.[32]

Welles highlighted the elite's aversion to Blackness and Black cultural forms. Fifteen years later, Camus celebrated the musical dimension but also presented one of the first serious recordings of religious songs and Afro-Brazilian religious practices. Camus visited the sacred places of worship (*terreiros*) and included elements of the religion such as the proper white attire, the ritual drumming, the cigar and greetings, and the trance, which leads to epiphany or possession. The film also shows the role of the medium who can channel the Orixás, or dieties, and the a *pai de santo*, a religious leader adorned with a feather-crown, which is associated with the Amerindian traditional spirits often found in Umbanda. Unfortunately, the film's association of Macumba with the underworld also may have left a one-dimensional impression since audiences do not necessarily perceive the importance of the religion in the life of believers. As Carlos Sandroni suggests, Christian audiences in Brazil and elsewhere might also have had negative reactions to this scene.[33]

The film script alludes to Greek mythology, for example, but African mythologies also abound in Brazilian culture. Nonetheless, from a musical perspective, by including the sacred ceremonial music, the audience experiences another manifestation of Black Brazil vicariously. As Sandroni insists, presenting "refined bossa nova together with sophisticated drumbeats of Macumba," invites us to rethink the connections that unite the different branches of Afro-Brazilian musical traditions. Moreover, in Macumba in Rio de Janeiro, worshipers sing and dance, inviting various African and Amerindian deities to come to earth and enter their bodies.[34] Nonetheless, at the center of those musical traditions is Orpheus, the protagonist who charms, seduces, and celebrates his audiences. Orpheus's face and voice resonate most powerfully in the movie.

Imagining Orpheus's Song Through the Global Media

The French producers had cast their ideal Orpheus for a global audience, but Breno Mello was not a professional musician. The director hired musicians off screen to perform voice and guitar. There is no evidence that the film producers paid any attention to the racial composition of the musicians behind the scenes as they did when forming the cast in front of the camera. However, Moraes indicated to Camus that since the film was about the Afro-Brazilian world, it was important that listeners identify the singer who portrayed the title character as an Afro-Brazilian. In stepped Agostinho dos Santos, an Afro-Brazilian crooner who represented a Black musical aesthetic in Brazil, although it is unclear if foreign audiences would have captured Brazil's racialized construction in the music industry.[35] In the film, Breno Mello appears to play the guitar and sing, but it is Agostinho do Santos's baritone that audiences will feel. Agostinho could sing in a soft, intimate style due to technological developments such as microphones that could amplify his voice when necessary.[36]

Agostinho dos Santos

Dos Santos was a *Paulista* from the Bixiga neighborhood who made a name for himself as a crooner because of his rich baritone voice. He performed in diverse locations, from social dancing halls to radio salons. He also recorded many 'hits' in the early 1950s. In 1955, dos Santos moved to Rio and recorded his first LP with music composed by Tom Jobim and Dolores Duran, one of the few early female bossa nova composers.[37] *Black Orpheus* had not been responsible for Agostinho dos Santos's initial success, but it was a pivotal moment in developing an international career. The movie allowed him to become a global ambassador when few Afro-Brazilian performers had platforms outside of South America. Dos Santos's work on *Black Orpheus* garnered him worldwide attention as the voice of Orpheus without ever appearing on screen. Thanks in part to dos Santos's voice, demand for the film's soundtrack album grew long after its 1959 release on the Epic label in the United States, leading to its rerelease in 1964 by Fontana Records.[38] Antônio Maria and Luis Bonfá's "Manhã de Carnival" became a popular music and jazz staple and a crowd-pleaser by the 1960s partly because of Agostinho dos Santos's original melodic interpretation.[39] Agostinho dos Santos's version in Portuguese also won widespread approval at the Carnegie Hall concert in 1962.[40]

After the concert, many performers secured recording and performing contracts and remained in the United States. Global audiences' admiration of dos Santos's performances and style continued until he died in 1973. He performed across South America and Europe, often teaming up with other singers who visited Brazil like Johnny Mathis.[41] The two baritones had similar timbres, and the collaboration enhanced dos Santos's visibility. Like Mathis, dos Santos could wrap his voice around melodies with his emotions while simultaneously controlling the song's character. Dos Santos had already accumulated cultural capital in the Brazilian musical world. He had collaborated with Jobim and Moraes on the album *Antônio Carlos Jobim and Fernando César na voz de Agostinho dos Santos* (*in the voice of Agostinho dos Santos*). His rendition of "Eu não existo sem você" ("I Don't Exist Without You") beautifully conveyed the feeling of Moraes's lyrics. His recordings on the film's soundtrack of the theme song "Manhã de Carnival" and "A Felicidade" made him a de facto global representative of Black Brazil well beyond 1958.[42]

Although dos Santos returned to Brazil after the famous Carnegie Hall bossa nova concert in 1962, he helped to inspire a broader interest and consumption of bossa nova and Brazilian culture in the United States and Europe. Other Afro-Brazilians at the concert, including Carmen Costa and Bola Sete, would also contribute to the circulation of Brazilian music outside of Brazil. Still, Agostinho dos Santos's role in *Black Orpheus* and his presence in the United States make him a pioneer on many fronts.[43] Moreover, Agostinho dos Santos's version in Portuguese also won widespread approval at the Carnegie Hall concert. Even though artists from the United States and France recorded covers in English and French, the original Portuguese also indicated that the globalization of Black Brazil was connected to the globalization of Brazil and the Portuguese language.[44] Dos Santos's trajectory underscores the importance of the *Black Orpheus* project as an opportunity for Afro-Brazilian visibility on a global level. Elizeth Cardoso's female voice on the soundtrack's record version also elevated the music's status and helped promote Afro-Brazilian music abroad.

Elizeth Cardoso: 'The Divine Voice'

Although many scholars credit her as the voice of Eurydice in the movie, Elizeth Cardoso's participation in the *Black Orpheus* project occurred almost exclusively in the recording studio for the production of the soundtrack. However, her relationship to the musicians and composers and her position as one of the pioneering Afro-Brazilian crooners of her time should not be overlooked. Camus had paid her 30,000 cruzeiros to record the voice of Eurydice in "Manhã de Carnival." Cardoso also recorded the first pre–bossa nova album, *Canção do amor demais* (*Songs of Too Much Love*), under the supervision of João Gilberto, who would release his own album, *Chega de saudade* (*No More Blues*), the first commercially successful and bona fide bossa nova album, in 1958. The experience also allowed her to work with Tom Jobim, Vinicius de Moraes, and João Gilberto in the same year as *Black Orpheus*. Like the *Black Orpheus* soundtrack, the album signaled a new way of understated performances that was distinct from her orchestrated *samba-canção* records. The single "Chega de saudade" is most indicative of this style and would become the name of the first recorded bossa nova album by João Gilberto one year later.[45]

Cardoso had already made a name for herself on Brazilian radio and in the cultural circles around Brazil when she received the invitation to record Eurydice's singing voice. She was an Afro-Brazilian crooner with a sweet earthy voice that resonated with the popular and middle classes of the country. Her rags-to-fame story also endeared her to her fans. "I was born very poor," she told Ronaldo Bôscoli in an interview for the magazine *Manchete* in 1979. She also confided that from her poor house with small rooms near the São Francisco Xavier train station, she made embarrassing choices. Before becoming a singer, Cardoso started working at eight years old and exercised various professions, including a factory worker, a street cigarette seller, and a taxi girl (a paid dancer) at clubs around Rio. A self-declared *Mulata*, or as she would often say, a *Mulatona* (a real Mulatta). Cardoso knew how to place her emotions in her music, which is what global listeners perceive on the *Black Orpheus* record.[46] *O Globo* attempted to praise her by calling her "a Brazilian distinguished mulatta" who became a symbol of a culturally mixed Brazil.[47] Moraes believed her voice possessed a particular Afro-Brazilian sensibility that connected her to Afro-Brazilian culture.

The magazine *Visão* declared that Cardoso was "The Divine One," a moniker given to her by Haroldo Costa, who directed her in the 1958 movie *Pista de grama* (*Grass Track*). Also known as *Um desconhecido bate a sua porta* (*An Unknown Person Knocks at the Door*), *Pista de grama* circulated in film houses and Rio and São Paulo and was received positively by critics. In Cardoso's short scene, she performed Tom Jobim's "Eu não existe sem você" ("I Don't Exist Without You") with João Gilberto on guitar.[48] *Black Orpheus* did not launch Cardoso's global career, but it was one of many instances in which her recording became part of the transnational Black Brazil. Cardoso became an ambassador of Brazilian music in seventeen countries in the Americas, Europe, and Japan, earning her comparisons to American performers such as Lena Horne and Sarah Vaughan.[49] At the same time, Cardoso remained a popular Brazilian figure who publicly celebrated her Afro-Brazilian roots, including her association with spiritualists and Macumba.[50] Long after the release of the official soundtrack of *Black Orpheus*, Cardoso continued to perform songs associated with the film, even though she was not credited on many of the records sold in France. She recorded and sometimes performed with Vinicius de Moraes, Tom Jobim, Luis Bonfá, and other emerging musicians such as Baden Powell.

Few Afro-Brazilian performers garnered contracts or opportunities to travel to the United States or Europe in the late 1950s or early 1960s due to segregation, discrimination, and economic barriers, even as the themes and images of Black Brazilian culture and bodies circulated because of the success at Cannes and at the Oscars. Ironically, the White musicians and composers initially associated with the film were responsible for promoting *Black Orpheus*. Luiz Bonfá was one of those musicians who worked closely with Camus and took the opportunity and responsibility to represent Brazil and promote *Black Orpheus* in both the United States and Europe. White advantage certainly allowed Bonfá to appear on multiple U.S. platforms not available to African Americans or Afro-Brazilians. This privilege does not diminish Bonfá's talents and his pioneering role as the original composer of the theme song of *Black Orpheus*.[51] Bonfá was known to be a professional and unsentimental musician with an international reputation, and Camus enjoyed working with him. He also did not feel the ownership rights that Jobim expressed.

Brazilians recognize the pioneering roles of Tom Jobim, Vinicius de Moraes, and João Gilberto in the global spread of bossa nova. Others acknowledge the impact of Baden Powell's *Afro-Sambas*. Brazilians generally do not recognize Bonfá's role in promoting bossa nova transnationally because he lived abroad for most of his life, before social media allowed for global communication.[52] In fact, Bonfá's international reputation preceded the bossa nova wave of popularity, though he benefited from it later. Bonfá already accumulated cultural capital due to his travels to the United States and a chance introduction into the American performance circles through Mary Martin, famous for her performance of Peter Pan on Broadway and just about to embark on a sixty-city tour. His association with Martin brought him unprecedented attention in the United States over the next two decades when he agreed to tour with her as his contemporaries developed their craft in the Zona Sul of Rio de Janeiro.[53]

Bonfá explained to *O Globo* in the 1990s that he left Brazil for the United States in 1956, shortly after his work with Camus, and struggled in the first few months, although his fortunes would soon change, particularly after the film's success. During one of his visits to Rio, Camus contracted him to write the tune for the main character's voice. After Bonfá created the theme song "Manhã de Carnaval" with lyricist Antônio Maria, he worked on his 1957 album *Alta Versalidade* (*High Versatility*), which pioneered songs from Brazil and the United States, including "Somewhere Over the Rainbow" and "Xangô."

The success of *Black Orpheus* meant that Bonfá's work received wider coverage, and he had opportunities to promote Brazilian music that often intersected with the globalization of Afro-Brazilian culture. As the bossa nova era developed and caught American and European media attention, Bonfá received invitations to perform in the United States and Europe. It helped that his English was excellent. Other White musicians associated with *Black Orpheus*, including Roberto Menescal, who played backup guitar on Bonfá's "Happiness." The Italian guitar player Henri Crolla, and the flutist Odette Ernest Dias also joined the Brazilian performers. Structural racism in Brazil, the

United States, and France continued to deter Black performers from pursuing possibilities. However, despite exclusion, many Afro-Brazilians found opportunities outside of Brazil in the aftermath of the success of *Black Orpheus*.

Afro-Brazilian musicians also utilized their small roles in the film as a springboard to continue the Orphic tradition abroad. A young Carlinhos Pandeiro de Ouro, a teenager at the time, appeared as an extra and contributed to the musical score. Although the film did not credit or compensate him for his involvement, Carlinhos acknowledged that the film was a critical moment in his personal career and allowed him to contact many musicians in the 1950s and 1960s. "One drum that can perform all the rhythms of the samba is the *pandeiro*," he explained in 2005, near his home in Culver City in Los Angeles. Like the tambourine but played differently, the pandeiro is tunable, and with the right technique, a skilled player can sound like a drum set. Carlinhos took up the pandeiro at age seven, starting with one of his mother's cake pans. He practiced and visited Mangueira, one of Rio's most popular samba schools. Carlinhos would also join in during rehearsals, and he soon came to the attention of Mangueira's legendary singer, Jamelão, who invited Carlinhos to become a performing member of Mangueira.[54] He believed that participating in the film profoundly impacted his life as he went on to play the pandeiro.

Other Black performers, including the three young children (Jorge dos Santos as Benedito, Aurino Cassiano as Zeca, and Maria Alice), also helped with the musical score. They appear throughout the film, enthralled with music and with Orpheus. At the end of the film, the three children provide an uplifting rendition of the song of hope after Orpheus's death at the hands of Mira, who threw a stone at him and killed him instantly. As the sad theme song fades in the background, Benedito beckons to Zeca to take Orpheus's guitar and play it to "bring the sun up." As he plays, Maria Alice dances with joy in the background. It is a new day, and the new generation will continue celebrating. The film ends with the four-note tune. The girl turns to Zeca and tells him, "Now you are Orpheus." A chorus sings "La la . . . la" in 4/4 time as the children dance.[55]

Conclusion

Children and older family members, vendors, and carnival-goers were critical to presenting an organic picture of a vibrant Afro-Brazilian community in flux. Rather than seeing these minor characters and unnamed extras as a mere backdrop to a European plot, Camus places their musicality, especially during carnival, the quintessential moment of national revelry, at the center of the theme of Brazilian Black joy and simplicity. As we have seen, the music is not all joyous or Dionysian. However, the film interplays the joys of samba with the melancholy and slowness of the samba song, which is different from the chorus-like singing of the samba group. The slow paired down formulation of samba would later become part of the central aesthetics of bossa nova.

In *Bossa Mundo: Brazilian Music in Transnational Media Industries*, K. E. Goldschmitt astutely traces the movement of bossa nova from *Black Orpheus* to widespread success in the United States. Goldschmitt argues that "even though the music was mostly created by White middle-class Brazilians from the Rio de Janeiro South zone neighborhoods, its mediation through the film conveyed a vague sense that bossa nova was other."[56] In fact, Afro-Brazilians such as Johnny Alf and Carmen Costa made important contributions to the early development of bossa nova. Baden Powell's intervention would take bossa nova back to its African roots. However, White Brazilians were the first to make careers in the genre abroad. It took two more years and a trip by jazz musicians to Brazil to create a formula that would allow bossa nova to break into the American mass market. In his discussions on bossa nova, Jean-Paul Delfino argues that the success of the Cuban revolution cut off the importation of Cuban music, prompting multinationals to search for other forms of popular music. *Black Orpheus* provided the impetus and the gateway to Brazil and bossa nova.[57]

4

Oblique Gazes

The Transnational Reception of *Black Orpheus*

According to Paulo Siquiera, "Everything began with the original Brazilian theatrical title 'Orfeu do Carnival'" (Orpheus from Carnival or Carnival's Orpheus). The celebratory Dionysian event and the Afro-Brazilian poetic performer are inextricably linked. The transnational French version for the silver screen explicitly racialized the title for a global audience, and carnival's Orpheus became *Black Orpheus*.[1] The idea of a Black Orpheus was not new. Marcel Camus's *Black Orpheus* may have been inspired by French writer Jean-Paul Sartre's 1948 essay "Orphée Noir" ("Black Orpheus"), which he published as the preface to a collection of Francophone African literature edited by Léopold Senghor. The magazine *Black Orpheus: A Journal of African and Afro-American Literature* emerged from Nigeria in 1957. Founded by German expatriate, editor, and translator Ulli Beier, the publication became one of the most influential Black cultural forums for emerging literary scenes in both Anglophone and Francophone Africa. Thus, the idea of a Black Orpheus singing to the world was part of the postwar zeitgeist. It influenced an entire generation, which included creatives such as Vinicius de Moraes and Camus.

Even though the idea of a Black Orpheus may not have been new, Camus's decision to project the Black Brazilian from a shanty town in Rio de Janeiro on the silver screen broke new ground. Camus and his team also diverged from the dominant Western film industry's racial and aesthetic norms. As with his

FIGURE 3 Photo of Léa Garcia with a panoramic view of Rio de Janeiro. Credit: Lopert Pictures/Photofest. © Lopert Pictures

first film, *Mort en fraude*, the French director wanted to take spectators on an exciting adventure using conventional forms of storytelling. Unlike his first film, however, Camus utilized Brazilian music as a central character to highlight Black Brazilian cultural aesthetics. Many European and American audiences had consumed aspects of Brazilian music through the Carmen Miranda films and records before the 1950s.

Sacha Gordine and Camus made a calculated artistic and commercial decision to promote images of a Black Brazil in the post–World War II era. In the process, Camus developed a deep and personal connection with the country he would later call his second home. His entry document to Brazil signed by Deputy Consul General in Paris Oswaldo Barreto e Silva on June 15, 1959, indicated that Camus was seeking "permanent" entry into the country.[2] He saw himself as an unofficial transnational cultural ambassador with a mission to encourage the promotion of the joyous aspects of Afro-Brazilian culture.[3] Camus's choices also helped continue the myth of Brazilian racial democracy, lusotropicalism, and Brazilian exceptionalism, advanced by a host of prewar writers, including Gilberto Freyre, Stefan Zweig, and the young Jorge Amado.[4] The French film producers understood that cinema was a type of popular culture designed for mass consumption, as Malcolm Bernard reminds us. This goal of reaching a mass audience often encourages passive consumption that reinforces dominant ways of perceiving and dominant structures as they relate to social constructions of race, nation, and gender.[5]

Black Orpheus engaged audiences' senses and emotions in the late 1950s and 1960s, but this does not mean that Camus's work was not political. His politics can be seen in his choice of subject and his celebration and collaboration with Black artists, limited as they may have been in a film industry where Blackness was hardly seen or celebrated. Still, for the 1950s Camus, who wanted to make commercial mainstream films, that spectator was 'universal,' which meant Western and White if not majority White. Thus, the decisions he made would resonate widely with Western viewers, shaped by White European patriarchal standards and ways of viewing. Camus would have been familiar with the black-and-white aesthetic examples of his fellow filmmakers from the Nouvelle Vague, including Jean Cocteau's *Orphée* and the emerging Brazilian filmmakers of *cinema novo*. However, he opted for a Technicolor production to celebrate a country and a people using a tried and true storytelling style that would include many elements of Aristotelian Greek drama. Given his cultural and personal background, Camus nevertheless relied on existing tropes of Blackness, albeit from what he thought was a positive perspective. The new imagery would engage Western audiences' penchant for transgressive pleasure in the dark collective privacy of the cinema, which was the only way to view films long before video cassettes, DVDs, and streaming services. Transnational spectators, critics, and journalists gave meaning to the film in multiple ways. An assessment of the transnational reception, including the criticism, must be understood as a type of epistemological seeking about Brazil and Blackness *and* about the viewers' quest to understand their racialized, gendered, and nationalized community's place in the world at a specific historical moment in the second half of the twentieth century.

Constructing Spectators: Beyond the Manichean World View

In early versions of the script, Camus had considered using a character that the writer calls "the professor." The professor was to serve as an omniscient commentator at the film's beginning and at select places throughout the narrative. For example, as Eurydice approaches the city by boat, the professor would have announced her arrival. This filming device would have created a different type of narrative that borrows from the documentary style or from Brechtian theater, which tries to provide some distance between the audience and the spectator. In the end, Camus decided to use the Aristotelian-inspired style of drama that relies on a connection with the audience, empathy, and a complicated drama that must be resolved at the end, providing audiences with a catharsis.[6]

Unfortunately, we have very little analytical data on the film's reception among Black audience members in France, Brazil, and the United States in the late 1950s and 1960s. Securing data about individual moviegoer experiences across three countries in the 1950s and 1960s is challenging. However, views from a cross section of journalists, independent writers, and critics including from the Black press in the United States, combined with anecdotal accounts provide us with windows into the audience experience. At the same time, Janet Staiger reminds us that ordinary audiences do not necessarily have additional cultural texts or analytical tools to deconstruct film but that "representations are developed in social circumstances and bear the ideological marks of the class or group that controls meaning."[7]

Communication between filmmakers and film viewers is largely based on a shared understanding of cultural meaning and cultural rituals. As Anna Siomopoulos explains in her work on Oscar Micheaux, filmmakers' chosen aesthetics reveal their political intentions. Micheaux, she argues, constructs a spectator who is more critically astute than previous filmmakers.[8] Manthia Diawara goes further by highlighting the fact that spectators are socially, historically, and psychologically constituted. He demonstrates that there are different types of viewing and different types of spectators. At the same time, individual viewers can do two things at once. It is possible to enjoy segments of a movie, resist the dominant narrative, and construct alternative meanings depending on a series of identification, including race, class, sex, and nationality.[9]

In general, transnational spectators of the era reveal an overwhelmingly positive view of the film *and* a tacit criticism of diverse elements such as exoticism, over-emphasis on Blackness, avoidance of social realities, and unpleasant reactions to the speed and rhythm of the film. Brazilian critics often expressed their surprise at French interest in the favela, while also showing a sense of postcolonial pride that Europeans were interested in Brazil. French and North American viewers in the 1960s were fascinated with the vibrant colors and a supposedly exotic culture. Spectators may be drawn to one element but repulsed by another in the same film. Viewers and critics alike focus on three major themes or issues: Black cultural production in the favelas, carnival, and Rio's natural landscape. All these themes relate to the circulating global symbols of postwar Brazil and the globalization of Afro-Brazilian culture.

Reception in France

Black Orpheus received quick approval from France's Ministry of Information to appear at the Cannes Film Festival. The international festival had only been launched in 1946, and the festival organizers only created the top prize, the Palme d'Or, in 1955. *Black Orpheus* was only the fourth film to receive that prize in 1959. However, it would be one of the first films to benefit from the newly created Film Market (the Marché du Film). This forum made the festival a commercially important venue for promoters and producers to buy and sell movies and make deals for transnational distribution.[10]

The key question for the producers was whether the film would represent France or Brazil in the festival since the film was in Portuguese with a Brazilian cast, but the financing and production were French. Gordine turned to the Brazilian embassy in Paris to determine whether Brazil would support the idea of *Black Orpheus* being presented as a Brazilian film. However, the Ministry of Foreign Affairs had not yet seen the film. Moreover, Ambassador Carlos Alves de Souza wanted to verify the protocol for choosing Brazilian films for international festivals. He telegrammed the Ministry of Foreign Affairs in Rio for advice. The telegram alerted the ministry that "Sacha Gordinis [*sic*], the producer of *Black Orpheus*, came to the Embassy, telling us that the French government had invited him to present the film as a French film, but that he preferred to present it as a Brazilian film."[11] After a series of exchanges, and before he could give Gordine a definite response, Ambassador Souza alerted the minister that the French press had already announced that *Black Orpheus* would represent France.[12]

Thus, *Black Orpheus* entered the festival as a French film, exposing the limited national framework and focus of the festival organizers and its early inability to account for transnational cinema. The nationalist lamentations began almost immediately after the news of the Cannes prize appeared in the press. A letter dated May 20, 1959, from Carlos Alves de Souza, the Brazilian ambassador in Paris, to the minister of foreign affairs in Rio summarized the events and his constraints and expressed his mixed feelings, but his ultimate approval that Brazil had been recognized:

> Dear Minister,
> Now that "Black Orpheus" has been consecrated as the best film of the year at the Cannes festival, there will be no shortage of critics in Brazil, as unfortunately, there is no shortage of last-minute patriots here to regret that "Black Orpheus" was not presented by Brazil. They will blame this Embassy and the Ministry of Foreign Affairs for that.
> 2. I don't really see what additional advantage there would be for Brazil, and particularly for Brazilian cinema, if "Black Orpheus" had been presented by us and not by France. The director would continue to be French, the production Franco-Italian-Brazilian production, the idea Brazilian from Vinicius de Morais [*sic*], and the majority of the actors Brazilian. But whether we present it or not is not important. What matters is knowing whether this Embassy or Itamaraty has not been carrying out its duties.
> 3. Having completed the film almost on the eve of the festival, the producers were not able to take care of the registration on time. As far as I know,

> the first request made regarding the inscription of "Black Orpheus" as a Brazilian film was the one sent to me by Mr. Sacha Gordini [*sic*] on April 14. I reported this to Your Excellency in a telegram of the same day. Gordini, however, took care of the registration, and there is nothing to criticize about "Black Orpheus" being registered as a French film. Once this was done, as I reported on April 21, the producers were no longer interested in obtaining our sponsorship.
>
> 4. "Black Orpheus" was in the Film Festival. That's what matters, and it was honored with victory. That should make us happy. This Embassy had the greatest sympathy for the case from the beginning, as Mr. Gordini [*sic*] himself and director Camus will certainly be able to testify. I went to see a special screening of the film, in which I congratulated Camus on his achievement. Even though "Black Orpheus" is officially French and not Brazilian, I sent a telegram to the festival's management stating our country's interest in the film and supporting the request for it to be presented in a night session. The Brazilian program on French radio, this Embassy and Itamaraty program dedicated no less than three sessions to "Black Orpheus."
>
> 5. I don't see what more could be demanded of this Embassy or from Itamaraty. There are those who, because of this victory, and many of them are in Brazil, instead of rejoicing, purely and simply, will go meanly looking for false arguments to criticize those who work honestly.
>
> I avail myself of this opportunity to renew the assurances of my respectful consideration to Your Excellency.
>
> Carlos Alves de Souza[13]

The presence of Marpessa Dawn, the non-Brazilian actress in the film, complicated the issue even further. Cannes relied on movie stars to promote the films it showcased. Sensing this, Gordine immediately sent a telegram to fly Breno Mello to France, but he was not able to travel. In the end, no Brazilian actor represented the movie in Cannes. Dawn, who was living in Paris, stood in for her fellow actors and played a critical role in promoting the film in the press and at events around the Cannes festivities in 1959. The French media splattered her image on newspapers and television for months, leading many to believe that she was Brazilian.[14]

Many Brazilians were present at the Cannes Film Festival. Vanja Orico, one of the stars of *O Cangaceiro*, was among them. Orico, who was not Black, had spoken openly on Brazilian television about her pride when the orchestra played the Brazilian national anthem in Cannes after *Black Orpheus* won the Palme d'Or. She also spoke about the "Brazilian racist opposition" to Camus's *Black Orpheus* because it had "too many Blacks."[15] Orico would go on to record music from the film for the Philips label in France, using the image of Breno Mello as Orpheus on the cover of the LP. Orico would also travel to the United States, where she performed at Carnegie Hall in 1971, earning praise for her "folk and pop-style pieces, including some fascinating chants in Indian dialect." Though "her sultry voice, expressive gestures, charming introductions, and infectious vitality proved inadequate for her incursions into Debussy, Respighi, and others."[16]

Although Camus was associated with members of the Nouvelle Vague, whose black-and-white films had gained critical acclaim, he knew those films did not reach mass audiences at the time. Filming *Black Orpheus* in Cinemascope would attract more viewers than most of the other French films. Spectators and commentators were impressed by the vibrancy of the colors that emerged from the first scene as the Brazilian characters and their music burst through the screen adorned by classical Greek images of Orpheus and Eurydice. Others were charmed by the scenic trolleys "in the small village of Santa Teresa" and "the "glorious view of the Bay of Guanabara," which many were seeing for the first time. *Black Orpheus*, color, vibrancy, and carnival once again became a major symbol of Black Brazil, Brazil as a nation, and the city of Rio de Janeiro.[17]

"Full of tenderness and beauty," exclaimed the French actress Michèle Morgan after viewing the film.[18] Marketing carnival and *Black Orpheus* was also going to be big business. The Brazilian magazine *Manchete* reported that American television representatives (Paramount, Columbia, United Artists MGM, and independent producers) were chewing peanuts and "licking their mouths and ready to negotiate." On the same day as the victory of *Black Orpheus*, the actress Marpessa Dawn became engaged to Georges Eric Vander, a Belgian actor whom she had met in Brazil. This event would hardly make news (especially in Brazil) if not for her success in *Black Orpheus*. The news of the romance and that the two got to know each other in Brazil gave Brazil a romantic power of a sort. *Manchete* also cited Robert Chazal from the French publication *France-Soir*, who remarked that *Black Orpheus* was an "obra prima that would make millions."[19]

Film Reception in France

The media attention in the wake of Cannes played a critical role in cementing the film's visibility and legacy and its original success among French audiences in 1959 and the early 1960s. According to *Le film français*, the Parisian French film magazine founded in 1944, from August 14, 1958, to August 13, 1959, *Black Orpheus* was the second most viewed film in metropolitan France after *Les tricheurs*, directed by Marcel Carné. They were the only two films seen by more than half a million viewers, with *Black Orpheus* attracting some 551,346 million, to Les *tricheurs*'s 556,203 viewers. *Les 400 coups* only received 261,145 viewers.[20]

When Gordine, Jacques Viot, and Camus arrived together in Rio de Janeiro in March 1957, carnival was already in the air. This energy, along with Camus's personal research and visits to favelas and Macumba ceremonies, would make it into the film. Camus wanted to capture this energy on film and share it with the French public and the world. Adapting the Orphic myth to the Afro-Brazilian milieu, Camus created a film that included death, mysticism, and rebirth. The film ends with a double death, symbolic of desperation. However, the final scene with the children commemorates rebirth.[21] The idea of death and rebirth resonated with many in a country where Catholicism had shaped the culture. André Besseges noted, for example, that *Black Orpheus* was the last great film of the season. He argued that the myth of Orpheus came from a religion founded by the transmigration of souls, and like Mardi Gras, the film was a "frenetic cortège put in place."[22]

For Catholic readers, the scene of Orpheus descending to hell and the carnival scene depicting Macumba were the most problematic. Despite this criticism, the positive review in the 1950s may be related to what bell hooks has called "transgressive pleasure." hooks relates that the idea of transgressive pleasure to fetishism, what she calls the "psychohistories of White racism, have always called attention to the tension between the construction of the Black male body as danger and the underlying eroticization that always then imagines that body as a location for transgressive pleasure."[23] Here again, Diawari reminds us that spectators have the power to engage in oppositional or resistance reading and viewing.[24] John Storey rightly points out that popular culture and the consumption of popular culture can be both conformist and transgressive.[25] For the peoples and communities depicted it can also be celebratory.

The tension in the dialogue is seen among writers and critics. One French critic focused on the prize and thought that *Les 400 coups* should have won the top award but could not deny the passion and skill of the director and the novel adaptation of the Orphic myth.[26] For critics like this, the prize was about perceived artistic beauty and not popular enthusiasm. Many critics focused on Mello's and Dawn's acting and their chemistry. "Marpessa Dawn is a superb woman with tenderness," claimed one writer. For this writer, from *Le Figaro*, Orpheus represented the disenfranchised people in the favelas of Rio. Special praise was doled out to Léa Garcia, who played Serafina, Eurydice's cousin in the film. She represented a "beautiful body animated with grace." In addition, the perpetual movement and its shifts were a door of rhythm and intelligence. The film is a "must-see."[27] Another newspaper illustrated that Camus's message was not lost in the spectacle: "This wonderful film is full of tenderness and love" and shows "the horror of vice and hate that we can do without."[28] The charm of listening to Portuguese was also important. "Listening to Portuguese is part of the magic" for many in the French audience, hinting at the desire to consume difference, if not perceived exoticism. Brazilian viewers also made similar observations from a patriotic perspective.[29]

The newspaper *Le canard enchaîné*, which still features a diverse spectrum of investigative articles, critiques, and cartoons, was direct with its praise: "Let's say it right away: the Palme d'Or that this film received was well deserved. Marcel Camus gives us Orpheus with frenetic energy and with talent and a diversity of images and rhythms that brings value to the cinema."[30] The positive view did not stop the writer from proposing another ending, illustrating Diawari's point that spectatorship and viewing can have multiple layers, even from the same viewer.[31]

Claude Mauriac, another writer from *Le Figaro*, highlighted the enormous energy of carnival that he and the producers experienced on the eve of the celebration in Rio. The writer, who was in Brazil, then documented the intense preparation that he witnessed as carnival approached and people prepared for it. He also wrote about the inversion of roles and how people engaged in fun behavior that would otherwise be viewed as ridiculous. According to Russian philosopher Mikhail Bakhtin, these practices by the popular classes allow them to subvert hegemony and authority.[32] In apparent agreement with Bakhtin, Mauriac argued that spontaneous shouting and dancing seemed normal and appropriate during the carnival merriment. For Muriac and many other viewers, everything in this film was new except for its traditional way of narrating. Like the viewer watching the film, carnival participants view and engage in transgressive pleasure right before the period of fasting, sacrifice, and introspection represented by Lent, the season when Catholics fast and make daily sacrifices. As *Le Figaroscope* noted, carnival itself is a transgressive ritual. Moreover, the audience's pleasure has turned the film into a commercial success and the record producers allowed consumers to enjoy themselves repeatedly. While some viewers saw the film multiple times to experience Brazilian joy, spectators such as Euzhan Palcy were also happy to witness Black representation.[33]

By focusing on Rio's carnival, the largest Brazilian public celebration when Brazilians are not working, Camus avoids discussing daily work or the racialized interactions among the working people who live in the hills and the mostly White employers who live in the city nearer to the beaches or in the *Zona Sul*, or southern zone of Rio de Janeiro. Jean-Luc Godard's stinging criticism of the film in the influential *Cahiers du cinéma* not only indicts Camus in a manner that seems personal but also contributes to the Manichean nature of film criticism rather than engaging in a dialogue with multiple transnational audiences. Godard's brilliantly written prose impacted journalists and scholars who continue to cite it, although it makes no mention of the film score, one of the most important contributions. "What would poetry be without a poet?" Godard asks rhetorically, only to answer, "Well, it would be *Orfeu Negro*, in which the Cannes jurors more or less recognized their friendly persuasion." He continues: "The kindness and sincerity of Marcel Camus are not in question. But is it enough to be kind and sincere to make a good film?" Godard is particularly critical of the attention that Camus has garnered, missing completely its racial significance and its possible impact on African descendants. He compares what he calls the inauthenticity of *Black Orpheus* to the cinema verité style of Jean Rouch in the 1958 film *Moi, un noir*, apparently wanting Camus to make an ethnographic film rather than a commercial one. Though Godard's criticism seems personal, it is also an indictment of unpoetic Hollywood filmmaking that quickly dominated global markets.

> And it was also very good to make a film in Brazil rather than in Saint-Germain-des-Prés, to film the tramways of Rio rather than the parties of Passy. But then, you don't direct your Black actors with the same words and gestures as Jean Boyer directing Line Renaud and Darry Cowl in a reconstructed guinguette on the Billancourt sets. It doesn't matter that *Orfeu Negro* is only faintly related to the Thracian bard. However, Cocteau (I ask again, have you seen *Orpheus*?) was careful not to make that mistake, the most important thing is that, compared to a film like *Moi, un noir*, Orfeu Negro is—to adopt the vocabulary of Madame Express—completely inauthentic.[34]

After criticizing the Cannes jury, Godard compares his own experience in Brazil, using his personal view as a better point of departure:

> With no money and waiting for a cheque from Sacha Gordine to finish his film, Marcel Camus had all the time in the world to walk around the rather prodigious city of Rio de Janeiro. It was then, he says, and thanks to these walks, that he really became aware of what Rio and its people were like. And it is at this point that I reproach him. It so happens that I found myself in exactly the same situation. And I'm surprised, and I'm very disappointed that I don't see anything of Rio in *Orfeu Negro*. I didn't see the wonderful small Santos Dumont airfield where Eurydice had to land between the ocean and the skyscrapers. And why didn't you make Orpheus (did you see Cocteau's film again?) a bus driver instead of a tram driver already seen in all the fantasies commissioned by MGM from a man named Pete Smith? Poetic were those little station wagon buses that sped from the Maracanã stadium to the Copacabana strikes. And poetic would have been Orpheus' way of holding his banknotes to give change: folded lengthwise between each finger of both hands. But in his fifteen years of kindly assisting others, Marcel Camus has lost his sense of poetry.[35]

After several other criticisms, Godard relents with small praise: "Let's be fair," he concludes. "There is a nice shot in *Orfeu Negro*: the one where Eurydice's friend, standing on her lover's feet, bends down to turn off the lamp. However, the scene would have been even better if Orpheus and Eurydice had played it, not their comrades. In short, what shocks me in this adventurer's film is that there is no adventure or poetry in this poet's film."[36] Godard's criticism is an important view from an esteemed French observer and writer, but it only represents one view of the reception in a particular cultural sphere. The view of filmmakers such as Euzhan Palcy provides us with another reading. Popular newspapers and magazines also present a broader reception that may also be explained through the history of the French penchant for the foreign cultural products that many in the post–World War II era deemed exotic. Exoticism, as Daniela Berghahn has noted, is a form of translation. It also reveals as much about the consumer's wants and desires as about the subject or subjects being consumed. These multiple viewings exist and dialogue with one another, ultimately contributing to the circulation of ideas about Black Brazil.[37]

A Note on Film Reception in Brazil

According to the National Cinema Agency (ANCINE), there were just over 2,500 cinemas in Brazil in 1971. Between 1958 and 1967, there were no more than 1,000 theaters. That number only increased after 1969 and reached its peak in 1975.[38] The lack of cinema houses limited the possibility for Brazilians to view any film. Unlike in the United States and France, where *Black Orpheus* was released in multiple movie houses, *Black Orpheus* was first shown at the headquarters of Itamaraty, the Ministry of Foreign Affairs, in downtown Rio. In his book, *Feliz 1958: O ano que não deve terminar*, Joaquim Ferreira dos Santos lists the fifty-eight most important events of that year. He ranks *Orfeu Negro* as number twenty-two and cites its historical importance, but it is unclear how many Brazilians saw the film in Brazil in 1959 or between 1960 and 1965.[39]

Two informants living in the middle-class southern zone of Rio de Janeiro in the 1960s report that small cinemas began to appear in many neighborhoods, but that *Black Orpheus* did not circulate for a very long time. On the other hand, moviegoers seemed amazed at Marpessa Dawn's appearance in the film. Not knowing the full story of the withdrawal of the Brazilian Eurydice, many wondered why the director had chosen an American actress to play the role.[40] Generally, the film's reception in Brazil can be divided into three major categories: First, Brazilian critics and newspapers, including the Brazilian ambassador in France, who initially praised the film when it was released in France. Second, by the early 1960s, Brazilian filmmakers and cultural producers began criticizing the film for its exoticism and lack of attention to political and social problems in Brazil. Many were probably influenced, in part, by Godard's essay in the *Cahiers*. Third, many Afro-Brazilians praise Camus for providing opportunities to Black Brazilians. This category also includes other Afro-descendant commentators who have recently recognized the film's historical importance, its documentary role of life in Brazil, and its music.[41]

Because of its transnational attention, the local press and local commentators paid attention to the film as a major event. As early as 1955, the *Diário Carioca* highlighted the unusual racial and gendered casting, reporting that "almost 1000 girls with skin color between dark *moreno* to dark brown to dark black will parade in front of Vinicius de Moraes in the next twenty days." The paper explained that the author would be choosing twenty *Cabrochas*, an old-fashioned word for Mulattas, who would appear in the film. The article ends with suggestive, if not sexist, language, stating that "Vinicius divides his time between the text that he wrote and the 'human material' that he should approve."[42] In another article, the journalist Borroró praised the film's colloquial style (presumably contrasting it to the play). He also suggested that Léa Garcia play the role of Eurydice.[43]

Before the film's release, major news outlets had documented the production process, including the recreation of carnival and the casting methods of the French team. Immediately after the release of the film in Cannes and before the arrival of the film in Brazil, however, most of the journalistic criticism focused on the reception abroad rather than direct observation since the film did not premiere in Brazil until August 1959, after the film had received the top award in Cannes.[44]

On August 20, the newly opened Opera Theatre in the Botafogo neighborhood exhibited the film with a gala reception that also marked the inauguration of the movie theater. The Pioneiras Sociais (Social Pioneers), a civil society association created in 1956 under President Juscelino Kubitschek and Rio's French Beneficent Society, organized and hosted the event.[45] On August 21, the newspaper *Ultima Hora* announced that the premiere of *Orfeu de Carnaval*, the Brazilian title of the film, was an "absolute success." Moraes, Camus, and other crew members were present, as well as French ambassador to Brazil, Bernard Hardion, producer Sacha Gordine, and the theater's owner Livio Bruni. Radio Nacional covered the event, and radio announcer Adolfo Cruz introduced the film to a full-capacity crowd. The newspaper had previously announced the arrival of Camus in the city and a presidential lunch with the actors and Miss Brazil 1959, Vera Ribeiro.[46]

Even before the Cannes Film Festival, newspapers like *Aurore* announced that *Orfeu Negro* was the favorite to win the top prize. According to the paper, critics had looked beyond some of the film's problems to "praise Rio and its beauty," "a beauty that is more splendid in the film than in reality." Marpessa Dawn and Breno Mello also conquered the critics in addition to the merriment of carnival, samba, and folkloric music. "It is an authentic cinematographic poem," affirmed Steve Passeur. He also praised Camus for ensuring that the film was totally spoken in Portuguese but seemed to be concerned that the actors seemed to be shouting.[47] Another paper, the *Jornal do Brasil*, underscored Moraes's contribution to helping bring Black Brazilians to the screen.[48]

The Brazilian press also took a keen interest in the French director and the American Eurydice. A reporter from the magazine *Manchete* followed Camus up the hill to the Babilônia favela, for example, and was thrilled to learn that he was learning Portuguese and had even learned the Brazilian slang spoken in the favela "as if he had been born in Meier or Madureira," working-class suburbs of Rio de Janeiro. The magazine also reported that the French director was studying the psychology of the Carioca. "Because of Camus' talent," the magazine argued, French cinema found a home in Brazil. "If he confirms his great talent with *Black Orpheus*, the film will constitute propaganda for Brazil comparable to what Lima Barreto had done with *O Cangaceiro*."[49] In France and Brazil, *Black Orpheus* had viewers who praised and criticized the film from different perspectives. Critics in the United States were not a monolith either, but the American writers and critics mostly praised *Black Orpheus* in the 1960s. As we have seen, the film inspired African American musicians and filmmakers alike.

Reception in the United States

In August 1959, the American press announced that *Black Orpheus* had been acquired for American distribution by Lopert Films. Lopert Films had only been created in 1947 to acquire and promote foreign films at a time when the art film houses were beginning to expand. As it had benefited from the creation of new organizations and ways of marketing films in Europe, *Black Orpheus* would also take advantage of new postwar developments and distribution channels in the United States. Lopert Films' founder, Ilya Lopert, was a Russian-born entrepreneur, film producer, and distributor who had worked for MGM before creating his own independent film distribution company based primarily on extensive transatlantic contacts. Lopert Films was also part of the recently created Screen Producers Guild, now the Producers Guild of America (PGA) after the merger with the Television Producers Guild. In April 1960, the guild nominated *Black Orpheus* for its best-produced film award in the year's first quarter. The nomination would guarantee more press coverage, more viewers, and more profits for the producers and the distributor. The guild also nominated three other films: *Our Man in Havana*, *Can-Can*, and *Home from the Hills*.[50]

Black Orpheus arrived in the United States in November 1959, but like their Brazilian counterparts, news outlets like *The New York Times* announced what was happening in Europe. The paper reported that France took the major prize at Cannes and that Marcel Camus, the youngster and newcomer who "was picking up international glories."[51] The U.S. papers highlighted the fact that Marpessa Dawn, an American, was playing the part of the Brazilian Eurydice.[52] Lopert Films also seized on Dawn's role to promote the film. Industry insiders raved about her beauty, and Lopert produced a brochure about her to promote the film. The agency paid less attention to Mello, the actor who played the title character, presumably because he was not American. *Motion Picture Daily*, the industry publication, announced to readers in the United States that:

> Marpessa Dawn, the star of Lopert's "Black Orpheus," is the daughter of a Black mother and a Fillipino (sic) father. According to *Life*'s March 14 issue, she is a lovely girl with a faunlike grace and disposition. Marpessa was born in Pittsburgh, grew up in New York, and hit success in Paris. Interestingly, her first big film, "Black Orpheus," was made in Portuguese in Brazil, which she had to learn. This Lopert film won the Golden Palm at the Cannes Film Festival, is an Academy Award nominee, and also received editorial recognition in *Life*. Lopert has published an impressive press book in attractive spring hues, which will be a splendid advertising aid to all managers playing "Black Orpheus."[53]

Lopert's investments in publicity guaranteed it an impressive initial reception among mainstream audiences in the United States. It was also bound to reach the Academy of Motion Picture Arts and Sciences. Ironically, the Academy awarded the best foreign language to a film in Portuguese to France, a country that did not speak the language of the film. The Academy had only created the Foreign Film Award in 1956, and, unlike other awards, it was presented to countries rather than to the director or producer. In 1960, Sacha Gordine accepted the Oscar for France alone. By that time, Camus, Breno Mello, and Marpessa Dawn were immersed in other projects.[54]

News of the Oscar nomination sent off a series of accolades praising aspects of the film from its poetry to its primitivism. In fact, these two elements appeared in the title of Mae Tinee's article about the film in the *Chicago Daily Tribune*: "Film Joins Primitive and Poetic." Tinee warned audiences that they might be hearing more about the film because it was "a masterful combination of the poetic and the primitive set against the colorful background of the annual carnival in Rio de Janeiro." "Carnival," she continued, was a time "when the poor forget their troubles," put on elaborate costumes, and "dance the night away." These descriptions about Afro-Brazilian customs come from the movie rather than research by the writer, indicating the power of Camus's construction of Black Brazil at a time when information was not as readily available as it is today.[55]

Tinee's article represented the transgressive audiovisual pleasure of the mainstream White American audience. The presence of Black Brazilians and the visual Dionysian spectacle of carnival constituted elements of Brazilian positive 'primitivism,' a pleasurable version of the 'noble savage.' Ironically, Americans such as Tinee consumed this positive yet static version of Brazil in the 1960s precisely because of its difference from mainstream (middle-class and White) Protestant America in the post-McCarthy era. Furthermore, this version of Black Brazil was a pleasant alternative to the tense racial relations in the United States, as President Barack Obama's mother related.[56] Aside from Mardi Gras parades in the United States, Rio's carnival in *Black Orpheus* also included merriment among the poor. Indeed, the "frantic gaiety, the pulsating music, and mad whirling runs as well as a somber thread of the ill-fated love in a slum section of the Brazilian city."[57] Like other critics, the *Chicago Daily Tribune* journalist lavished praise on Breno Mello and his American costar, who emanated an "appealing," "mellow," and "gentle" presence, the customary gendered tropes.[58]

Black Orpheus was destined for popular success, and Lopert Films expected to gross considerable economic returns. According to Leon Brandt, Lopert's general sales manager, the movie was on track to gross between $800,000 and $1,200,000. In the fifteenth week at the Plaza Theatre in New York, *Black Orpheus* will do more business this week than in its engagement's second and third weeks.[59] Because of a prior Plaza commitment, *Black Orpheus* was going to move into two other Manhattan art houses. In addition, according to *Motion Picture Daily*, the film would receive a booking increase of 50 percent. "Forty key city situations are anticipated by April 15, and while these are restricted to specialty houses, Brandt said he already has been approached by heads of a general circuit here to dub the film into English for mass patronage."[60]

A Note on the Black Press in the United States

Reactions in the Black press in the United States were similar to those in the mainstream press. However, individual responses from African Americans often highlighted a diasporic connection while also mentioning the spectacle. In early April, *The Chicago Defender* simply informed its audiences that *Black Orpheus* had been selected for the best foreign picture of the year by the Academy of Motion Picture Arts and Sciences at the thirty-second annual awards event.[61] Meanwhile, the *Pittsburgh Courier* focused more attention on its African American daughter, Marpessa Dawn. Staff writer Phyllis Garland reported that Marpessa Dawn had achieved the highest peak of her career and hoped that Pittsburghers would have an opportunity to see the girl who jumped from Redstone to Paris and stardom in just a few short years. Garland claimed that the film "throbs with sex, color, and music."[62]

The focus on "color" and "music" was consistent with other reviews.[63] However, the film had no actual sex scenes, although Camus filmed intimate scenes of Orpheus and Eurydice in bed and with Serafina and her visiting boyfriend, both of which implied loving and consensual sexual relations among Black characters. These scenes, depicting Black love in organic ways, were new for mainstream audiences in the United States. The short 1898 film *Something Good-Negro Kiss* by White filmmaker William Selig, also an owner of a minstrel company, manages to depict one of the earlier moments of intimacy between two Black characters. Not until the 1950s and 1960s would American mainstream films feature films depicting intimacy between Black characters. Consider the 1954 *Carmen Jones*, featuring Dorothy Dandridge and Harry Belafonte, and later *Paris Blues* (1961) with Sidney Poitier and Diahann Carroll. Music was central to both films. Afro-Latinx characters were nonexistent. The newness of Afro-Latina beauty depicted by a Black American actress was also novel. Garland described actress Dawn as a "dusky ethereal beauty," a Black version of the Greek myth. She described Mello as "ruggedly handsome" while misidentifying him as "one of Brazil's top football players."[64]

American journalists and audiences, Black and White, associated *Black Orpheus* with Brazil and not France. The film became a reference and later a point of comparison with other films with Brazilian themes.[65] Because of its global reach, *Black Orpheus* created a transnational dialogue around national and racial representations. Different writers spoke differently to their national audiences about exoticism, beauty, and the meaning of carnival. Brazilian and French discourses differed from one another and from the language that described the reception of the film in the United States, the largest potential audience and movie-viewing market. As President Obama's memoir indicates, *Black Orpheus* continued to leave a mark on audiences with different sensibilities and in different geographical spaces. The film also inspired party themes, Halloween, and masked balls like the one at Club Allegro in Chicago in 1972. It continues to inspire debates online, on Facebook and on YouTube.[66]

Conclusion

The reception of *Black Orpheus* in the United States, France, and Brazil in the 1960s constitutes an integral part of the circulation of ideas about Brazil and Afro-Brazilian culture. This chapter presents a window into the press and thousands of local and national newspapers and magazines that covered movies from the 1950s to the 1970s. In an era before widespread digital data and opinions, reporters and commentators in major newspapers and magazines helped to disseminate impressions of the movies for national audiences. They helped to construct an imagined spectatorship. However, as we have noted throughout this work, audiences and viewers are not a monolith. Nor was there just one imagined Brazil. Nevertheless, the dialogue among the different ways of viewing *Black Orpheus* enhanced the circulation of the film, ideas about Brazil, and consumption of Afro-Brazilian cultural products.

Many Brazilian writers in the 1960s were interested in foreign perceptions of Brazil. They were curious about the French 'foreign' producers' interest in Brazil and their insertion into the Carioca landscape. They also wrote to national audiences in Portuguese about the attention Brazil received abroad. Meanwhile, *Black Orpheus* emerged in the American and French press, inspiring joy and excitement. American and French periodicals gravitated toward descriptions and images highlighting what their national audiences perceived as 'exotism.' Even those views that had common points of view were not comparable. Instead, they constituted oblique views, different ways of seeing the same images and listening to the same songs based on national, racial, and gender sensibilities. French and American writers were curious about Brazilians' different relationships to music and dance. Foreign newspapers also highlight images of sensuality, excitement, and impressive landscapes in the film. Others praise or criticize the acting. American writers highlighted their 'home girl,' Marpessa Dawn. One French publication places the film within the Catholic carnival ritual of merriment, alluding to the symbolic resurrection of Orpheus.

This chapter does not provide a complete comparative analysis of the Brazilian, French, or American views about *Black Orpheus*. Rather, the chapter highlights the importance of reception to the dialogues around *Black Orpheus*, focusing mostly on a sample of prominent newspapers in the United States and France and a smaller sample from Brazil. We highlight Jean-Luc Godard because of the cultural and intellectual importance and respect of the *Cahiers du cinéma*. Godard dialogues with voices from other more popular publications, including opinions from the Black press in the United States. Articles and images of the film and its actors also appeared in the vanity press in France and the United States. U.S. magazines *Jet* and *Ebony* and the French magazines *Ciné-Révélation* and *Chez nous* featured Dawn in photoshoots, presumably because of her accessibility outside of Brazil compared to her co-stars.[67] The juxtaposition of opinions by the respected periodicals and writers is inherent to the analysis and contributes to the globalization of Afro-Brazilian popular culture.

Part II

Black Orpheus Legacies and the Globalization of Afro-Brazilian Culture

Part II looks at the continued circulation of Afro-Brazilian images as a part of the constructed ideas of Brazil in the United States and France. Chapter 5 analyzes the images and sounds of Black Brazil in U.S. American and French commercial film production in the 1960s and 1970s and provides an analysis of the Afro-Brazilian presence in Brazilian films of the era. Compared to *Black Orpheus*, few films centered the Black experience or hired a majority Black cast. Unlike *Black Orpheus* constructed narrative around Black life, the majority of American and French films present Black Brazil through music and dance. There are a few exceptions that employ Black actors in compelling roles. Yet, here again rather than dismiss the images related to music and dance only as one-dimensional (some of them are), this chapter invites readers to ask how those images gave audiences a glimpse into the continued saliency of Afro-Brazilian talent. It implicitly engages ideas about the contested and multilayered nature of Black popular culture from Stuart Hall, Michael Boyce Gillespie, bell hooks, Daniela Berghahn, and Manthia Diawara as it relates to ideas about diaspora and the transnational circulation of popular culture.[1]

Chapter 6 uses the 1962 Carnegie Hall concert as a springboard to examine the collaborative role of African diasporic collaboration. It looks at the trajectories of Afro-Brazilian artists who migrated to the United States in the wake of *Black Orpheus*'s success. It highlights the influence of three Afro-Brazilian performers and the trajectory of Brazilian music abroad through their collaborations with African American jazz performers in the 1960s. It also presents information on other Afro-Brazilian performers who followed in their footsteps in the 1960s and 1970s. Finally, chapter 7 follows two Afro-Brazilian performers in Paris and provides readers with an analysis of their contributions to the circulation of Afro-Brazilian culture. It ends with a survey of diverse Afro-Brazilian performers who also made their way to Paris. Afro-Brazilian performers in the United States and France represent new incarnations of the metaphorical Orpheus, who influenced the global musical and cultural legacy in the 1960s and 1970s.

5

Transnational Lights Beyond *Black Orpheus*

Based on the novel *Samba pour la France*, the 2014 French film *Samba* focuses on undocumented workers in France. At the center of the narrative is the romantic relationship between one of the White female immigration workers (played by Charlotte Gainsbourg) and Samba, an undocumented Black man from Senegal (played by the actor Omar Sy). Audiences follow Samba as he attempts to legalize his status in France.[1] He interacts with an undocumented Algerian worker who pretends to be Brazilian because he believes people will treat him better. There are no actual Brazilian human characters in the film, but Brazilian sounds, images of carnival, and Brazilian merriment pervade the script. The title "*Samba*" comes from the name of the main character in the film and not from the Brazilian musical form and dance.[2] French filmmakers Olivier Nakache and Éric Toledano's film reminds us that France's image of Brazilians as joyous, sensual, and fun-loving remains strong. Moreover, *Samba* attests to the enduring legacy of Brazilian cultural influences in the Atlantic world's popular culture half a century after the success of *Black Orpheus*.[3]

In the 1960s and 1970s, images and tropes from *Black Orpheus*, often without Black characters, continued to inspire filmmakers and producers in the United States and France. While it is impossible to provide an exhaustive assessment of all the American and French films shot in Brazil, this chapter provides a sample of the major films of the long 1960s. Many filmmakers developed or utilized similar images to those in *Black Orpheus*. Others incorporated Brazilian music, tropical landscapes, or versions of Afro-Brazilian religious

FIGURE 4 Still of the actress Ruth de Souza, who plays a "voodoo priestess," from the American film *Macumba Love* (1960), directed by Douglas Fowley. Credit: United Artists/Photofest © United Artists

practices in various film genres from adventure and romantic comedies to horror. Most American or European films did not employ Black casting, and none used Portuguese as the primary film language. Yet, many representatives and cultural products from Black Brazil continued to circulate in cinema productions in France and the United States after *Black Orpheus*. We can see direct influences from *Black Orpheus* in films such as *Copacabana* (1962), but more often filmmakers use Brazilian references in storylines that are not

FIGURE 5 Still of the main White female protagonist (the actress Françoise Dorléac) dancing with a community of Afro-Brazilians in Rio de Janeiro from the French film *That Man in Rio* (1964), directed by Philippe de Roca. Credit: Courtesy Photofest

about Brazil. Many actors and musicians connected to *Black Orpheus*, the Black Experimental Theatre, or one of the producers worked on other transnational projects. They continued to contribute to the globalization of Afro-Brazilian culture. However, few films produced in the United States or France focus *exclusively* on Black Brazilians or Brazilian popular culture. Often, many films include or reference Black Brazil through music, carnival, or by employing Afro-Brazilian performers and actors.

Other movies filmed on location in Brazil utilized tropical landscapes where Afro-Brazilians serve as backdrops. Nevertheless, these references constitute Afro-Brazilian cinematic signposts that tell audiences where they are. They also remind spectators of the African presence in Brazil, mainly when Black actors are present implicitly or tacitly through sounds, styles, and other audiovisual cues. Any films shot in Minas Gerais, for example, may not directly reference the work of the Afro-Brazilian sculptures of Aleijadinho or other monuments constructed by Afro-Brazilian labor, but they are nonetheless there for observers to discover. Viewers must search for such references since, as Ed Guerrero notes in *Framing Blackness*, commercial cinema is a "monopolistic, capital-intensive film business," which, despite narrative innovation and exploration, has been formula-bound and conservative, delivering commodified entertainment to a broad middle class, predominantly White audiences. For Guerrero, this means continued subordination of Blacks and a "hold in place" of the White-dominated symbolic order beyond the actual film artifact.[4] Yet references, signs, and symbols are often present. In many movies shot on location in Brazil, the Afro-Brazilian presence may be 'hidden in plain sight.'

Sacha Gordine's acceptance speech for Best Foreign Film at the 1960 Academy Awards symbolizes the White-dominated symbolic order. Gordine appeared on stage alone.[5] No Afro-Brazilians were present, and Gordine does not mention Black Brazil in his speech. This absence is at odds with the purported goal to showcase Afro-Brazilian culture. Afro-Brazilians remain invisible in many global spaces where power brokers gather even as their images and cultural products circulate globally. At the same time, as we have seen, actors like Breno Mello enjoyed some initial success in front of the camera after *Black Orpheus*. Mana de Xangô, Mello's ex-wife, attested to his newfound fame and the subsequent limitations imposed on her ex-husband.[6] Marpessa Dawn had initial success in Paris as well. By the late 1960s, she pursued roles in the cinema and in the theater, although her dream was to perform on Broadway, which *Ebony* calls "The Great White Way." Nonetheless, she remained in France for the rest of her life.[7]

Black Orpheus provided actors and musicians with the visibility necessary in the entertainment industry. Filmmakers and producers also took notice of the film's success and developed new film and musical projects that relied on Brazilian popular culture. Yet, fewer film projects consciously aimed to invest in exploring Black Brazil. Many were capitalizing on the demand for exotic themes about Brazil, including popular Brazilian culture. Laurent Dubois points out that most of the Brazilian images circulated among French audiences cast the country as an unknown exotic land of adventure.[8] American filmmakers trafficked in these types of images well before the release of *Black Orpheus*. Images of fun-loving, racially ambiguous people with a joy for life, symbolized by Rio's carnival, circulated widely on both sides of the Atlantic. The nonthreatening Brazilian exotic image remained a staple well into the 1970s, often without the details and cultural nuances in *Black Orpheus*. The perceived widespread Brazilian cultural and racial intermingling contrasted with the official segregation in the United States.[9]

French and American Commercial Movies After *Black Orpheus*

Images of Brazil, Brazilian culture, and Afro-Brazilians continued to appear in French films after *Black Orpheus*. However, no film focused exclusively on a Black community or employed Black casting. Indeed, none of the French mainstream movies replicated the racial representation in *Black Orpheus*, although many films employed musicians and actors or referenced actors and cultural products, particularly Brazilian music. Paris also allowed for cross-African diasporic connections due to the presence of African descendants from Africa and across the diaspora. The 1961 American film *Paris Blues* almost had a connection to *Black Orpheus* with the possible participation of Léa Garcia, who was in Paris when the crew was shooting. Actor Sidney Poitier approached Garcia to appear in the film, but she could not accept the invitation because she had to return to Brazil. Gestures such as Poitier's represent a tacit connection to *Black Orpheus*,[10] and the possibility of African diasporic transnational exchange and dialogue in the 1960s.

French filmmakers included Brazilian music in their film scores more than any cultural product. French films about Brazil also showcased Afro-Brazilian music in the plot and the soundtrack, including Brazilian drumbeats and sounds from other instruments, *cantigas*, guitar playing, ballads, religious music from Candomblé and Macumba, and especially samba, a quintessential symbol of Black Brazil.[11] As Carlos Sandroni tells us, before its institutionalization as a type of national music, Brazilians considered samba, whether referring to music or dance, a "Black thing."[12] Samba was the central Black symbol in *Black Orpheus*, and it continued to play that role in subsequent French films.

The 1965 film *Arrastão: Les amants de la mer* (*Doomed Lovers*) has many parallels with *Black Orpheus*, though the main protagonists are White. Vinicius de Moraes once again wrote the script that transported the Celtic story of Tristan and Isolde, made famous by the Richard Wagner opera, to Itaipu, a small fishing village across Guanabara Bay in Rio de Janeiro. The two lovers, Geronimo and Emaësa, face a familiar dilemma as Emaësa is already committed to Geronimo's cousin Marcus. Directed by the Parisian-born Antoine d'Ormesson with dialogue in French, the movie featured the musical film score of Brazilian composer Ubirajara Quaranta Cabral.[13]

Many Afro-Brazilians appear in the film, including the great Grande Otelo, who plays the vindictive fisherman Focinho, who is also deeply in love with Emaësa.[14] Unable to attract her attention, he turns to a Macumba priestess to no avail and then tries to manipulate Marcus into killing Geronimo. In an unexpected moment, Marcus throws Focinho off the cliff to his death.

Afro-Brazilian actress and dancer Iolanda Braga also represents Black Brazil. She plays the role of Mana, another character in pursuit of someone who does not reciprocate her feelings. She has feelings for Geronimo and lies to him as he dies on the floor and insists that Emaësa does not love him as she does. There are also many other Afro-Brazilians among the fishermen. The child actor Cosme dos Santos plays a small but important role as he dances the samba in a public square of musicians who utilize matchboxes and tin cans to create sounds. Here, as in *Black Orpheus*, the viewer experiences an endearing scene of an innocent young boy dancing samba, a symbol of Black joy. At the same time, the young dos Santos is performing for the camera, allowing for multiple ways of viewing. When there are no other Black characters, the persistent and singular connection to dance and music enforces the stereotypes, but to its credit,

Arrastão includes several Black characters in diverse roles. Incidentally, the other two prominent Black characters use deception to pursue White characters romantically, but they fail.

While Black representation was vital to the globalization of Black Brazil, *Arrastão* centers on the relationship of the protagonists Geronimo and Emaësa, played by White actors Pierre Barouh, of Turkish-Jewish ancestry and Duda Cavalcanti, who was born in Rio de Janeiro and later moved to Paris. Nonetheless, Otelo's talent was on display as he played the story's villain. The Brazilian actor was happy to work with the French crew and play a character who was different from the comical characters he consistently played in Brazilian films. In a television interview at the end of his career, Grande Otelo was candid about the racism he experienced in Brazil as a performer, having to enter the stage through the backdoor, among other indignities. He also reminisced about the good times, such as working with Josephine Baker at the Cassino da Urca and befriending the filmmaker Orson Welles and the French singer Henri Salvador, another important promotor of Brazilian music in France.[15] Grande Otelo relished working with foreigners who brought a different sensibility to filmmaking. On November 26, 1993, he died in Paris en route to the northern Atlantic city of Nantes, where he was to be honored for his work in Brazilian cinema.[16]

Throughout the 1960s, Barouh would play an important role in highlighting Black Brazil to global audiences. Before leaving Rio after shooting *Arrastão*, Barouh created the French version of Baden Powell's composition "Saravá," which pays homage to the pioneers of Brazilian popular music. He later used the song in the 1966 *Un homme et une femme* (*A Man and a Woman*). *A Man and a Woman* focuses on the relationship of a French widow and widower as they continue to think of the memories of their deceased spouses. The widow, Anne Gauthier (played by Anouk Aimée), reminisces about her deceased husband (played by Pierre Barouh), who appears in flashbacks. Anne talks about how samba entered her husband's life in one scene, and the film flashes to him talking about Brazil. Barouh convinced composer Francis Lai to include a French translation of "Saravá" in the film score at this critical moment in the narrative.[17] Thus, this transnational project references Afro-Brazilian and Black Brazil through sound.

Referencing a joyous Brazil that has changed his life, Barouh's translated version of "Saravá" salutes many Afro-Brazilian musicians and samba: The lyrics pay homage to many Brazilian musical pioneers. It celebrates Black Brazil by sending blessings to Afro-Brazilian musicians Dorival Caymmi, Baden Powell, and Pixinguinha, among others. He ends the song by referencing Bahia, samba's original birthplace. It concludes with an uneven gendered image of racial mixture:

The samba has the grace of whiteness in her form
But she has the soul of Blackness in her heart
I am enchanted by her call,
My heart loves the samba best of all.[18]

Two additional issues in the lyrics deserve special mention. First, Barouh indirectly points to Brazil's complex relationship between race and nation when he sings that Moraes is the Blackest White man in the country. Moraes repeated that description about himself on many occasions and reiterated his love for Black culture. Afro-Brazilian icon Gilberto Gil defended Moraes's version of racial drag, insisting that this description was accurate because Moraes "was touched by Black culture aesthetically, morally and culturally." Gil also claimed that Moraes lived with affection for others. "He wanted all Whites to be Black and all Blacks to be White."[19] However, if he were speaking today, Moraes would probably find a different way of expressing his affection for Afro-Brazilians and Afro-Brazilian culture. Even then, Moraes was performing a type of drag since he was not Black and could not experience life as a Black man, though he tried to understand it. Moreover, to paraphrase the title of Greg Tate's work, Moraes could celebrate and experience "everything but the burden."[20]

In an interview recorded by the National Library, Moraes explains that he is deeply attracted to Black Brazilian culture, especially after encountering Candomblé in Bahia and working with Baden Powell on the *Afro-Sambas*. He then lists all the Black musicians with whom he worked before adding that if he had the choice, he would have liked to have been born Black.[21] Finally, Barouh's celebration of samba ends with an often-simplistic dualistic racialized version that purports that "the poetry of the samba is White, but its soul is Black." Here again, with an intent to celebrate Black Brazil, the essentialist lyrics end up robbing Afro-Brazilians of their contribution to poetry, which, in fact, is central to the Orphic myth. Similarly, Barouh talks about himself as the most Brazilian Frenchman, a moniker clearly meant to express his enthusiasm for Brazil. Incidentally, the early Negritude poets initially utilized essentialist language within a historical context of post–World War I when authors such as Oswald Spengler were writing about the decline of the west and searching for spiritual and poetic references elsewhere.[22]

As noted above, when filming in Brazil, many directors invariably highlighted tropical landscapes, beaches, and forests, similar to images promoted by Brazilian tourism. However, it is still unclear whether the films about Brazil directly influenced the expansion of French tourism to the country in the 1960s and 1970s when French international aviation developed. We know that because of rising demand throughout the 1960s, Air France established an office in Brazil with one employee in 1976. Tourism brought foreign currency to the country but also contributed to foreign gentrification. The case of Brigitte Bardot in Búzios, a multiracial fishing village, is a case in point. "And Bardot Created Búzios," the title of the 2004 article, attests to Bardot's power since Búzios began to rapidly develop after she visited the sleepy fishing village with her boyfriend Bob Zagury in 1964. That same year, Bardot, already a global film personality, recorded Carlos Lyra's Brazilian song "Maria Ninguém" in Portuguese. The song had been a part of the bossa nova repertoire ever since João Gilberto recorded it on his album *Chega de saudade* in 1959. Brazilian critics apparently loved it because of her "delicious French accent in Portuguese."[23]

Today, the main strip of land in Búzios is called the Orla Bardot. The only cinema is called the Cinema Bardot, and the actress's bronze statue adorns the seafront on the Praia dos Ossos.[24] Her trip to Brazil directly impacted the small town as streams of Europeans and Brazilians flocked there, transforming it into a global tourist destination while displacing the fishermen. It was a Brazilian example of transnational gentrification. Bardot's story is relevant to the circulation of Black Brazil because it provides a context in which *Black Orpheus* flowed as part of the currency of Blackness and Brazilian popular classes. Travel to Rio de Janeiro increased because of the film and the global gaze of White celebrities. The Brazilian elite's neocolonial gaze and pleasure in receiving attention from Europeans is also part of the dynamics of cultural circulation. Búzios soon became an acceptable local destination for the elites and the middle class.[25]

Other French filmmakers had a less intimate relationship with Brazil yet utilized the Brazilian landscape and ordinary Brazilians as backdrops to their main stories. Director Philippe de Broca collaboration with film actor Jean Paul Belmondo in the 1963 *L'Homme de Rio* (*That Man from Rio*, 1963) is an excellent example. Broca wanted to make a naive adventure film about a man who goes to Brazil to rescue his fiancée who had been drugged and kidnapped. The main actors' dialogue is in French, and French translators dub all the Brazilian Portuguese into French. The action showcased Belmondo's wit and the actress Françoise Dorléac's talents. The protagonists travel through the Brazilian landscape, allowing audiences to vicariously experience Brazil's geography and parts of its culture. The film crew had unprecedented access to the major landmarks across the country and Brasilia as the capital was being built, making the film an important document for students interested in the construction of the new capital city.

An hour into the film, Belmondo visits a favela in Rio de Janeiro and witnesses the Afro-Brazilian community playing music and dancing samba. Audiences see and hear the unique sound of the *cuica*, the *pandeiro*, and the beating of drums and clapping. Belmondo's young Black friend Milton shows his talent by dancing in the circle as Dorléac's character (Villermosa) joins in. The camera focuses on her as the Afro-Brazilians serve as a cultural backdrop. Viewers have no information about the Afro-Brazilian community or why they are celebrating. It is as if the producers added the community dancing scene as a short respite for the protagonist, who has just endured an arduous chase. The Brazilian actor Milton Ribeiro from *O Cangaceiro* plays one of the villains in the film, and as in Luis Carlos Barreto's film, his racial identity fits within a Black-*Mestiço* continuum. While the film visually documents aspects of Black Brazil in the 1960s, the critic James Martin from *Film Quarterly* shows his ignorance of Brazilian music, referring to the soundtrack as a series of "likable variety of Calypso music."[26]

The film references and parallels *Black Orpheus*: the favela, samba, dancing, and the inclusion of children. In one instance, the film also samples a musical phrase directly from the *Black Orpheus* soundtrack. In general, the film utilizes popular Brazilian music to provide local touches. *Batucada* drumming also helps provide a sense of adventure. The film featured the musical talent of Aníbal Alves de Almeida, brother of the famous Afro-Brazilian singer Aracy de Almeida.[27] An uncredited singer also performs "Chorando sim," in the style of many of the decade's Afro-Brazilian crooners.[28]

In 1965, André Hunebelle directed *Furia à Bahia pour OSS 117* (*Fury in Bahia*) about the adventures of Agent 117 and his investigation of a criminal organization developing a drug to control human behavior. Like Belmondo's film, this adventure allows audiences to explore Brazil, but Brazilian culture and personalities are not central to the plot. References to Afro-Brazilian culture appear as a part of the musical scenes and soundtrack by Michel Magne, one of Henri Salvador's favorite composers. For Magne, the movie's musical score is essential for the overall effect on the viewer. It can highlight certain aspects of the plot or even transform the intention.[29] In *Fury in Bahia*, Magne includes jazz, bossa nova, and samba. "Batucada de Bahia," for example, is emblematic of that mixture with the distinct sound of the *cuica*. Magne also includes carnival music for a samba scene with Afro-Brazilian dancers as the character Hubert Bonisseur de La Bath (alias OSS) eats with his date (Anna-Maria Sulza). The short scene features Afro-Brazilian performers dancing in the street in red and white costumes. The film again highlights the uniquely Brazilian instrument: the *cuica* and the compositions "Samba de Furioso" and "Batucada de Bahia." The typical plot also uses the local landscape and culture as a backdrop.

In *Pour un amour lointain* (*For a Distant Love*, 1969), Luiz Bonfá, from the *Black Orpheus* project, returned to Brazil to create the soundtrack for a movie about a French star who falls in love with two *Carioca* twins. Despite Bonfá's presence in Brazil, Brazilian culture becomes the backdrop for the French main narrative. Bonfá created the decidedly bossa nova soundtrack without referencing Black Brazil or *Black Orpheus*. He collaborated with the White singer

Maria Toledo for the only ballad in the score. Five years earlier, Bonfá had teamed up with fellow musicians Tom Jobim and João Gilberto for an appearance in *Copacabana Palace* (1962), the French-Italian and Brazilian coproduction by the Italian director Steno. With dialogue in Italian, *Copacabana Palace* followed the pattern set by *Black Orpheus* without placing Afro-Brazilians at the center of the narrative. However, the drama takes place over the three main days of carnival. The chic decor of the Copacabana Palace Hotel replaces the favela. The film directors also ventured into the streets of Rio to provide glimpses of urban life and capture scenes with Afro-Brazilians.

All the leading Brazilian characters are White. Yet one short scene presents a sexualized European gaze of Black Brazil even as they make up a part of the cultural backdrop. A group of shirtless, muscular male Black characters appears briefly in a scene as they navigate a boat carrying the White Italian princess lounging lazily on the deck. The nameless men, who have no speaking role, appear in white shorts as the princess stretches, providing viewers with a gaze onto Brazilian Black male bodies. The camera moves back and forth between the men to the princess, who moves her body around and eventually releases the strings from the bikini. The sexually suggestive and racially charged scene would have gotten the audience's attention. It would have been censored in the United States because of the Hays Code.

French-produced films benefited from France's global distribution network, which also helped in the global circulation of Brazilian images in French films. The French government's Development Act of 1953 instituted a small surcharge on French ticket sales to create a development fund that assisted French filmmakers (including in coproductions) in producing and distributing their films. With the impending expiration of the act on December 31, 1959, filmmakers rushed to finish projects in production in 1959.[30] As Isabelle Vanderschelden points out, France has continued to develop robust mechanisms for governing and supporting French film production.[31] Governmental support of French cinema has continued since the 1950s, although sources of income have expanded to include other venues as cinema options have expanded. In 2021, France launched a 10-million-euro modernization fund for the film, TV, and videogame sectors. Exact data for film subsidies for specific films in the 1950s and 1960s are difficult to obtain, but producer Sacha Gordine was an able fundraiser through his many production companies, including Dispat Films.

Camus and Brazil Post–*Black Orpheus*

Throughout the 1960s and early 1970s, no French-Brazilian production received as much widespread transnational attention as *Black Orpheus*. Nor did any film center Black Brazil or demonstrate the commitment to work with Afro-Brazilians that Marcel Camus demonstrated. After the success of *Black*

Orpheus, Camus made two more Brazilian-themed movies. He had also developed deep connections to Brazil. Later, he married the Brazilian Lourdes de Oliveira (who played Mira in *Black Orpheus*). Oliveira also collaborated on his two other Brazilian films. In *Os Bandeirantes* (*The Pioneers*, 1960), Camus followed the formula of the adventure film genre and used the Brazilian landscape beyond Rio de Janeiro. However, this time, the main characters were European, although Afro-Brazilian characters played important roles and did not merely serve as backdrop like in many other French productions.

In *The Pioneers*, Camus included Brazilian actors and musicians as he explored the interior of Brazil and the Amazon region. He relied on the music from the multitalented Afro-Brazilian composer and musician José Toledo (Zezinho) and the White Italian musician Henri Crolla, who had worked on the *Black Orpheus* film. *The Pioneers* centered on an excursion into the Amazon. The audience follows Jean, the main character, intent on seeking revenge. As he traverses the Brazilian landscape and meets Brazilians along the way, he discovers himself, joy, and the value of human generosity. Lourdes de Oliveira plays the role of the Brazilian woman, Suzana. Léa Garcia, another Brazilian actress from *Black Orpheus*, also appears in the film in a supporting role as Herminia, along with the young Maria Alice, who plays Suzana's daughter. Afro-Brazilians such as Edgar Freire, a world-class long-distance runner known as the Paulista Locomotive, also appeared in the production, showing Camus's desire to connect with Brazilians by continuing to feature famous Brazilian personalities. Freire also appeared in the transnational film production *Le tout pour le tout* (1962), produced by Sacha Gordine, who continued looking for film opportunities in Brazil. Despite Afro-Brazilian and other Brazilian representations, this French film follows the hackneyed formula, placing Brazilians as supporting characters to the central French story.

Fifteen years later, Camus returned to Brazil to focus on Black Brazil with the film *Otália da Bahia*, his last Brazilian film. Camus focused on Brazilian characters in this project and worked closely with the Bahian writer Jorge Amado, whose work inspired the film. The film also allowed him to work with musician-composer Tom Jobim once again, the Bahian Mestiça singer Maria Creuza, and Afro-Brazilian composer Emilio Santiago. *Otália* was an important intervention in the construction of Black Brazil for a new generation. Yet, the film uses similar images from Black Brazil, including songs, dances, and religions. It takes place in Bahia, often called the 'Black Rome,' where African culture flourishes in multiple dimensions. The influence goes back generations, leading many Brazilians to refer to White people from Bahia as '*branco de Bahia*,' connoting that somewhere in the family's ancestry there are African family members. Camus's collaboration with Jorge Amado parallels his earlier work with Moraes in many ways. In a call-in interview on Brazilian TV, Amado defended himself against criticism that he chose *Mestiço* characters over Black ones by claiming that he was a follower of the Afro-Brazilian religion, Candomblé, and had celebrated Brazil's African heritage more than any other writer in Brazil. At the same time, Amado proclaimed that the only solution to racism was mixture.[32]

Camus also addressed the criticism leveled at him for the exoticism in his films. He emphasized that he would continue to celebrate the Afro-Brazilian community's cultural production while helping to preserve and document that culture, which was slowly disappearing due to industrialization. According to Camus, laughter and joy cannot erase the profound loss, but he confessed to the newspaper *O Globo* that his film was inherently nostalgic. Camus recognized his pioneering role in exposing many people around the globe to Black Brazil. The IMDb statistics demonstrating *Black Orpheus*'s popularity in France support that assertion.[33] Despite the criticism about his apparent exoticism, Camus was not repentant about his choices for *Black Orpheus*:

> I did not come to make a portrait of the Brazilian people . . . or a type of report about the favelas. *Orpheus* was born from Vinicius' marvelous idea based on a Greek legend, and I tried to make a film against racism. I took advantage of carnival to show that people of color can live better with the same intensity as [w] hite people . . . I perhaps knew more about Brazil than many Brazilians. I can talk about all the places of Brazil that I went to at least once, if not twice, when I accompanied Orlando and Claudio Villas Boas . . . when they discovered the Indians of Xingu . . . Brazil is a homeland for me despite this accent that I have.[34]

Camus spent several weeks in Salvador with Jorge Amado as he filmed *Otália*, and he developed great affection for the city and for Amado. Amado's use of laughter to express freedom resonated with his vision of the world. Camus's filmic gaze had similarities with many films made by Brazilians, including those inspired by Amado's work, such as *Dona Flor and Her Two Husbands* and *Tent of Miracles*. As with *Black Orpheus*, Camus's plot was fast-paced, and he employed Afro-Brazilian music as a central character. "*Orpheus* was a challenge," Camus conceded. However, he believed he succeeded in bringing Brazil's musicality to audiences worldwide. He hoped that *Otália* would do the same fifteen years later. However, the world had changed, and Brazil was now in the middle of a military dictatorship.[35] Camus expressed his desire not to disappoint Amado in his production of *Otália* since Amado had chosen all the locations and many of the people who appeared in the film. Through Amado, Camus met the Candomblé *mãe de santa*, or priestess-advisor, Mãe Mirinha, who agreed to be filmed with all her daughters to show an authentic version of Candomblé.

Afro-Brazilian actress Mira Fonseca plays the protagonist Otália. The film includes other Black actors, including Grande Otelo, as well as other well-known actors, such as Antonio Pitanga and the *Mestiço* actor Jofre Soares. As in *Black Orpheus*, Camus also relied on many nonprofessional actors. For Camus, the characters displayed generosity and the capacity to love life despite their challenges and difficulties. The French director was also cognizant of the danger of exhibiting sensuality and sentiments that may fall into stereotypes. He lamented that some of the characters appear only briefly in the film. He was also aware that the characters pass by so rapidly in the film that they cannot develop as they do in Amado's novel. At the same time, Camus intended to show real people such as the *mãe de santa* and the Bahians who practice the Afro-Brazilian religion Candomblé. "I did not invent these people who go to the temple and enter the church, nor did I invent the sense of rhythm that they show when they begin to dance. Somebody just needs to appear with a guitar," he once declared.[36]

Brazilian actors enjoyed working with Camus, and many Brazilians recognized his role in promoting Brazil abroad. When he died in 1982, filmmaker Luis Carlos Barreto expressed his remorse, noting that "he was the foreign filmmaker who best understood Brazil and its people. I do not think it is a big loss for national cinema because he represented France more than anything else, however, I do not have any doubt that *Orpheus* propagated the most important Brazilian party internationally."[37] For Léa Garcia, Camus's death was an incomparable loss from the artistic and human perspective:

> As a filmmaker, he was my father: I am indebted to him for my initiation into my film career because *Orpheus* was my first film. As a person, he was one of my best friends, the type that you know you will never lose and that you will never find another like him. We wrote a lot, and when I found out today that he died, I could not stop crying because the pain was so great. I really lament this very much because we have lost a filmmaker who loved Brazil very much so much so that he married a Brazilian. I lost my friend who called me 'my angel.'[38]

Camus resisted depicting misery and instead chose to depict joy even though he was clearly cognizant of the more socially engaged and political depictions of Brazil. "I don't think that I should be the one to make this type of film," he remarked. "I'm French. To say that Brazilians have this misery in their homes. No. This is for Brazilians to say, and in addition to this, authors such as Nelson Pereira de Santos and Glauber Rocha have already done this." "There's something else," he continued:

> I don't believe in cinema as a direct political instrument. Who will go and watch these austere, politically committed films? Only people who are already convinced and who have money (because cinema is expensive) can dwell on alienating misery while comfortably seated in the cinema. The people who

> spend the entire day in a factory want to laugh and relax when they go to the cinema. On TV, there's another problem. There, one can try with reports to show a certain reality and hope that that reality touches new people. But pay attention: I live among the poor, and I have the right to say this. I am not one of those people who condemn progress. I believe that only industrialization can create a middle class and bring material goods to everyone. What I regret is that this extraordinary communication and this generosity will disappear. Because for all the architects and directors, the construction of a modern city is obligatorily connected to this indifference.[39]

Camus's familial and emotional ties to Brazil, his intuition, and his deep affection for the country and its people are undisputed. Brazilian film scholar Tunico Amâncio affirms that Camus knew that his film aesthetics and his natural impulse as a filmmaker were distinct from the politically engaged filmmaking of Brazil's new cinema movement.[40] Yet, Camus shared similar points of view with other non-Brazilian filmmakers who were making films for their national audiences. Unlike many of them, he made deep connections with Brazil, including establishing legal residency. Amâncio, who participated in the documentary *In Search of Black Orpheus*, is convinced of Camus's historical importance and his impact on Brazilian filmmakers. However, Amâncio argues that Camus's greatest contributions were his documentation of the Brazilian reality of his time and his incomparable affection for a country that he called his second home.[41]

Other members on Camus's production team followed his lead and continued to develop professional relationships with Brazilian actors and performers. Robert Mazoyer, one of the assistant directors on *Black Orpheus*, directed his own transnational film in 1964. *O Santo Módico*, starring several actors from *Black Orpheus*, was one of the first transnational French-Brazilian commercial films to feature the northern state of Bahia, even before Camus's *Otália*. The film centers on the poor fisherman Bento, played by Breno Mello, who comes to the aid of Maria das Dores, a woman who dislocated her collar bone. When he fixes it, das Dores sees an opportunity to make money and spreads the word that Bento can cure any ailment for a price. Crowds eventually follow him pleading for miracles, but Bento, who fears punishment from God, eventually leaves. Mello attests to going to Bahia to make the movie but no copies of the film have been found in Brazil or France. IMDb lists Moacir Santos, Tom Jobim, Luis Bonfá among the collaborators.[42] The credits also boast the presence of Hilda Campos Soares da Silva, better known as Leny Eversong. Eversong, who dyed her hair blond, represents another transnational performer whose racial identity remained ambiguous inside and outside of Brazil depending on the context and historical era. Her 1957 appearance on the Ed Sullivan show performing "Jezebel" with her bellowing operatic and gospel-like voice earned her praise in the United States and Brazil. She also recorded music in France in 1958.[43] Neither Eversong nor any other non-White Brazilians made major appearances in Hollywood movies after the death of Carmen Miranda in 1954. U.S. racialization practices may have also affected other White Brazilian actresses in the United States such as the Lia Torá (1907–1972), Eros Volúsia (1914–2004), Leonora Amar (1926–2014), Leonor Rodrighero, (1926–2014), and Laura Suarez (1909–1990). Hollywood tended to prefer White-looking or White-presenting female actresses. American moviemakers did not develop as robust of a production schedule in Brazil as their French counterparts, and their representations of Afro-Brazilian culture reveal similar trends.

Afro-Brazil Culture in U.S. Hollywood Films

The success of *Black Orpheus* in the United States did not lead to more Afro-Brazilian representation in Hollywood films. Hollywood was grappling with its own challenges with Black American representation and had little interest in Black transnational collaboration or imagery. In fact, American filmmakers did not follow the example of their French counterparts. First, Brazil had strong historical cultural links with France that it did not share with the United States. Second, American governmental support for commercial cinema was limited. However, Brazilian and Afro-Brazilian cultural elements were still present in the American films set in Brazil made for North American English-speaking audiences. Brazil also appeared in American adventure or exotic film stories.

Hattie McDaniel received the Academy Award for Best Supporting Actress for her role in the 1939 film *Gone with the Wind*. Donald Bogle documents the challenges and triumphs of Black actors in Hollywood in the 1940s, including in race movies and what he calls "Black Hollywood." He highlights the talents of McDaniel and Ethel Waters and describes the ascendance of actresses and personalities such as Lena Horne and Hazel Scott.[44] By the 1950s, African Americans had begun to make strides in mainstream American films in the United States. Bahamian American actor Sidney Poitier was a Hollywood pioneer of the 1950s. Poitier appeared in films such as *The Defiant Ones* (1958), *Porgy and Bess* (1959), *Raisin in the Sun* (1961), and *Lilies of the Field*, the 1963 movie that garnered him the Academy Award in 1964 for best actor. Poitier was the first Black person to receive the award for best actor. Poitier's on-screen characters represented a new middle-class protagonist equal to his White peers. Other actors such as Harry Belafonte, Dorothy Dandridge, Ruby Dee, and Ethel Waters also gained wide acclaim in the 1960s.[45] Meanwhile, the dominant image of Brazil in American film production in the immediate post–World War II era was still being shaped by Carmen Miranda's legacy, a formula that American audiences knew. No other Brazilian actress or actor would gain mainstream attention and promote Brazilian culture in the United States until the arrival of Sônia Braga in the 1980s.[46] By that time, demographics and inter-American relations had changed significantly. There were very few specific roles for Brazilian characters. Braga would play various 'Latin' characters in a host of films, from *Kiss of the Spider Woman* (1985) to *The Milagro Beanfield War*, where she plays a Mexican woman.

In the post–World War II era, few opportunities were available for African American actors in Hollywood, much less for Afro-Brazilians. Moreover, Afro-Latinx or Latin Blackness would remain largely invisible in film production until the twenty-first century. Afro-Brazilian or Brazilian culture was not altogether absent in U.S. film production. After the war, for example, Alfred Hitchcock's 1946 *Notorious*, which starred Ingrid Bergman and Cary Grant, featured Rio de Janeiro as a backdrop. Viewers see studio-made images of downtown Rio and the Zona Sul. Viewers get a glimpse of Brazilian extras; some are Afro-Brazilians, but the film is not interested in Brazilian culture. Michael Curtiz's 1948 film *Romance on the High Seas* also focuses on American White main characters who travel on a cruise to the Caribbean and South America. Shot in Technicolor, this comedy-musical features music and dance and relies on the choreography of Busby Berkeley, whose extravagant numbers appeared in many Hollywood films.

Romance on the High Seas samples from Brazilian composer Ary Barroso's 1939 "Aquarela do Brasil," which celebrates *Mulato* Brasil: "Brasil, meu Brasil brasileiro/Meu mulato inzoneiro." The cruise features various Black performers along the Atlantic. The first stop was Cuba, where African American Broadway performer Avon Long sings and dances to "The Tourist Trade" in a scene that recreates a fictitious fruit market. The stop in Trinidad features calypso music led by the Afro-Trinidadian performer Sir Lancelot. On the boat, a lively group called the Samba Kings also perform in Spanish, but there is no connection to Brazil. Ironically, no local Brazilian talent appears when the ship finally arrives in Rio. Instead, Georgia Garret (played by Doris Day) sings in the finale accompanied by a local orchestra. There is an obligatory carnival scene, but no Afro-Brazilians are visible in the orchestra or the indoor carnival. This movie is part of a familiar Hollywood practice of sampling Black culture without Black people. In this case, transnationally.

After *Black Orpheus*

The 1960 American film *Macumba Love*, directed by Douglas Fowley and written by Norman Graham, is emblematic of the continued foreign fascination with Afro-Brazilian spiritual practices. Fowley also showcases Black Brazilian talent, particularly with Afro-Brazilian Ruth de Souza, one of the cofounders and actresses of the Black Experimental Theatre, and Cléa Simões, an actress from Belém in the northern Brazilian state of Pará. Only this time, Hollywood continued a tradition of mixing diverse cultural influences into a fictional space for the American gaze. The film is about a trip of an American writer, who specializes in debunking religious and superstitious beliefs, to an unnamed South American island. Because the movie promoters billed the project as a horror adventure film, the fabricated local "voodoo culture" served that end. The plot centers on the central White characters Venus de Viasa (played by the Israeli actress Ziva Rodann) and J. Peter Weils (played by Walter Reid). The model, June Wilkenson, also appears in seminude shots. Ruth de Souza plays a central character as the voodoo priestess Mama Rata-Loi.

Contemporary advertisements for the movie highlighted the most sensational aspects of the imaginary island inhabited by Black natives. One poster emphasized the "blood lust of the Voodoo Queen" and the "weird, shocking savagery of the native jungle." The poster also enticed audiences with the new technology, advising that the film was entirely "shot in *flaming* Eastman color."[47] The movie trailer contains constant screaming and drumbeats as the narrator asks viewers to bow their heads for those who have lost their lives "on an island in the South Atlantic where voodoo is practiced today . . . See the bloodlust of the voodoo queen wreaking a terrifying vengeance on those who disbelieve . . . in the witch goddess." However, the film's focus on spells, voodoo dolls, and sensationalism avoids discussing organized religious practices. It is emblematic of a particular Hollywood vision of exoticism in horror films. Still, here too, in spite of the script, viewers may be able to appreciate the performances by de Souza, Simões, and other Brazilians.

The 1964 military coup in Brazil stymied and censured national and transnational film production, especially after the ascendance of the military hardliners in 1968. However, in 1965, *The New York Times* reported that foreign film production was booming in Brazil. Low production costs, including the availability of qualified technicians, the variety of scenic opportunities, and the cooperation of the local government, were apparent attractions. Brazil was also an ally amid the Cold War since the United States had actively supported the 1964 coup. In 1967, director Robert Day Shagan produced the fourteenth Tarzan movie, *Tarzan and the Great River*, on the heels of Italian films such as *Kiss the Girls and Make Them Die* (1966) and *A Rose for Everyone* (1967) featuring the Tunisian-born Italian actress Claudia Cardinale.

Although *Black Orpheus* had less of a direct impact on film production in the United States, its legacy emerged in the music for the silver screen and for television. Collaborations and occasional musical performances of *Black Orpheus* and other Brazilian tunes began to appear, although references to Afro-Brazilian culture were either unnoticed or simply viewed as Brazilian.[48] However, opportunities for adventure films would continue for the next few decades, as the James Bond film featuring Roger Moore, *The Spy Who Loved Me* (1977), indicates. Director Lewis Gilbert took advantage of magnificent views of beaches and landscapes, including Sugar Loaf. The city again serves as a backdrop rather than a protagonist, as in Camus's film.

A Brief Survey of Afro-Brazilian Images in Brazil in the 1960s

By the mid-1960s, Brazilian *cinema novo* had pushed forth a new committed aesthetic that challenged international and national film production from companies such as Vera Cruz and Atlátida. It is doubtful that *Black Orpheus* played a role in this change, but many Brazilian filmmakers were intent on creating images that contrasted or inverted the Dionysian worldview just for celebration. The Brazilian *cinema novo* filmmakers tended to dislike Camus's type of filmmaking, as Glauber Rocha's essay "The Aesthetics of Hunger" clearly indicates.[49] Nonetheless, Blackness or Afro-Brazilian characters was not necessarily essential to *cinema novo*. However, many *cinema novo* filmmakers showcased Afro-Brazilian talents. Although not part of the *cinema novo* movement, Haroldo Costa's 1958 film *Pista de grama*, directed by one of the few Black directors, Odilon Lopez, shows Elizeth Cardoso and João Gilberto performing.

To date, Afro-Brazilian directors, producers, technical staff, and actors constitute a small percentage of the workers in the Brazilian film industry. Black directors and writers have suffered from the limited access to federal, state, foundation, and private funds necessary to make films in Brazil. Nevertheless, Brazil has produced several directors. Afro-Brazilian writer, producer, and director José Cajado Filho worked on several films in the late 1940s and early 1950s, although the works of Black directors such as Odilon Lopez and Waldyr Onofre deal more specifically with Afro-Brazilian issues. Add to this a host of documentaries by Afro-Brazilians such as Zózimo Bulbul. Black actors and actresses have played roles in both the cinema and television. Benjamin de Oliveira, one of Brazil's first clowns and the actor in the silent film era, leads the list of talented pioneers.

Dialoguing with *Black Orpheus*

Carlos Manga's 1953 movie *Dupla de Barulho* (*A Great Pair*) showcased the talents of Grande Otelo with his partner Oscarito, following a comedic genre full of mishaps as the main characters travel through Brazil searching for fame and adventure. As we have seen, the early 1950s also brought several dramatic movies to audiences. *Sinhá Moça* (*The Plantation Owner's Daughter*, 1953), made before *Black Orpheus*, and *João Negrinho* (1958), made the same year, provided viewers with nuanced representations of Afro-Brazilians. Based on the nineteenth-century work by Maria Dezonne Pacheco Fernandes, *Sinhá Moça* (directed by Tom Payne and Osvaldo Sampião) was a dramatic period piece about the abolition of slavery. However, the film centers on the conflict between a slave-owning father and his abolitionist daughter. Simultaneously, the film offers complex views and performances by many talented actors, not least of whom was Ruth de Souza. The film also received several national and international awards in 1953 and 1954 for its directors and the principal actress.

In *Black Orpheus*, foreign audiences see one of the first film representations of the syncretic religion, Umbanda. Brazilian films from the 1960s offer more complex assessments of Afro-Brazilian religions and syncretism. Films such as Glauber Rocha's *Barravento* (1961) and Anselmo Duarte's *O Pagador de Promesas* (*The Given Word*, 1962) are two examples. *Tent of Miracles* (1977) also addressed the topic. *The Given Word* and *Tent of Miracles* focus directly on syncretism while illustrating the tensions and prejudice of White society. *Barravento* examines the Afro-Bahian religion on its own terms, although not without exposing the limitations of organized religion.

Black Orpheus does not explicitly present, address, or contend with any racial tensions, racial hierarchies or issues related to racial intermingling. Camus presents a convivial view of Brazilian society. Brazilian filmmakers often make those tensions visible, especially through a class lens. In the 1960s and 1970s, under the watchful eyes of the censors, Cacá Diegues produced films that came close to Black casting as he created historical dramas around African slavery and rebellion. *Ganga Zumba* (1964), *Xica da Silva* (1976), and later *Quilombo* (1984) covered Brazilian historical themes and employed Black actors and actresses. *Ganga Zumba*, which relies heavily on historical sources as well as myth, lore, and fantasy, recreates the life of Ganga Zumba, nephew of Zumbi, the famous leader of Palmares, the seventeenth-century self-emancipated community-turned-republic that Diegues focuses on in *Quilombo*. *Xica da Silva*, on the other hand, tells the story of an enslaved Black woman, Xica (played by the Black actress Zezé Motta), and her alliance with João Fernandes, a Portuguese diamond official sent to Vila Rica (Ouro Preto in the state of Minas Gerais) in the eighteenth century. The film emphasizes the plight of a Black woman held in bondage in a contradictory manner. It utilizes the stereotype of the erotic Black woman while illustrating the limits of sexual unions as a social ascent. Today we know much more about the historical eighteenth-century Xica, whom colonial society called a *Mulata*. Because of her romantic relationship with a wealthy Portuguese, Xica gained her freedom and lived with uncommon privileges. She also raised twelve or thirteen children, two of whom went to Portugal.

Four years after the 1965 film *Arrastão,* Joaquim Pedro de Andrade's 1969 *Macunaíma* brought Grande Otelo back to the silver screen, albeit after the military dictatorship censured the film and asked for modifications to the script. Based on the 1928 Mario de Andrade novel of the same name, *Macunaíma*, the film, tells the story of a Black Tapanhumas Indian from the interior of Brazil who migrates to the booming city of São Paulo. The protagonist is an antihero who succeeds using magical powers, wizardry, and a sense of independence, combined with modern technology. At one point, Macunaíma finds a magical spring that turns him into a White prince, an identity he will eventually wear permanently. The racial allegories and criticism of whitening represents a revision of the modernist celebration of cultural syncretism and racial mixing. The movie treats Brazilian national identity and Blackness and the idea of whitening with humor. According to Robert Stam and Randal Johnson, the movie is also an indictment of cultural and economic imperialism.[50]

Overall, the 1970s also brought Brazilian films that often present racial intermingling and mixing with class complexities rather than focusing explicitly on the Black population. Films such as Waldyr Onofre's *As aventuras amorosas de um padeiro* (*The Amorous Adventures of a Baker*, 1975) lighten any possible interracial tensions with humor. Onofre's film focuses on two working-class men's adventures with a White woman from the middle class. Odilon Lopez's *One Is Not Enough, Two is Good* (*Um e Pouco, Dois e Bom*, 1971) and Pereira dos Santos's offer complex visions in *Tent of Miracles* (1977) and *Na boca do mundo* (*In the Mouth of the World*, 1979). *In the Mouth of the World*, Afro-Brazilian actor Antônio Pitanga exposes a love triangle between a Black worker (Antônio), a White bourgeois woman (Clarisse) with whom he has an affair, and his *Mulata* girlfriend (Terezinha). Race and class intersect with urban and rural tensions in a film that ends in the main character's death and a surprising alliance between Clarisse and Terezinha.

It is important to recall that Brazilians were living under a military dictatorship from 1964 until 1985, and filmmakers relied heavily on government financial support to produce films. Any analysis of movies, film scores, or cinematic choices must consider the role of censorship and the dictatorship's overtly nationalist leanings. The regime's aversion to criticism and anything it deemed 'anti-Brazilian' meant that directors, producers, actors, and other creatives had to tread carefully and be prepared to edit or not make their film at all. Cinema novo productions and other films often escaped the censors by using satire, allegory, irony, and creative musical choices.

Conclusion

Music, revelry, and religion constituted essential aspects of *cinema novo* and the more commercial films that treated issues related to Afro-Brazilians. Black discontent or social marginalization were also present implicitly or explicitly in films before and after the release of *Black Orpheus*. Consider Roberto Farias's 1962 *Assalto ao trem pagador* (*Attack on the Pay Train*), which was based on a 1960 train robbery. Despite the title, Farias provides an engrossing story about the relationship among the multiracial robbers, interweaving race and class issues. Tião, one of the Black thieves, stands in contrast to Grilo Peru, one of the White robbers, who not only iterates the only explicit racial slur in the film but also can spend his money conspicuously without drawing attention to himself. *Assalto ao trem pagador* boasts a talented multiracial cast that brought the film more critical acclaim than other films dealing with the favela's inhabitants.

This work has focused on commercial films, but filmmakers in France, the United States, and Brazil have also made compelling and exquisite documentaries, experimental films, and shorts that have focused on the Black experience. In fact, Afro-Brazilians have turned to documentaries, shorts and other experimental genres because of the paucity of resources in Brazil and the barriers to securing them. Zózimo Bulbul's work in the 1960s and 1970s represents an important example. Bulbul participated in many theatrical pieces and films, including Cacá Diegues's *Quilombo*, but he also began to produce his own shorts and documentaries. In 1973 he directed the short *Alma no Olho* (*The Soul in the Eye*), and in 1988 he directed the documentary *Abolition*.[51]

Afro-Brazilians such as Zózimo Bulbul and his quest to create a space for Black cinema ironically have a direct legacy from Camus's foreign vision. In an interview in Rio in 2016, Bulbul confessed that he always wanted to create something different in Rio. When he visited Paris, he saw different clubs for different ethnic films and wanted to create a space for Black films.[52] Zózimo Bulbul also believed that it was important for people to see *Black Orpheus*. It was a moment for foreigners to see Blacks dancing and expressing joy. Bulbul had played Orpheus in a production directed by Cacá Diegues in a theater in Copacabana in the 1970s and spoke candidly about how the film *Black Orpheus* motivated him and other Black actors.[53] Overall, Bulbul acted in at least fifteen films. He was also a consequential Brazilian filmmaker. In 2007, at seventy years old, he created the Centro Afro Carioca de Cinema to promote Brazilian cinema and celebrate the contributions of Afro-Brazilians in dialogue with filmmakers, actors, and others in the African diaspora and Africa. He showcased films from Africa and the diaspora at annual gatherings in Rio. Bulbul curated the first gathering, which focused on Black cinema in Brazil and Africa, in 2007 with an exhibit that included forty-eight Brazilian films and twelve African productions. The festival honored Ousmane Sembène (1923–1977), a pioneer of Black cinema in France and Senegal. Sembène believed that cinema could be a way to awaken Black conscience and encourage Africans to fight for better conditions. Thus, the first Centro Afro Carioca de Cinema in Rio de Janeiro included screenings, talks, and seminars and instituted a diasporic dialogue that continues today.

Bulbul's own trajectory began after his dialogue with Afro-Brazilians and African descendants across the Atlantic.

> In short, it all started when my film "Abolition" was selected for a film festival of African Diaspora directors in New York in 1995. At that time, I was surprised that half of the audience for this festival was Black. At that time, I did not know what Burkina Faso was, nor did I have much knowledge about Africa, and these Africans who were at the festival did not know that there were Blacks in Brazil. It was an excellent opportunity to exchange information. In the last days of the event, I was invited to go in 1997 to participate in the FESPACO—Pan African Film Festival of Ouagadougou, in Burkina Faso. I felt very honored, as this festival is the most important in Africa and one of the most important in the world. "Abolição" had won the Brasilia festival in 1988 and also won an award in Cuba, and in that festival in Cuba, they asked me to go to New York.[54]

Bulbul returned to Brazil, saddened because he had received international attention but none in Brazil. "I came back very sad with this thing about the film having won several awards at festivals and here in Brazil nothing happened, neither with me nor with the film . . . I wanted to put my face on the street, discuss not only Brazilian Black cinematography, but also the theme of the film, and there was something very 'shut up, (racial slur)—that doesn't exist!—you are making these things up!'"[55] In this way, Bulbul agreed with Camus: films were made for the elite, not ordinary Black people. His idea to create the Centro Afro Carioca de Cinema was born out of disappointment and frustration, but his determination created an Afro-diasporic space for exchange. Bulbul was also inspired by the history of the samba schools, which created innovative community space for exchange at the beginning of the twentieth century. Bulbul was clear: "I knew that this was a weapon and that it would bear fruit. Instead of buying a '38' or a machine gun and going to the favela, I chose to bring the favela inside to study the audiovisual. Cinema is the most modern weapon that exists today."[56] When Bulbul passed away in 2013, the city honored him with a funeral in the Municipal Congress in Cinelândia, and he was buried in the San Francisco cemetery in Cajú, in the port area of Rio de Janeiro, where Blacks had toiled for centuries. Camus filmed and referenced Cajú in his 1958 film.

Bulbul's project has become a reference point for Brazil and for the diaspora. Black film festivals and city and university screenings in the United States, Europe, and Africa constitute important venues for sharing images and discussing connections across the Atlantic. Almost seventy years later, screenings and discussions of *Black Orpheus* continue to resonate with audiences and engender discussions. Brazil continues to inspire filmmakers. Its imagery and its music continue to move audiences. The old stereotypes have not entirely disappeared, but foreign and Brazilian filmmakers have embraced Afro-Brazil in multiple ways. Afro-Brazilian filmmakers, producers, and actors have helped to create new images. They have also inspired many White filmmakers to become more conscious about representations of Afro-Brazil. New global films have begun to emerge in the digital age. Multinationals such as Netflix, Amazon Prime, and HBO often feature productions directed and produced by Brazilians that feature Afro-Brazilians and Afro-Brazilian culture.

In recent decades beyond the 1960s, Brazilian actors in Hollywood have also begun to play roles in fashioning images and ideas of Brazil for global audiences. Afro-descendants such as Seu Jorge have also left their mark. Afro-Brazilian Alfred Lewis Enoch, one of the few Black boys in Harry Porter and the American TV series *How to Get Away with Murder*, is another example. These examples attest to the global diversity of Afro-Brazil on the heels of *Black Orpheus*.

6

Bossa Negra in the United States

The soundtrack of *Black Orpheus* first promoted the melodies that would later become bossa nova, the new wave of Brazilian music. However, the major talents who took bossa nova global were White. Nonetheless, Black performers represented Black Brazil and left their mark transnationally on the bossa nova era in multiple ways in France and the United States. Jean-Paul Delfino theorizes that the Cuban revolution cut off the flow of Afro-Latin American rhythms that had captivated American audiences and commercial interests since the 1930s.[1] Bossa nova emerged to fill the Latin-inspired void, and the 1962 bossa nova concert in Carnegie Hall became an important global launching path for that to happen. In fact, in the United States, the media labeled a myriad of Brazilian-themed genres "bossa nova," including performances that were clearly samba, jazz, or even rock and roll. They were part of the Brazilian new wave. Musical forms were transformed across borders as they adapted to new audiences, cultures, and languages, even though musicians clearly understood the new bossa nova aesthetics.

The differing aesthetics were clearer back in Brazil. That evolution had racial implications that Black performers like Elza Soares understood. On the cover of her 1961 album *Bossa Negra*, Soares defiantly stares at the viewer, directly challenging the racial aesthetics of the predominantly White Copacabana-based middle-class musicians responsible for the transnational media attention given to bossa nova.[2] Three years after the release of *Black Orpheus*, Soares's album represented an intervention in the discussions on

FIGURE 6 Photo of Carmen Costa performing in Rio de Janeiro in 1957. Credit: Public domain / Arquivo Nacional Collection

music and representation. She mainly sang sambas but told audiences she was also a part of the new bossa. Implicit in the title and the album was a market and social distinction between samba, associated with working-class Afro-Brazilians, and bossa nova, perceived as coming from and for the predominantly White middle-class sectors. The dissonance is also musically palpable in the *Black Orpheus* score, between the many musical numbers in public spaces and those that have an acoustic guitar accompaniment.

In the early 1960s, market forces grappled with the audible dissonance among the diverse musical styles in the film. Collaborations among American jazz musicians and emerging Brazilian musicians, including composers made famous by the movie, forged a visual and audible new cosmopolitan aesthetic that joined jazz with Brazilian music in multiple ways. This new wave created excitement among the middle-class youth in Brazil, the major consumers of film, radio, and records, primarily because it represented a new generation distancing itself from traditional percussive samba and the *samba-canção* of the early 1950s. It also excited jazz musicians and aficionados in the United States. Samba relied on drumming and other percussion instruments, and the *samba-canção* depended on orchestras and powerful singing voices. Bossa nova restrained the percussion and the vocals, creating a more intimate aesthetic. This also created a distance from the Afro-Brazilian aesthetics of the samba. Although bossa nova spread in predominantly White middle-class forums in Rio, Afro-Brazilian musicians such as Johnny Alf, Baden Powell de Aquino, Jair Rodrigues, and Agostinho dos Santos contributed significantly to the genre.

If we consider the transnational face of bossa nova, however, most ambassadors of the bossa nova in the United States—Tom Jobim, João Gilberto, Astrud Gilberto, and Luiz Bonfá—were all White. We know very little about Black Brazil and the Afro-Brazilians who made their way to the United States. Afro-Brazilians such as Agostino dos Santos, Djalma de Andrade (affectionately called Bola Sete), Carmen Costa, and José Paulo (often written as José Paula, José de Paulo or Paula) performed at the Carnegie Hall concert in 1962. They also played essential roles in propagating the bossa nova transnationally in the 1960s through collaborations with American interlocutors and producers interested in producing bossa nova or Brazilian-themed music in the United States. African American musicians played a vital role in helping to promote Black Brazil. This chapter examines the ways in which Afro-Brazilian performers at the 1962 bossa nova concert in Carnegie Hall propagated Afro-Brazilian popular music through collaborations with African American jazz musicians in the United States.

By focusing on the collaborations of three Afro-Brazilian musicians who attended the 1962 Carnegie Hall concert and their collaborations with African Americans, this chapter highlights the diverse and complex ways that Afro-Brazilian performers helped propagate bossa nova in the United States in the 1960s after the success of *Black Orpheus*. Afro-Brazilian collaborations with African American jazz musicians created an Afro-diasporic visual and cultural medium, furthering the idea of a *Black Orpheus* tradition represented by Black people. Studying them also provides insights into transnational practices, borrowings, and furthering the Afro-Brazilian global musical scape.

Ironically, Bola Sete, Carmen Costa, and José Paulo were not part of the bossa nova circle in Brazil. Yet, they contributed to the advancement of Brazilian popular music through jazz by traveling to the United States. *Black Orpheus* also constitutes a metaphor for the global Black artist as Jean-Paul Sartre argues in his essay "Black Orpheus."[3] The transnational trajectories of migrant performers such as Bola Sete, Costa, and Paulo in the United States in the 1960s and 1970s represent one stream of Afro-Brazilian global performance, while the migration of performers such as Maria d'Apparecida and Baden Powell in France (chapter 7) represents another. The Brazilian performers in the United States adapted to the vibrant jazz market in multiple ways. Unlike their French counterparts, none became famous musicians with access to the mainstream American media, and two returned to Brazil to pursue their careers.

For their part, American jazz performers embraced bossa nova in multiple ways, often reproducing or combining the Brazilian-inspired rhythm with other Latin-inspired ones to create a distinctly North American *bossa* in the instrumentation, harmonies, inflection, and style. Black jazz artists also attempted to establish or maintain ties to Marcel Camus's film by explaining its impact on them. Others claimed Afro-diasporic connections or established Brazilian roots through travel to Brazil or collaboration with Black Brazilian artists. North American musicians also used Portuguese and created personal narratives emphasizing their relationship with Brazil and Brazilians.

Examples of the bossa nova creations of Dizzy Gillespie, Lionel Hampton, and Ramsey Lewis and their collaborations with Afro-Brazilians Carmen Costa and José Paulo provide us with a window into the cross-diasporic transnational dimension of bossa nova in the wake of *Black Orpheus*'s popularity. While initially being criticized by respected Brazilian biographer Ruy Castro for his "non-bossa nova" performance during the Carnegie Hall concert, Bola Sete performed and promoted bossa nova and other types of Brazilian popular music in the United States as a part of his eclectic repertoire.[4] The narratives of Ella Fitzgerald and Horace Silver also highlight the personal connection of the other performers to Brazil.

Reassessing the Dynamics of the 1960s

Bossa nova gained currency in an age of enormous racial strife and social transformation in the United States. Racial segregation remained the norm in business establishments and entertainment venues across the United States. The Carnegie Hall concert occurred less than a year before Martin Luther King's March on Washington in August 1963 and two years before the 1964 Brazilian military coup. President Lyndon B. Johnson signed the Civil Rights Act in July of that year. Johnson acquiesced to Black activists' complaints that the government had not done much to enforce comprehensive civil rights since the landmark desegregation of public schools in 1954. Racial violence continued in Watts, Los Angeles,[5] and across the South. In more liberal East Coast cities such as New York and Boston, discrimination against African Americans continued.[6] Musicians were not immune to these changes. As African Americans pursued civil rights and modernity, their music accompanied them. Jazz remained prevalent in some quarters, but its general consumption among African Americans had declined by the time bossa nova began to gain visibility in the United States in the early 1960s.[7]

Social access and diplomatic restrictions in Brazil and race codes in the United States continued to deter many Afro-Brazilian musicians from performing there.[8] Although White and non-White Brazilian musicians collaborated and performed in many forums across Brazil, Afro-Brazilians rarely represented Brazil abroad. Until the 1950s, few Black musicians showcased their talents internationally or in the most prestigious performance venues in Rio de Janeiro, the Brazilian capital.[9] Thus, the presence of four Afro-Brazilians representing Brazil in the United States in 1962 should not go unnoticed.

The White urban middle class may have been the most influential consumer market of bossa nova in Brazil and the United States. Still, African Americans consumed various music genres, including bossa nova, and Black and Latin jazz musicians consumed, tinkered with, and produced their bossa nova sounds much like their White counterparts.[10] Jazz performers' consumption and reproduction of bossa nova guaranteed the Brazilian musical genre a place in the jazz and U.S.-based Latin music repertoires. At the same time, the improvisational dimension of jazz meant that there would be many strands and types of bossa nova in the United States, including forms that Brazilians may not have recognized.[11]

Brazilian performers, such as Sérgio Mendes, one of the 'non-Black' performers at the Carnegie Hall concert in 1962, were able to capitalize on their experience. Mendes created several successful Brazilian-themed bands and performed multiple types of samba and bossa-nova fusions in the United States. Mendes's story also merits further study, primarily because he celebrated Afro-Brazilian rhythms like Carmen Miranda before him and transformed them for global audiences. He also collaborated with non-Brazilians creating musical fusions with lyrics in English, Portuguese, and Spanish. Unlike Miranda, his paternal ancestry was Afro-Brazilian, and he performed *with* Afro-Brazilians in Brazil and the United States, particularly in the 1970s. It is worth mentioning that Jorge Ben Jor also arrived in the United States but was frustrated by the racism he experienced. He eventually returned to Brazil. By the early 1970s, Afro-Brazilian migrant performers experienced a better welcome.[12]

Sérgio Mendes presents an interesting challenge for scholars studying Black Brazil. Mendes celebrated his mixed cultural background. In the 2021 documentary *Sérgio Mendes: In the Key of Joy*, Mendes explained that his father was Black, and that his mother's side was Portuguese. Although Blackness and Portuguese are not mutually exclusive, Brazilians of Mendes's generation perceived them as different racial identities. More importantly, American readers will quickly note a different way of speaking about racial identity since in Brazil, Mendes would have referred to himself as White (Branco) based on his skin complexion. Other Brazilians would also have referred to him as White based on skin color rather than ancestry. In recent decades on college campuses in the United States, students have begun to use terms such as 'White presenting.' In Brazil, many Brazilians have long identified as Brown (Pardo) long before the term became fashionable in the United States.[13] Here again, racial identity and cultural identity diverge. Mendes was well aware that he was celebrating Afro-Brazilian rhythms and various Afro-Brazilian fusions. In the 1960s, outside of Brazil, consumers and marketers labeled this music bossa nova.[14]

The consumption and reproduction of bossa nova present a complex and varied history. Structural racism in Brazil and the United States partly explains the relative privilege and exposure of talented White performers over their talented Black counterparts in the United States and Brazil. Being in the right place at the right time also helps explain the opportunities of artists such as Carmen Costa and José Paulo compared to other talented Brazilian artists who never received invitations to travel to the United States. State and private support of diverse American artists, from Charlie Byrd to Dizzy Gillespie, helped open travel opportunities to explore Brazil.[15] As American musicians consumed and reproduced bossa nova, they also attempted to make connections with Brazilian performers—some because of personal connections. The Afro-Brazilian presence in productions allowed non-Brazilian performers to claim a level of authenticity or legitimacy whether the Brazilian performers were White or Black. Carmen Costa's and José Paulo's participation with Gillespie, Hampton, and Lewis represented examples of transnational Afro-diasporic connections. However, these productions were American, and the Brazilians played secondary but essential roles in celebrating the music's Brazilian roots.

Jazz Musicians and the Brazilian Inflection

The idea of "tinge," or inflection, is an important notion in the history of Brazilian American cross-musical influences.[16] It is also more nuanced than the contentious idea of authenticity. To be sure, many musicians "cashed in" on the bossa popularity. In November 1962, *Down Beat*, the U.S. premier jazz magazine, published the "Bossa Nova Band Wagon" column featuring and rating seven works. The magazine criticized how record labels marketed their records as bossa nova, including the rerelease of the Brazilian Laurindo Almeida's 1953 album and Cal Tjader's presentation of Brazilian and Mexican-inspired work *Cal Tjader Plays the Contemporary Music of Mexico and Brazil*, which producers called a bossa nova album. *Down Beat* predicted that "the population on the bandwagon is increasing so rapidly that it can only be hoped its springs will withstand a breakdown."[17]

In a January 1963 article called "Bossa Nova Ad Absurdum," the magazine assails the trend: "Already this bossa nova business has gotten out of hand. Since nobody wants to be left out in the cold, we will soon be seeing albums like Gene Ammons, and Sonny Stitt's *Bossa Nova Boss Tenor Battle*, Ornette Coleman, *Shape of Bossa Nova to Come,* the Duke of Dixieland's *Rampart Street Bossa Nova*, Meade Lux Lewis's *Bossa Nova Boogie,* Max Roach's *We Insist Bossa Nova in 5/4 Time*, and Les McCann's *Goin' to Meetin Bossa Nova*."[18] Moreover, the magazine admitted that all the albums were "strictly bossa nova in their intent or effect." Still, all are products of interest in cross-pollination between Latin and jazz rhythms in a manner less aggressively rhythmic than that of the more commonly combined Afro-Cuban elements.[19] This fusion is akin to a bossa nova or Afro-Brazilian tinge because it illustrates the desire of many jazz musicians to engage with and perform new Brazilian rhythms while acculturating them into the earlier Latin jazz tradition after the global circulation of *Black Orpheus*.

African American and Latin performers had already created Latin jazz fusions before the 1960s. Many jazz artists saw bossa nova as an exciting extension or example of the already rich Latin jazz repertoire. African American and Latino performers (predominantly if not exclusively male) began including bossa nova songs in their gigs and their albums. Many also created new fusions while maintaining a Brazilian inflection, even if only in a composition's title. Tito Puente's *Bossa Nova* album was more Cuban-inspired Latin jazz than Brazilian bossa, for example. Gene Ammon's *Bad! Bossa Nova* combined soul-jazz style with catchy grooves with his use of Portuguese in titles such as "Moito Mato Grosso [*sic*]." He also fused bongo playing with Latin rhythms and soul music. Bossa nova inspired a generation of musicians for varied reasons, from pure exoticism to understated phrasing. Others liked the harmonic approaches. Still others wanted to take advantage of the economic opportunities to meet the growing demand to hear bossa nova. The attempt to create a bossa nova dance was an extension of these inspirations.[20]

Jazz performers often connected with Brazilians through their use of the Portuguese language, their travels, and their personal contacts. Others forged narratives based on personal experience. For example, Ella Fitzgerald and Horace Silver drew on their personal family histories to make deeper connections to Brazil, Brazilian music, and Black Brazilians. Fitzgerald, who began to perform bossa nova tunes in the 1960s, dedicated her 1972 album to Tom Jobim. She also spoke of her connection to the Portuguese language through Joseph da Silva, her Portuguese stepfather. Horace Silver drew on his Cabo Verde roots to forge connections with Portuguese-speaking Brazil in a similar fashion. After returning from a trip to Brazil in 1964, Silver produced his bossa nova album *Song for My Father* (subtitled in Portuguese "*Cantiga para meu pai*") and dedicated it to his father, John Tavares Silva, of Portuguese origin from Maio, one of the Cabo Verde Islands.[21]

Like their White counterparts, talented and well-traveled African American musicians such as Dizzy Gillespie, Lionel Hampton, and Ramsey Lewis recognized a distinctive quality that they wanted to add to their already impressive repertoire. The African diasporic elements were essential, but so was the creative impulse as they searched for inspiration. Gillespie claimed that he performed the bossa before it became popular. He and many other jazz musicians incorporated Brazilian influences into their eclectic performances. For example, American musicians adapted their compositions into the bossa nova phrasing or rhythm in ways that allowed them to be loyal to the main principles of bossa nova and create new compositions at the same time. Other jazz musicians also engaged and dialogued with Afro-Brazilian performers Carmen Costa and José Paulo, which helped achieve the desired Brazilian inflection.

Afro-Brazilian Musicians in the United States

Brazil's different modes of racial identification notwithstanding, most Brazilians who traveled to the United States before the 1960s identified as White. Despite the 1951 Brazilian anti-discriminatory law, the Brazilian diplomatic service rarely hired Black Brazilians. Likewise, very few Afro-Brazilians received official support to travel from Brazil to the United States in the 1960s.[22] Because of his global reputation, Agostinho dos Santos, the Afro-Brazilian crooner from *Black Orpheus*, was an exception. The guitarist Bola Sete, singer Carmen Costa, and percussionist José Paulo were already living in the United States.[23] U.S. racial codes before the 1960s also made it difficult for Black Brazilians to perform there. Given the changing racial climate in the early 1960s, however, the Brazilian embassy probably invited Bola Sete, Costa, and Paulo to perform even though they were not a part of the bossa nova crowd in Rio because they were already in the New York area.[24]

Black Orpheus garnered widespread accolades from the mainstream White press and the Black press in the United States after it won the Academy Award for Best Foreign Film in 1960. Demand for the soundtrack album grew long after its 1959 release on the Epic label in the United States, leading to its rerelease in 1964 on Fontana Records.[25] Antonio Maria Araújo and Luis Bonfá's "Manhã de Carnival" became a staple and a crowd-pleaser, thanks in part to Agostinho dos Santos's original melodic interpretation.[26] Agostinho dos Santos's version in Portuguese also won widespread approval at the Carnegie Hall concert.[27]

Unlike the other Afro-Brazilian performers who remained in the United States, dos Santos traveled to New York from Brazil with the financial support of his record label, Specialized Radio Recordings or RGE Discos. After the show, dos Santos returned to South America to fulfill other contractual obligations, including in the Argentine and European markets. The American audience's admiration of dos Santos's performances and style continued until he died in 1973. As noted, he received frequent American visitors in Brazil, including Johnny Mathis, with whom he performed his celebrated "Manhã de Carnival" in 1964 and again in 1971.[28] Long after the film, dos Santos's voice is still inextricably connected to Orpheus's voice.

Costa and Paulo

Carmen Costa took a different path to the United States. After working with Francisco Alves, one of Brazil's greatest crooners, and singing backup for many singers in Rio de Janeiro, she launched her solo career in 1942.[29] Even though Costa was a samba singer, she began to sing in a more colloquial style that used the popular vernacular, anticipating the bossa nova style. This mannerism distinguished her from many of the samba singers of the 1940s. Costa lived in the New York area between 1946 and 1950 and returned in 1958 to perform in contracted venues. When the Brazilian consulate began organizing the Carnegie Hall concert, they invited her and guitar players Bola Sete and José Paulo. Carmen Costa eventually sang in many U.S. productions but never became the center of any like the White performer Astrud Gilberto did. Gilberto's image of a Brazilian woman with an understated voice and manner became perfect for the mainstream bossa nova image in the 1960s.

According to Costa, the bossa nova artists who had arrived from Brazil treated her with suspicion: "The bossa nova crowd did not want to mix, and they looked strangely at those who were not from their clique. I was considered 'bossa-velha' (old bossa)." Nonetheless, according to Costa, "bossa nova was easy," but "what was difficult was doing bossa and being Black."[30] For many African Americans, however, Carmen Costa and José Paulo represented the "new sound" in the United States because they were Brazilian and understood Brazilian music. This view allowed her to collaborate on several albums as a part of the rhythm section, including productions by Stan Getz, Gary McFarland, and Lalo Schifrin.[31] Black Brazil was on display even as the mainstream image ushered in by Gilberto, Jobim, and others received more attention.

José Paulo also collaborated on many recordings while in the United States.[32] Brazilian biographer João Carlos Viegas noted that Costa hired José Paulo to perform with her in the United States when she left Brazil in 1958.[33] Paulo played piano, guitar, and several Brazilian percussion instruments to add Brazilian sounds to many performances. Carmen may have originally hired Paulo, but then they both started collaborating with American musicians. Paulo's expertise and presence could take multiple forms and help a group or band achieve a desired Brazilian sensibility or tone using Brazilian percussion. Paulo, who is credited as José Paula, also participated in Quincy Jones's 1962 *Big Band Bossa Nova* album.

Bola Sete

Bola Sete's role in propagating Brazilian music in the United States took a different path. As a part of a transnational Black Brazil, his story is equally compelling. It also represents bossa nova's acculturation to the jazz milieu despite biographer Ruy Castro's claim that Sete had nothing to do with the new musical form. Bola Sete, who hailed from Rio de Janeiro, had already toured Europe and South America. He was the only Afro-Brazilian artist from the Carnegie Hall concert who remained in the United States for the rest of his life. Executives from the Sheraton had contracted Bola Sete to perform at the New York Park Sheraton and the Sheraton Palace in the early 1960s. Like Costa, he was conveniently in the area as the organizers began to put the Carnegie Hall program together.[34]

Bola Sete's performance and style may have departed from what had become the classic bossa nova aesthetics, but like his compatriots in France, his virtuosity and flexibility demonstrated Black Brazil's ability to adapt and innovate. During the Carnegie Hall concert, his rendition of "In the Mood" with Costa and Paulo celebrated that versatility. He was a more high-spirited representation of the metaphoric Brazilian 'Black Orpheus,' playing the guitar on his shoulder. Classic bossa nova enthusiasts would have described him as 'over-the-top.' In fact, he did not limit himself to the classic aesthetic. Beyond Carnegie Hall, Bola Sete left his mark on the jazz and pop community in the United States. He performed at the 1962 Monterey Jazz Festival and released his bossa nova album with the Berkeley-based Fantasy Records label. The record helped him to circulate more globally. Entitled *Bossa Nova*, Bola Sete recorded his version of "Manhã de Carnaval," a "Brazilian Bossa Galore," the Tom Jobim-Duran tune "Por causa de você" ("Because of You"), and several other Brazilian-inspired tunes. In his review and promotion description in the liner notes of the album, music critic Ralph G. Gleason praised the Brazilian's bossa nova repertoire as well as his versatility: "Bola Sete makes his debut album before the national U.S. audience with this L.P. He is a versatile performer and although proficient in the bossa nova genre (and one of the first bossa nova musicians to play in this country), he is also a first-rate guitarist in the classical, jazz and popular music fields. His music usually blends music from several Latin American nations in authentic styles with jazz overtones. I once heard him do a set that included flamenco, bossa nova, fado, and Bach!"[35]

Critics wrote positively about Sete's 1964 LP Tour de Force with its eclectic mix of Bach, Dizzy Gillespie, Brazilian samba, and bossa nova. At the same time, he continued the connection and legacy of the film *Black Orpheus* with his rendition of "Samba de Orfeu." *Down Beat* called the album "impressive," arguing that "the bossa nova and the jazz numbers are equally served." His "melodic inventiveness" never pales, yet "his bossa novas are as they should be."[36] That same year, *Down Beat* readers elected Bola Sete as the eleventh most popular jazz guitarist in the United States.[37]

Bola Sete's move to San Francisco led to many collaborations with jazz artists on the West Coast. His partnership with Vince Guaraldi produced many memorable performances and recordings, including renditions of bossa nova standards such as "The Girl from Ipanema."[38] Sete continued performing jazz, bossa nova, other Brazilian genres, and other international styles while touring the United States. He also performed regularly at the Sheraton Palace in San Francisco and in nightclubs such as The Matador and The Trident, in addition to touring around the United States. In 1966, Sete's live performance at the Monterey Jazz Festival cemented his stature as a bossa nova and jazz musician in the United States. The same year that Verve released the album, *Billboard* magazine honored him with a "special merit" award. The magazine declared that: "Bola Sete is going to be heard from in months to come. He is a South American jazz guitarist that, after six years, is beginning to come into his own, evidenced by his performance on this L.P. Sete gives a refreshing version of the overworked 'Manhã de carnaval' as well as other Latino jazz things at his powerful Monterey Jazz Festival performance."[39]

While opportunities opened for Carmen Costa, José Paulo, and Bola Sete because of the bossa nova craze after the concert in Carnegie Hall, the connection to African American jazz artists, particularly Dizzy Gillespie, cannot be understated. Gillespie, already an icon of jazz by the 1960s, brought Black Brazilian musicians into his sphere, as did Lionel Hampton and Ramsey Lewis after him. Gillespie had also raved about Bola Sete's talents and insisted that he be included in the 1962 Monterey Festival. Before returning to Brazil, Costa and Paulo also played important roles in several productions. That jazz artists integrated Brazilian musical forms into the jazz repertoire attests to the unspoken diasporic, transnational connections. These collaborations also indicate that bossa nova's survival in the United States depended on fusion. Black Brazilian and Black American collaboration provided a particularly poignant statement on Afro-diasporic connections produced by and directed at an American audience. Fusion allowed Black Brazil to enter the American market, sometimes to the chagrin of bossa nova purists.

Back to Jazz: Dizzy, Hamp, and Lewis

Many of the jazz musicians who worked with Brazilians and Brazilian music were less interested in imitating bossa nova as it was performed in Brazil than in translating bossa nova to create new music while still promoting and fusing the sounds with forms of jazz. This was true for African American musicians such as Ike Montreal, Quincy Jones, and Dizzy Gillespie. Dizzy Gillespie's penchant for originality and new creations with what he called "Latin rhythms" is well documented. Along with alto saxophonist Charlie Parker, Gillespie's development of bebop involved experimentation with unconventional chromaticism, discordant sounds, and irregular phrasing. Moreover, Gillespie had collaborated on many Latin jazz albums at the height of the Latin jazz scene in the 1940s. His collaborations with Cuban musicians created some of the era's most enduring transnational African diasporic collaborations.

Gillespie was also no stranger to Brazil. Like many of his generation, his first exposure to Brazilian music was through the film *Black Orpheus*: "My first exposure to samba was through the film *Black Orpheus*, and when I first started getting into it, I thought, 'Those are some brothers down there?' Arriving in Brazil, I found out that there were and that our music had a common bond."[40]

For Gillespie, "samba was the bossa nova, rather the bossa nova is a watered-down version of samba."[41] Samba, the music of his Afro-Brazilian "brothers," was the "real thing." Brazilian music, whether Gillespie called it bossa nova or samba, deeply affected him. He wanted his audiences to know that he was among the avant-garde and not a part of the bandwagon. "We were the first in the United States to play that music, samba, in the context of jazz. We had a lot of samba music, and Stan Getz used to bug me to death trying to get some of those tunes.... But the fact remains that I was the first one on the North American continent to play that kind of music."[42] Gillespie solidified his pioneering status by connecting Brazilian rhythms to other Latin American rhythms, broadly constructed, which he mastered while underscoring the importance of individual creativity and the inevitability of transformation when any musical form is imported. "I know Latin rhythms, you see, and always put my individual stamp on the music. I don't play it just like they do. Mine goes with theirs but isn't exactly like it because I figure you have to live a music, an ethnic music. You have to live that life to play it well, exactly like they do."[43]

Gillespie's 1963 LP *New Wave!*, which features live and studio recordings, includes four tunes with Portuguese titles: "Chega de saudade" (Jobim [music] and Vinicius de Moraes [lyrics]), "One Note Samba" (Jobim and Newton Mendonça), "Manhã de carnaval" (Bonfá and Antônio Maria), and "Pergunte ao João"; the first three were bossa nova standards and the latter a famous Brazilian *cantiga*. Gillespie played with Bola Sete on guitar on three of the tracks and Carmen Costa and José Paulo (vocals and percussion) on another three. Carmen Costa played the *cabaça* and the *güiro*, two folk instruments with which American audiences would not have been familiar. *New Wave!* did not enjoy the widespread commercial success of the Getz productions. However, it was one of the first albums to be released after the Carnegie Hall concert and included three Brazilian musicians who performed in that concert.[44]

As we have previously noted, Gillespie did not record his most celebrated bossa nova album in the United States. Nor did it feature any Brazilian performers. Gillespie released *Dizzy Gillespie on the French Riviera* only months after Stan Getz and Charlie Byrd's album, *Jazz Samba*, on the Verve record label.[45] By this time, Gillespie was aware that bossa nova was widely emulated and reproduced, and like his Brazilian counterparts, he continued to draw the connection to samba. "The average cat cutting the tune doesn't know what he's doing," he declared. "They don't know how to play the samba, and that's all bossa nova is."[46] He saw the early connection in favorable terms, almost as a badge of honor, all the while dismissing the musicians riding a popular wave.[47]

Gillespie was an early promotor and exporter of Brazilian popular music in Europe. For this bossa nova–inspired album, the trumpeter assembled a cast of renowned artists, including Argentine Lalo Schifrin on piano, Leo Wright on flute, and Erik Bacsik on guitar. The album opens with a rendition of Jobim's

"No More Blues," uniting the French Riviera's sound with Ipanema's, as one can hear children on the beach with the ocean in the background. The other Jobim tune, "Desafinado," featured the flute and Dizzy's understated trumpet, evoking a romantic, almost melancholy mood. The two bossa numbers set the mood for the entire album that includes a samba with the Portuguese title "Pau de Arara." While bossa nova dominates the work, like so many bossa nova albums in the United States, the LP is more than a bossa nova album, as Gillespie includes four other tunes that vary in style. The last tune, entitled "To the Gypsies," ends with the same sound of the beach that Dizzy uses to open his first bossa tune, only this time one hears a child call out for his mother in Spanish.[48] The use of Spanish in Brazilian-themed tunes continues today.

Like Gillespie, Lionel Hampton is one of the towering legends of jazz with an affinity for innovation. His contribution to bossa nova in the United States is even less known than Gillespie's since his bossa nova album was not released on CD or digitally. Since his early days, Hamp, as his friends called him, was the personification of the jazz showman. He exuded a style that was in many ways opposite to the understated motif of the classic Brazilian bossa nova performer. He was a vibraphonist, a drummer, and a bandleader interested in a host of styles. Hampton played with a huge broad smile, often jumped onto his drums, and played the piano in a unique two-finger style. He also played the vibes with energetic theatrical flair. Indeed, Hampton's style and propagation of bossa nova and Brazilian music, in general, paralleled many of Bola Sete's innovations.[49]

Entitled *Bossa Nova Jazz* and recorded in New York in the fall of 1963 on Hampton's label, this record represents an exciting production on many fronts. First, Hampton, the consummate showman, played melodic solos and promoted the album personally, including at stores such as Macy's.[50] Second, Hampton collaborated with Carmen Costa, José Paulo, and several other musicians. In addition, he decided to feature a picture of Costa and Paulo on his album jacket, highlighting the Afro-diasporic and Brazilian connections. Carmen Costa performed on this album the year before Stan Getz released his highly acclaimed collaboration with Astrud Gilberto.

Side one of the LP includes three bossa nova–inspired songs, all with Portuguese titles: "Recado (Message)," "Bossa Nova York," and "Sambolero." The second track, "Bossa Nova York," is the same title that Sérgio Mendes would give to his 2004 CD. The album highlighted Carmen Costa's low but melodic voice as Hampton played vibraphone. All but one of the songs (the jazz standard "St. Thomas") have Portuguese titles: "Palhacada [*sic*]," "Estranho" ("Strange"), "Bossa Nova Jazz," "Una Nota Sol [*sic*]," and "St. Thomas." The tune "Bossa Nova Jazz," which gives the record its title, flaunts this creative production's transnational nature under Hampton's direction. Even with the occasional misspellings and Spanish, the Portuguese titles gave the album the necessary Brazilian connection. In several of the numbers, Carmen Costa and José Paulo provide more than just the background. Costa sings on four tracks and provides added percussion while Paulo plays percussion—usually tambourine and cabassa—and guitar.[51]

Ramsey Lewis's venture into bossa nova territory was similar to Hampton's. Like Gillespie and Hampton, Lewis forged a personal and creative connection to the music that inspired him. A pianist, composer, and radio host, Lewis dabbled in various musical genres over his career, expanding the jazz repertoire and helping to bridge jazz and popular music in the United States. In the 1960s, his Ramsey Lewis Trio, with Eldee Young and drummer Redd Holt, recorded his only bossa nova album, *Bossa Nova*.[52] Like Gillespie and Hampton, Lewis forged his style of bossa adaptation featuring his piano jazz virtuosity while maintaining a Brazilian connection through instrumentation and by hiring Carmen Costa and José Paulo.[53]

Lewis includes Portuguese titles and lyrics and stays close to the standard bossa on two of the tracks from the *Black Orpheus* soundtrack: "Samba de Orpheus" ("Orpheus's Samba") and "Manhá de carnival [*sic*]" ("The Morning of Carnival"). The other Portuguese-titled songs are sampled from various rhythms and feature the trio members, in addition to Costa and Paulo. *Down Beat* praised the album, calling Lewis and his trio "well suited for bossa nova." *Down Beat* argued that "bossa nova may not be of any intrinsic value to jazz . . . but it proves once again jazz's marvelous pliancy."[54]

Bossa nova's harmonies and syncopation migrated to the United States when Brazil was optimistic and promoted itself as a new modern industrial nation. Jazz artists like Ramsey greeted the musical form with enthusiasm and excitement. Transnational collaborations ensued as American musicians traveled to Brazil and Brazilian performers traveled to the United States. In the United States, the major Brazilian and American mainstream proponents were White, including Tom Jobim, João and Astrud Gilberto, Stan Getz, and later Frank Sinatra, Perry Como, and others. African Americans and U.S.-based Latin performers contributed to bossa nova in the 1960s. As late as 1971, crooners such as Johnny Mathis sought out Agostino dos Santos for their programs.

In 1962, jazz performer Herbie Mann argued that bossa nova "will never make it unless it scores with the Negro market."[55] He may have been partly right. Mann made the statement when jazz was becoming less popular among Black audiences in the United States. Jazz, which emerged from African American fusions, gravitated toward bossa nova just as it had previously imported Caribbean and South American melodies and styles. African American jazz performers such as Gillespie, Hampton, and Lewis represent three of the most critical players in creating and forging links with the new Brazilian form and Brazilians. In the 1960s, interracial collaborations were rare, particularly among men and women and racial tensions were often high. Within this context, Bola

Sete's contributions are even more remarkable at a time when few Afro-Brazilians were traveling to the United States.[56] The jazz world was hardly immune to racism, but musicians and producers were actively involved in open discussions to promote racial unity.[57]

Beyond the 1960s, Beyond Jazz

Bossa nova attracted jazz musicians from many backgrounds, invigorating the jazz scene in the United States, and in turn transforming what bossa nova was in the United States. As more jazz artists jumped on the so-called bandwagon, a backlash from jazz enthusiasts emerged, criticizing the trend, but by the late 1960s, many bossa nova tunes were already jazz staples. Bossa nova numbers had already become a part of many jazz repertoires, continuing to be performed long after the craze had subsided. *Down Beat* said it best when it wrote that bossa nova enticed people to jazz and, in so doing, helped expand the number of jazz listeners in the United States. Some musicians undoubtedly looked with disdain at the popularity of bossa nova. According to *Down Beat,* if a more extensive audience hears a Stan Getz, a Dizzy Gillespie, a Bud Shank, or a Sonny Rollins because of bossa nova, jazz reaps the benefit. Curiosity about a new form of jazz could lead to curiosity about other forms.[58] The same also holds for the curiosity about Brazilian music in general.

As with many artistic creations on a theme or idea, there were many bossa nova variations in the United States in the 1960s. African Americans and Afro-Brazilians played essential roles in promoting the musical style in many ways. The Afro-Brazilian performers at the Carnegie Hall concert contributed to the propagation of bossa nova in the United States in diverse forums. Bola Sete's diverse and extensive career in the United States epitomized how Brazilian performers celebrated bossa nova through multiple fusions and cultural exchanges. These processes have been at the center of Brazilian and American cultural history since the creation of both nations. Yet, just like other Brazilian performers in the United States, such as João Gilberto and Luiz Bonfá, Carmen Costa, José Paulo, and Bola Sete left their marks on the bossa nova genre in the United States. Dizzy Gillespie underscored the importance of individual creativity and the inevitability of transformation when a musical form is imported.

The transnational consumption of bossa nova in the United States continued to develop and change at a moment of social transformation when Black artists began to gain more visibility and economic opportunities in the mainstream media. Because of these changes, Carmen Costa and Bola Sete were among the first Afro-Brazilians to gain access to desegregated American audiences. Their major recorded contributions resulted from collaborations with jazz artists. At the same time, a series of markers, including songs in Portuguese, accented English, and the presence of Brazilian instruments and sounds (for an American audience) marked them as Brazilian and/or Latin, and not American. Costa recognized her initial sense of exclusion by the White bossa nova performers in New York, although the archives do not record her views on American segregation. Afro-Brazilian performers such as Jorge Ben Jor, who also visited the United States in the 1960s, complained about the racial climate more directly.[59]

Was there a "bossa negra"? If the term "bossa negra" highlights the importance of Afro-Brazilians to the genre and expands the view that equates bossa nova with White artists, then the answer is yes. But did Afro-Brazilians create a new style of "Black" bossa nova? Not exactly. Carmen Costa, José Paulo, and Bola Sete contributed to producing a diverse repertoire of bossa nova. They performed standard bossa nova tunes celebrating the new sense of romanticism and poetry present in foundational albums such as João Gilberto's *Chega de Saudade* (Columbia Records, 1959) and the tunes from the soundtrack of *Black Orpheus* (Epic Records, 1959). However, all three performed other renditions that included different percussive sounds and vocals. They also performed sambas, *marchinhas*, and fusions as part of productions billed as bossa nova.

The early presence of Afro-Brazilian musicians in the United States on the heels of the success of *Black Orpheus* merits further investigation. We know, for example, that other Black or non-White Brazilians, such as Moacir Santos and Sivuca, performed in the United States during the bossa nova era. According to biographer Dominique Dreyfus, the guitarist Baden Powell also visited the United States briefly. He performed with João Gilberto informally in New York as well as in one show with Stan Getz in Buffalo, New York, before he moved to France.[60] Many other musicians would join them in later decades, developing new transnational styles. While the 1960s represent a particular period of cross-national collaboration and fusions, in their introduction to *Brazilian Popular Music and Globalization*, Christopher Dunn and Charles Perrone argue that these borrowings have been a part of the development of Brazilian popular music since the nineteenth century. The 1960s represented a critical juncture when Black bodies traveled along with the Afro-Brazilian cultural products. To be sure, the authors also highlight the fact that Brazilian music, however viewed, is largely *Mestiço*, not only because of the African, Portuguese, and Indigenous influences in melodies, instruments, and aesthetics but also because of other non-Brazilian influences as well.[61]

The evolution of Brazilian bossa nova relied on African American influences, as did many of the popular music traditions that emerged out of the United States by mainstream White artists. Other borrowings continued as new musical forms such as soul, funk, and rhythm and blues began to circulate. Tim Maia's transnational experience reinforces the fact that Afro-Brazilians in the United States pursued different avenues in the development of global Black Brazil. The 2014 biopic film *Tim Maia* includes the musician's experience on the

U.S. East Coast, where he discovered new music that he would incorporate into his own style and transform Brazilian soul music in the 1970s. As Stuart Hall reminds us, in the African diasporic tradition, often the innovative style is the point.[62] Maia arrived in the United States in 1959 at age seventeen and was interested in exploring Black popular music beyond jazz. During this time, he lived in Tarrytown, New York. "Jimmy the Brazilian," as people called him, participated in various bands. Authorities arrested him for possession of marijuana and deported him in 1964. Maia's transnational experience needs to be adequately studied. He did not record any music in the United States. References to him are difficult to find, but he returned to Brazil to transform Brazilian popular music and influence the emergence of a movement called Black Rio.

The U.S. experience of Antônio Viana Gomes, better known as Toni Tornado, adds yet another dimension to global Black Brazil. Like Tim Maia before him, Tornado engaged in illegal activities while living in Harlem as an undocumented migrant. While the archives do not verify the exact dates of his experience, Tornado participated in various interviews, locating his experience in the second half of the 1960s. Tornado's contact with soul music and with the Black power movement in the United States transformed his views of Black music and social engagement.[63] Indeed, like Maia, he would incorporate those lessons into developing Brazilian soul music. According to Michael Hanchard, Black Brazilian soul music "brought consternation to both Brazilian military and civilian elites."[64] While there may not be any evidence of Tornado's cultural production in the United States, his presence nonetheless constitutes a part of the larger Black circulation and borrowing throughout the African diaspora.

The enduring influence of Afro-Brazilian performers in the United States continued in the 1970s. The dismantling of racial segregation in the United States made travel by Afro-Brazilians to the United States less complicated. At the same time, the Brazilian military coup of 1964 and the establishment of the military hardline dictatorship in 1968 created a larger Brazilian diaspora. Afro-Brazilian intellectuals and performers were among them. Abdias do Nascimento arrived in the United States in 1968, for example. He eventually secured a post as chair of African studies at the University at Buffalo, the State University of New York. Alberto Guerreiro Ramos left Brazil for the United States two years earlier, in 1966. Black performers continued the Orphic tradition and were able to find opportunities in this new era, although the performers were predominantly male. Afro-Brazilian pianist Salvador da Silva Filho, affectionately called Dom Salvador, was also an important contributor to the globalization of Black Brazil from the United States.

Dom Salvador moved to the United States in 1974. In 1976, he released his first U.S. album entitled *My Family* on the Muse label. Muse was founded by record executive Joe Fields in 1972 and promoted its artist as part of a new contemporary sound. According to Robert Kaz, Dom Salvador was a consummate innovator willing to experiment while continuing to perform Brazilian musical compositions. According to Dom Salvador, he tried jazz and often changed his repertoire according to the clients who went to hear him play.[65] He also became the band director for Harry Belafonte and inaugurated the River Side Café in 1977, where he was still playing in 2024.[66]

Dom Salvador's contribution to Afro-Brazilian cultural production inside and outside of Brazil merits further attention. He was a pioneer who created one of the first all-Black bands, Dom Salvador and Abolição, in Rio de Janeiro. The 1971 album also demonstrated a racial and Black consciousness that would galvanize his generation before he left for the United States.[67] According to Harry Belafonte, Salvador was "a great leader touched by genius," a perfectionist who paid great attention to detail, traits that attracted other musicians who wanted to work with him. On the other hand, the Afro-Brazilian musician Ed Motta argued that that genius developed even more away from Brazil. "He was right to migrate," according to Motta, because it would have been difficult for Dom Salvador to develop the type of authorial music that followed his intuition rather than fitting within national parameters.[68] Others have compared Salvador to Thelonius Monk. The cover of the CD of Salvador's Carnegie Hall concert with the Rio 65 trio featured his portrait and his hands on the piano keys with the words "Dom Salvador & the Rio 65 Trio." According to Salvador the image celebrates him, Blackness, and Brazilian music for a global audience.[69]

Afro-Brazilian performers in the 1970s in the United States also performed beyond the jazz scenes on the East Coast. Popular performers such as Paulinho da Costa and Carlinhos Pandeiro de Oro have contributed to the repertoires of various North American artists and created their own transnational and global imprints.[70] Like the other migrant performers of Black Brazil, Costa was exceptional, showing the transnational reach of what Michael Hanchard called Black exceptionalism in Brazil. Costa, who played many instruments, went on to perform with scores of American groups and performers, including Earth, Wind and Fire, Michael Jackson, and Prince.[71] Carlinhos Pandeiro de Oro had a direct connection to *Black Orpheus* since he appeared in the film as an extra, playing the *pandeiro*. The multiple contributions of Carlinhos Pandeiro de Oro to Black Brazilian popular culture were not limited to the United States. He traveled to Europe, South America, and Asia. He also collaborated with African Americans, White Americans, and other Brazilians who had gained a foothold in the United States. His trajectory is also a testament to the extensive reach of Afro-Brazilian culture beyond the national borders.

Conclusion

Non-Afro-Brazilians (Whites, other Latinx performers, African Americans, and other ethnicities) celebrated and performed Black Brazilian popular culture as Brazilian culture. Many knew the roots of bossa nova from samba. Many did not. Herein lies the challenge of defining authenticity and assigning ownership and appropriation based only on identity. Afro-Brazilian popular music moves and evolves over time. Its survival through transformation and fusions is a testament to the ingenuity of Afro-Brazilians. Yet representation matters. Afro-Black representation matters at home and abroad, despite barriers to transnational movements. Black Brazilian performers and their cultural products were the root of popular Brazilian sounds in the United States and beyond.[72] Those roots can be traced to *Black Orpheus*.

7

Baden Powell and Maria d'Apparecida in Paris

Global Black Brazil celebrated a milestone with the release of the LP *Maria d'Apparecida chante Baden Powell*. The French production brought together Maria d'Apparecida and Baden Powell, two Afro-Brazilian musical talents who had moved to Paris. The collaboration featured d'Apparecida singing in Portuguese and Powell's guitar arrangements over ten tracks. The record was an instant success for the transnational artists. As in the case of movies, this collaboration featured Black and non-Black actors and French and Brazilian interlocutors working in tandem for a product that celebrated Black Brazil. Indeed, talented Brazilians of all backgrounds often joined their Afro-Brazilian compatriots in promoting the music of Black Brazil, including popular Afro-Brazilian rhythms and Brazilian cultural products in general. Powell and d'Apparecida were indirectly connected to *Black Orpheus* and Vinicius de Moraes. Moraes had wanted d'Apparecida to play Eurydice in the film and she reached out to him in the 1970s about performing popular Brazilian music. Powell performed songs from *Black Orpheus* on multiple occasions in France and recorded his "Manhã de carnaval" arrangement in 1970. Four years earlier, he and Moraes had embarked on a project that would return bossa nova to its Afro-Brazilian roots. That collaboration resulted in the 1966 recording *Os Afro-Sambas*.

While many scholars have explored African American experiences in France before and after World War II,[1] few have explored the Afro-Brazilian cultural presence in metropolitan France. Afro-Brazilian performers and Afro-Brazilian

FIGURE 7 Photo of Baden Powell with his guitar. Credit: Public domain / Arquivo Nacional Collection

cultural products circulated in France because of a robust record industry and the diverse venues for live performances. Powell and d'Apparecida moved to France to pursue those opportunities. The transnational migration of Black Brazilian performers such as Baden Powell and Maria d'Apparecida to France provides insights into the global circulation of Black Brazil in the 1960s and 1970s. Their transnational trajectories at a time of racial exclusion in Brazil and often limited possibilities abroad are also testaments to the visibility of Afro-Brazilians outside of Brazil. D'Apparecida and Powell developed their careers, made international connections, and expanded the idea of Brazilian popular culture abroad beyond *Black Orpheus*. They represent two poignant examples of the metaphorical transnational Orpheus in the early Brazilian diaspora in France. Other Afro-Brazilians would follow, bringing their own styles and audiences. While in the host land, to paraphrase Kim Butler and Stéphane Dufoix, performers are constantly dialoguing with the homeland. They were also navigating their connection to Blackness and the African diaspora, certainly examples of a kind of triple consciousness (racial, national, and migration status).[2]

Brazilians and Brazilian Popular Culture in France

Afro-Brazilians in France in the 1960s joined a long list of Brazilian migrants and sojourners in France. White modernist intellectuals such as Oswald de Andrade and Tarsila do Amaral had made connections with French intellectuals and publishers in the 1920s and 1930s. After the war, the novelist Jorge Amado and composer Heitor Villa-Lobos frequently traveled to Paris. Neither identified as Black or White, although Amado often referred to his Afro-Brazilian or *Mulato* background. In 1952, Villa-Lobos made the Hotel Bedford his home at 17 Rue de L'Arcade in the eighth arrondissement. It was the same hotel where Emperor Pedro II lived after his exile in 1889. Amado resided in the Hotel Saint Michel between 1947 and 1950, where he frequently received French and Brazilian friends. He often hosted feijoadas, traditional Afro-Brazilian-inspired meals with black beans and rice and other Brazilian foods, at his residence and made friends with many performers in Paris, including the Greek-born singer George Moustaki, who referred to Amado as a South American brother.[3] He continued this tradition in his apartment on the Quai des Célestins, next to Bastille Square. Amado also appeared on many French television programs, including the programs *Apostrophes*, *Thalassa*, *Ex Libris*, *Droits d'auteurs*, and *Le cercle de minuit*.[4]

France-based interlocutors also traveled to Brazil, forming a cross-Atlantic cultural circulation between the two countries that continues today. George Moustaki, for example, traveled to Brazil, stayed at Jorge Amado's home in Bahia, and was responsible for importing and translating many Brazilian songs into French, including "Aguas de março" ("Les eaux de mars").[5] The list also included others, such as actor and musician Pierre Barouh and teacher Michel Simon, who created the radio program "Aquarelles du Brésil" ("Brazilian Watercolors") in France and the French territories in 1957. The program was a significant forum in the globalization of Brazilian popular culture and symbols of Brazil.[6]

The friendly diplomatic relations between the governments of French president Charles de Gaulle and Brazilian president Juscelino Kubitschek in the 1950s helped bolster cultural exchanges between the two countries. France remained a crucial Western ally even as Brazil and the United States forged ties during the Cold War. The *Harvard Crimson* reported on this important alliance: "When President de Gaulle visits Latin America in three weeks, he will be making his boldest bid for leadership of a separate bloc of free nations since France began its independence strategy. De Gaulle carefully laid his groundwork: Five members of the French Parliament are currently touring Latin America, emphasizing the advantage of closer cultural and economic relations with France. Last week, de Gaulle announced with some fanfare that Germany and France would cooperate on aid to Latin America, giving increased credence to his claim that alternatives to dependence on the United States exist."[7]

De Gaulle visited Brazil in September 1964 and called for closer economic, political, and cultural ties. He employed the rhetoric of Pan-Latinism, which emphasized the deep historical connections between the two countries as "Latin brothers." The construction of the new capital, Brasilia, also brought together French and Brazilian architecture, which brought widespread attention to modernist Brazilian urban planning. President Kubitschek sent his wife Sarah to the opening of the Maison du Brésil in Paris in 1959, naming her the house's godmother, a gesture indicating the importance of the Brazil–France cultural partnership.[8]

French television played a role in promoting Brazilian culture, often emphasizing Afro-Brazilian cultural influences. Baden Powell and Maria d'Apparecida performed on multiple shows in the 1960s and 1970s, as did others such as Eliana Pittman, Tânia Maria, and the duo Les Étoiles in the 1970s. Television programs such as *Dim Dam Dom*, news broadcasts, and award shows featured Brazilian dancers and singers. In 1969, the television show *Dim Dam Dom*, for example, featured a special "Rio sur Seine" ("Rio on the Seine") with intellectuals and artists exiled in France, among them the filmmaker Cacá Diegues, avant-garde cinema producer Maria Lucia, and singer-songwriter Tuca Andrade, who later worked with French cultural icon Françoise Hardy.[9] Tropicália creators Caetano Veloso and Gilberto Gil also arrived in Paris in 1968, but they found the climate too stifling and headed to London.[10]

French producers, artists, and intellectuals such as Sacha Distel and Pierre Barouh were interlocutors for Brazilian performers and artists. Distel's television programs and records helped introduce many Brazilian performers to a French audience. Barouh knew many of the Brazilian performers personally. His recordings, films, and record label Saravah Records, which he created in 1965, also provided a space for many emerging artists. Barouh explained his decision to create the record label between 1965 and 1966 to promote Brazilian music in France.[11] These interlocutors contributed to the globalization of African-influenced cultural products based on European consumption patterns. In the process, a genuine intermingling and exchange among international performers took place. Black performers, especially from the United States, took advantage of the new possibilities in the European capital, having been disregarded by the local cultural elite at home for decades.

Promoting Afro-Brazilian Culture and Afro-Brazilians in France

During the Cold War, American cultural diplomacy played an important role in exporting American popular culture abroad. American jazz musicians who traveled back and forth between France and the United States played important roles in the circulation of American jazz and Brazilian music in France in the post–*Black Orpheus* era. Many musicians often included Brazilian musical influences in their repertoires. Jazz trumpeter Dizzy Gillespie was among the first musicians to record a bossa nova album in France, for example. John Storm

Roberts has documented Gillespie's experimentation and new creations with what he calls "Latin rhythms" in the 1940s, involving unconventional chromaticism, discordant sounds, and irregular phrasing. Gillespie cocreated several Latin jazz projects with Cuban musicians Chano Pozo, Mario Bauzá, and Machito, forging enduring transnational collaborations of the day, often with American government support. Gillespie also forged relationships with Brazilian musicians and with Brazil.[12]

French executives at Philips in Paris sought out the American Quincy Jones to produce and promote *Dizzy Gillespie on the French Riviera* only months after Stan Getz and Charlie Byrd's *Jazz Samba*.[13] Jones had moved to Paris in 1957 and became musical director of Barclay Disques, where he built an early reputation as a performer and producer. Eddie and Nicole Barclay had established the Blue Star record label in 1945 and later changed the name to Barclay. Barclay produced French chanson records and jazz while distributing music by various American labels in the 1960s and 1970s, until 1978. Eddie Barclay also recorded and produced various Caribbean artists such as Tito Puente and Henri Salvador before Baden Powell's first French album in 1962.

American interlocutors such as Gillespie and Marpessa Dawn, with knowledge of Brazil and access to French market producers, also played an important role in promoting Brazilian popular culture outside of Brazil. Marpessa Dawn's Brazilian productions also continued for almost a decade after the release of *Black Orpheus*. In 1959, Philips Records released five versions of the soundtrack for *Black Orpheus* with images of Dawn as Eurydice and Breno Mello as Orpheus. Dawn released her first Brazilian record in Portuguese and French the following year on the Bel Aire label. Two years later, she released her second Brazilian album with the Brazilian accordion player Sivuca, who was traveling through Paris. Sivuca later joined the South African performer Miriam Makeba in the United States. These exchanges and collaboration were part of the global circulation of Brazilian music.[14]

Baden Powell and Maria d'Apparecida made their cultural contribution as the global circulation of musical sounds and rhythms, which would later be called world music, developed. Powell emerged as a global Brazilian performer on the heels of the success of *Black Orpheus* and d'Apparecida, an Afro-Brazilian opera singer, also became a popular Brazilian singer, providing another story and image of Brazilian music abroad. Powell's and d'Apparecida's transnational stories expose the limitations and opportunities for Black performers in Brazil and abroad. French and European exoticism and racialization notwithstanding, both created successful Brazilian careers outside of Brazil. Paris became a point of encounter and a springboard for other collaborations inside and outside Brazil. In the late 1960s and early 1970s, Paris also offered opportunities to perform for a host of exiles, including Tuca, Ricardo Vila, Les Étoiles, Eliana Pittman, Vanya Orico, Naná Vasconcelos, and others.

American and Brazilian performers did not necessarily intermingle or perform together in Paris. The jazz clubs of Saint Germain-des-Prés on the Left Bank mostly featured U.S.-inspired jazz, blues, and other styles. Brazilians performed in places such as the Brazilian-inspired restaurant A Feijoada and the club Discophage. Anaïs Fléchet reminds us that Brazilian music in France was becoming increasingly diverse. By the early 1970s, the diversity of musical possibilities in France, from the Caribbean to Africa and the United States, had provided the French public with many global choices. Brazilian culture performances in France also flourished without the political overtones inherent in many of the performances from former French colonies. Many Brazilian influences have been fully incorporated into French repertoires by singers from Dario Moreno, who sang Brazilian and other Latin American-inspired songs in French, to Françoise Hardy, Georges Moustaki, and Serge Gainsbourg.[15]

Baden Powell Goes to Paris: An Orpheus with a Guitar in the Real World

The same year that *Black Orpheus* won the top prize at the Oscars, Baden Powell released his first album, *Apresentando Baden Powell e seu violão* (*Presenting Baden Powell and His Guitar*). It came one year after João Gilberto released *Chega de saudade* (*No More Blues*), a work that many critics argue was the first official bossa nova album.[16] Powell's album combined classical guitar with jazz harmonies in innovative ways that place him in dialogue with his bossa nova peer. Powell had already made connections with American jazz players with international reputations in Brazil. Herbie Mann recorded his tunes "Deve ser amor" ("Must Be Love") and "Consolação" ("Consolation") on his album *Do the Bossa Nova with Herbie Mann*. Mann had also invited Powell to play guitar on both numbers. On the back cover of the album sleeve, Mann saluted the player, claiming that there is "no way better to play the bossa nova than to perform it with Brazilians."[17] Indeed, Powell's talent and unique style allowed Mann to claim authenticity and a connection to Black Brazil in an era when *Down Beat* claimed that many musicians in the United States were hopping on the "bossa nova bandwagon" without understanding the Brazilian sound.[18] Soon, other artists including Stan Getz and Charlie Byrd were covering Powell's compositions. In 1963, Powell recorded *Baden Powell Swings with Jimmy Pratt*, an album collaboration with African American jazz drummer Jimmy Pratt. It was Powell's first album on the Elenco label. The album demonstrated Powell's capacity for cross-cultural and linguistic collaboration. It also helped the African American musician create a Brazilian record.[19]

Powell did not travel to perform in the 1962 bossa nova concert at New York City's Carnegie Hall, but his musical collaboration with Vinicius de Moraes awakened his interest in France. Meeting the French musician and producer

Pierre Barouh was also important.[20] Powell arrived in Paris in 1964, already connected to the Brazilian Orphic tradition, and emerged as an essential Afro-Brazilian creator and producer in the wake of the success of *Black Orpheus*. In less than a year, Powell became the opening act for Jacques Brel, one of the most influential performers in France in the 1960s. He also landed on Sacha Distel's popular television variety show, performing "The Girl from Ipanema" with Distel and the American singer Dionne Warwick. French audiences already recognized Powell as an ambassador and performer of Brazilian music. He celebrated samba and bossa nova and began to make his own imprint on the emerging global Brazilian musicscape in the post–*Black Orpheus* era.[21]

Powell remained in Europe for twenty years, helping cultivate and promote Brazilian culture in nightclubs, concert halls, French record labels, and television. In addition to Brel, Warwick, and Distel, Powell collaborated with diverse performers in Paris, including Stéphane Grappelli, Michel Legrand, Liza Minelli, and Claude Nougaro.[22] Powell's talents allowed him to forge alliances and find a niche in the Parisian cultural scene. His position, creativity, and attitude allowed him to expand his creations throughout the Atlantic world.

According to his son Philippe Powell, the main reason Baden Powell did not go to the United States was that his father had become very ill. The guitarist had decided to remain in Brazil, thus missing opportunities in the United States after 1962. The possibility to move to France opened two years later, and Moraes and Pierre Barouh helped Powell transition from Portuguese to French. His initial residence at the Hôtel du Levant, a place that had become a haven for Brazilians, allowed him to develop his instincts and cultivate a new home even as French society was changing. Barouh was also instrumental in getting Powell to open Jacques Brel's 1964 musical show at the Olympia and introducing him to French and American performers with whom he would collaborate. Powell played regularly at the Bilboquet nightclub and at other venues. He also participated in film and television shows. His most famous recording was "Samba da benção" for the soundtrack of Claude Lelouch's 1966 film *Un homme et une femme*, winner of Palme d'Or at the Cannes Festival in 1966.[23]

During this period in Paris, Powell's integration into the Parisian music scene was dramatic. He benefited from the growing demand for Brazilian music after *Black Orpheus*. Powell soon joined the artists at Eddie Barclay's company Barclay, where he released his first French album. Recorded in the Hoche studios in Paris, *Le monde musical de Baden Powell* (*Baden Powell's World*) garnered positive reviews, and the Brazilian newspaper *O Globo* noted its successful release and reception.[24] Powell's world included popular Brazilian music and his remakes of classical compositions and jazz in an impressive fashion that *O Globo* called "the best album of the magnificent guitarist from Varre-Sai." *O Globo*'s Sylvio Cardoso praised Baden's musical sensibilities on all ten tracks, boasting that "his performance on the record transcends the borders of what we know as popular music." The journalist only regretted that Baden had recorded "his best album outside of Brazil,"[25] while the *Jornal de Brasil* reported simply, "Baden Powell conquers Paris."[26]

Le monde musical de Baden Powell (*Baden Powell's World*) became Powell's first commercial and critical success in the French market. Moraes called it a beautiful LP, "an absolute 'must' for those who like Baden."[27] He later added that Powell's guitar was an extension of his arms. Powell's connection to Moraes and the *Black Orpheus* project was also apparent on the album since he recorded two compositions from the soundtrack: "Euridice" (with the participation of Françoise Walch) and the "Samba de prelúdio" ("Samba prelude").[28]

By 1967, Powell's growing fan base allowed him to launch a successful second French album, *O mundo musical de Baden Powell No. 2*, accompanied by the Paris Symphonic Orchestra. Despite winning the prestigious Golden Record Award in Paris, French audiences in the 1960s and 1970s, like audiences today, often obliged Brazilian artists such as Powell to play the same "hits," satiating their appetite for familiar vibes.[29] Powell resisted the limitations. He expanded notions of Black Brazil's musical and cultural production through constant experimentation. According to Moraes, Powell was not interested in performing for the market. He explained that neither audiences, tourists, nor the French bourgeoisie who went to concert halls would sway Powell to change what and how he performed.[30]

On one occasion, Moraes met Powell to discuss his career at the Hôtel du Levant on Rue de la Harpe. Powell confessed that his most serious concern with performing in Europe was that he would become a concert player. He could easily have earned free passes to the best salons in Europe and a secretary to carry his instrument, but Powell begged Moraes not to let him become a concert player. "What I want to do is what I do, mix popular with erudite playing the jazz bar, a little like listening to you and Tonzinho,[31] that's the thing I want," he insisted.[32]

In 1964, Rodrigo Coutinho, a journalist from the famous Brazilian magazine *O Carioca*, visited Paris to interview Powell and to get a sense of the Brazilian community of performers. Powell was the lone Afro-Brazilian among them. Coutinho emphasized the essential Brazilian-ness of performers abroad, claiming that underneath the European refinement, sleeps rooted Brazilians who cannot forget the food from his childhood or the brutal Brazilian landscape.[33] Moreover, Coutinho noted that "there was a Brazilian rhythm in Paris that the photographer cannot capture. Brazilians are learning to sing in chorus, a thing only dreamed by Mario de Andrade. The guitar that does not rest is that of Baden Powell's as it plays Brazilian songs."[34]

For Moraes, Powell represented Black Brazil and Brazil in general, reflecting what W.E.B. Dubois called "double consciousness."[35] Powell was also an immigrant adapting to a new Francophone world. In his interview with *O cruzeiro*, Moraes reminded Brazilian readers that Powell's initial entry into French life was not easy: "The Mulatto landed in Paris with his wife Heloisa on his right hand and his Di Giorgio on his left."[36] Since Moraes was working in his post at UNESCO in Paris, he took it upon himself to connect Powell to the Parisian power brokers and people connected to promoting Brazilian culture in France, including Michel Simon, who directed the radio show called "Watercolors of Brazil," and French performers such as Jean Sablon who had toured in South America. They also frequented the Brazilian restaurant A Feijoada, owned by a French antiquarian and located in the Quai L'Hôtel de ville, where he met other French musicians.

Soon afterward, Powell began to call France his second home, though he traveled widely, including to the United States.[37] Powell also performed with Stan Getz in the United States and on the same stage with Thelonius Monk while on tour in Japan, though Paris remained his home outside of Brazil.[38] At the same time, Powell maintained ties with emerging performers in Brazil. For example, he composed tunes for Elis Regina for the first Samba Biennial in 1968.[39] That same year, his Brazilian LP *Baden Powell* came out on the Brazilian Elenco label. The record demonstrated Powell's continued association with *Black Orpheus* since he included an interpretation of Luiz Bonfá and Antônio Maria's theme song. It was also an indication of his transnational existence that involved a continued attachment to his homeland.

By the late 1960s, Powell had become a global phenomenon. Between 1969 and 1974, Powell continued to record in France and Brazil for Philips and Barclay (later RGE) and in Brazil for the Elenco label, under the guidance of Aloysio de Oliveira, who had performed with Carmen Miranda in the United States. Powell also performed and recorded in Germany, including in 1967 at the Berlin Festival Guitar Workshop and for the 1975 LP *Baden Powell Trio & Opéra de Frankfurt*. While France remained his second home, Powell also spent time in Baden-Baden in Germany to rest and recuperate from his hectic schedule. According to his son Philippe, Powell also encouraged his children to become global citizens who were rooted in the Afro-Brazilian culture.[40]

Powell's afro-samba compositions with Moraes represented a significant change in the direction of bossa nova, one that represented an Africanization and recognition of the enduring legacy of the African influences in bossa nova.[41] When Powell and Moraes worked on the record that would become *Os Afro Sambas* (1966), classic bossa nova tunes focused on harmony and melody. They downplayed percussion historically associated with samba and Afro-Brazilians. Powell had researched the African traditions in Bahia for six months and included elements from Candomblé and Umbanda rituals in his *Afro-Sambas*. Those influences are audible in compositions such as "Tristeza e Solidão," "Bocoché," "Canto do Xangô," and "Valsa do amor que não vem."

Although Powell would later downplay his interest in Afro-Brazilian religion after becoming a born-again Christian, he explained that his interest was cultural more than religious. Afro-Brazilian religious influences were also a part of the Brazilian heritage. When reporters asked Powell where the "Afro" influence in his *Afro-Sambas* came from, Powell explained that people thought he was making music for the Afro-Brazilian religion Macumba or Candomblé. "There was none of that," he insisted, justifying his choices to a middle-class audience who may have looked critically on any associations with African religions. Powell explained that he had been studying Gregorian chants and liturgical customs and became impressed to learn that African chants were identical to Gregorian chants. He composed his *Afro-Sambas* over the Gregorian chants when he studied with Guerra Peixe, the arranger and conductor of the *Afro-Sambas* LP.[42]

Powell revealed a deeper truth when he said that the African influence was "in the blood, and the imprint was all over Brazil." While distancing himself from the religion, Powell affirmed his affinity toward the African-derived culture in Brazil but insisted on his research and understanding of African musicality in Brazil. "You have to study," he claimed: "Don't think you're going to have two bottles of beer and go out playing the guitar. Nothing will happen." At the same time, Powell declared his sympathy for Black culture in general. Out of this appreciation, he began to create songs with the berimbau after intense research with Guerra Peixe on the Gregorian chants, allowing him to celebrate Afro-Brazil and the universal human longing. Powell explained that "it was very much like the mermaid song of the sea. [On the LP], it became 'Canto de Yemanjá' ['The Orixá of the Sea']. It is an image that has existed in Japan, in China, for more than 10,000 years."[43] For him, 'Afro-Samba' had a stigma among middle-class Brazilians. However, it was a type of music that existed in Brazil, like the slow samba, the *samba-canção*, and the *samba-lamento*. The latter slow lamenting *samba-lamento* was linked to what he called *Afro-Samba* and shared many harmonistic and melodic with bossa nova.

While Tom Jobim and João Gilberto lived in the United States, neither of them ever declared their belonging or desire to honor their temporary place of residence. It was clear that they were in the United States for economic reasons and for opportunities to perform. Baden Powell developed a different relationship with France. It was like that of many African Americans, including Josephine Baker, who declared her love for France in her song "J'ai deux amours." In the song, Baker declared, "I have two loves/My country and Paris/Forever/My heart is overjoyed."[44] In an interview on French TV in the 1990s, Powell expressed his love for France and the French people when he declared, " I do not like the United States. I love Europe. I prefer Europe. We did not expect the warmth that surprised us . . . I hate giving interviews. Ever since arriving in Paris, I felt like I was in my own country. From my heart, I am the most French Brazilian in the world."[45]

Powell also admitted that as much as he loved France, he still needed to return to Brazil for inspiration and to create new material. Indeed, wary of playing the same hits repeatedly, he often returned to compose. "Baden Powell, here again," one news article read, helping to solidify his relationship with the Brazilian public. According to the article, Powell had tried to stay abroad, where he was able to make in one show what he made in an entire season in Brazil, "but he was not able to stay away because he was not able to compose any new material, one of the most important activities of his life." He was also happy to be back in Brazil, composing the "Opera of the Northeast" with Moraes.[46]

Powell had opened pathways for many Brazilians after him, just as Brazilians and French interlocutors had opened doors for him. By the 1980s, hundreds of performers had covered Powell's music in the United States, Brazil, and France, including Elizeth Cardoso and Sivuca on their CD *Baden Powell Live at the Rio Jazz Club*. Powell continued to celebrate and discuss his Afro-Brazilian heritage. As a musician, he celebrated the African cultural legacy in his work. Fábio Eduardo Matias de Siqueira notes that neither Baden Powell nor Moraes joined political organizations fighting for Black rights in Brazil. Indeed, their transnational life in the 1960s and 1970s would have made any sustained connections difficult, although not impossible. Powell expressed his opinions through his music.

Maria d'Apparecida also used her music to express herself and connect with her country abroad. Her family history and struggles as a Black woman in opera provide a different outlook on the Afro-Brazilian experience abroad. Her transnational role in promoting Brazilian culture is equally important in the 1960s and 1970s. Powell returned to Brazil permanently with the democratic opening in the 1980s, and he died in Rio de Janeiro on September 26, 2000, at the age of sixty-three. Powell had returned to Brazil from Europe in 1997 and had become ill in the years before his death. His two Franco-Brazilian sons, Louis Marcel Powell, a guitarist, and Philippe Baden Powell, a pianist, would later go on to honor their father's legacy while pursuing their own transnational careers in a new globalized era. Powell's friend and fellow Afro-Brazilian performer and partner Maria d'Apparecida remained in Paris long after Powell left Europe. She passed away in her apartment in Paris seventeen years later, on July 4, 2017. D'Apparecida was buried in the Cimetière de Bagneux in Paris on September 8, 2017. The small gathering honored her with a short ceremony and read words she wrote: "I am Maria d'Apparecida: A Brazilian singer." "She was always proud of her Brazilian origins," one of the speakers remarked, and "she was a pioneer of classical music and important to the Brazilian music in France," he reminded the gatherers.[47]

The Globalization of Maria d'Apparecida

D'Apparecida's collaboration with Powell in the 1970s represented one aspect of her transnational experience and her contribution to the globalization of Black Brazil. *Maria d'Apparecida Sings Baden Powell* settled within the familiar ethnoscape of Brazilian popular music. The project featured recorded musical compositions with clear influences from the Afro-Brazilian repertoire. Black Brazil presents itself in the aesthetics and in the bodies of two Afro-Brazilians. As we have indicated, however, non-Black producers, technicians, and others helped Powell and d'Apparecida bring their visions to fruition. However, d'Apparecida came to popular music after a long career in classical music. Her training and performances in classical music, a field associated in Brazil and elsewhere with Europe and Whiteness, allow us to revisit the question of aesthetics, representation, and definitions of Black culture.

In his article on African Americans and the history of classical music in the United States, Joseph Horowitz argues that American classical music did not necessarily have to be associated with Whiteness. The Slavic composer Antonín Dvořák predicted that the genre would eventually include what he called "Negro melodies" and influences. Persistent institutional racism, prejudice, and racist, if not racial, bourgeois sensibilities diminished those influences and the opportunities of talented Black composers and performers, solidifying an identification of classical music as White.[48] A similar history of aesthetics and representation in modern Brazil allowed audiences to associate classical music with Europe and Whiteness. Unlike the United States, and thanks in part to the modernist revolution of the 1920s, Brazilian intellectuals celebrated the mixture of Brazilian culture in its classical music. The famous Afro-Brazilian intellectual Mario de Andrade praised classical composers such as Heitor Villa-Lobos and Camargo Guarnieri for including the musical influences of the people.[49] Still, in terms of representation and social practice, classical music audiences and performers were primarily White. What did this mean for an Afro-Brazilian performer such as Maria d'Apprecida Marques? Her presence allows us to ask new questions about Black Brazil.

Maria d'Apprecida Marques was born in Rio de Janeiro in 1930. She worked as a primary school teacher and radio announcer in the city. In 1948, she entered and won the *Rainha das Mulatas* (*Mulatta Queen*), a beauty contest organized by the Black Experimental Theater (TEN) to promote different types of Black beauty.[50] TEN was a rare Black organization that challenged White society, White aesthetics, and the marginalization of Afro-Brazilians of all colors and backgrounds. The beauty contest that d'Apparecida won did not mirror the superficial contests of mainstream society, but instead judged contestants based on creative talent, intellect, and ethical attitudes.[51]

When d'Apparecida realized she wanted to sing, she enrolled in the Brazilian Music Conservatory and began her career as an opera singer, an uncommon choice for Afro-Brazilian performers of the era. She developed her skills and soon distinguished herself as a talented performer. Soon, d'Apparecida began recording songs by various Brazilian composers, including Waldemar Henrique (1905–1995), Hekel Tavares (1895–1969), Villa-Lobos (1897–1959), and Jaime Ovalle (1894–1955). However, opportunities to perform live in Brazil were rare, mainly because of her skin color and lack of acceptance by the Brazilian elite who attended opera.

At age twenty-five, d'Apparecida moved to France to exercise her profession there. She arrived in Paris in 1955, seven years before Powell. Once there, d'Apparecida eventually found success and became the first Black performer to play the title role of Carmen in the Paris opera, earning her the title "The Brazilian Maria Callas." Ironically, her success in Paris allowed her to display her talents in Brazil when the Paris Opera performed at Rio de Janeiro's Municipal Theater. Still, the experience was painful after a racist incident when a White woman asked her, "what a Black woman was doing in the opera."[52]

According to d'Apparecida, this attitude differed from those in Paris, where she received invitations to perform in opera houses, theaters, on television, and the radio. She promoted Brazilian lyrical and popular music on the mass media platforms of communication. She also spoke openly about Brazilian racism in Brazil in ways that Powell had not. Gender played an important part in that difference, but so did her isolation within opera's bourgeois milieu. Powell had emerged from the more racially tolerant and racially diverse bohemian circles. During an appearance in April 1960, she performed the composition "Tamba-Taja" for French television.[53] A year later, on May 26, 1961, she performed "Sem seu," a Brazilian composition by Brazilian classical composer Waldemar Henrique, on the popular *Discorama* show ahead of her opera performance at the Odéon. Henrique explored Afro-Brazilian folklore in his compositions and the "Sem seu" lyrics directly referenced Candomblé and the Orixá of the Sea, Yemanjá. D'Apparecida took advantage of her television appearance to explain to audiences that she was delighted to sing the marvelous wonders of her country.[54] When asked about Brazil and her experiences there, d'Apparecida emphasized the difficulty for Black Brazilians at a time when the image of Brazil as a tropical paradise free of prejudice remained powerful: "Things for Black singers are very difficult," she declared. "We arrive, but with a great deal of effort." At the same time, d'Apparecida remained patriotic and praised the beauty of the Brazilian country she loved.[55]

After an accident forced d'Apparecida to abandon her career in opera, she turned to popular music and reinvented herself in the French media and recording industry. As we have seen, Baden Powell was instrumental in that transformation. When one French radio program announcer asked her about her views on opera and popular music, she declared that for her, "there are no borders." "Mozart, Gershwin, popular Brazilian music were all possible," though she still preferred opera.[56] As an opera singer, d'Apparecida recorded music by Brazilian and European lyrical composers. Her 1966 *Chants brésiliens* (*Brazilian Chants*), for example, introduced listeners to a variety of Brazilian classical composers from Villa-Lobos and Waldemar Henrique to Ernani Braga and Catulo da Paixão Cearense.[57]

As a popular music performer, she focused mostly on Brazilian music, as her albums from 1966 to 1980 indicate. Her first collaboration with Baden Powell, *Maria D'Apprecida Chante Baden Powell*, features compositions that fall within the bossa nova/jazz spectrum with songs composed by Powell, Vinicius de Moraes, and the carioca poet and composer P. C. Pinheiro.[58] In her 1978 album *Construction*, d'Apparecida engaged the music and lyrics of diverse famous Brazilian composers such as Chico Buarque, Ataulfo Alves, Noel Rosa, and others. In her 1980 record dedicated to Brazil, she repeated that formula while adding songs in French.[59]

D'Apparecida also became a regular personality in the French media. Throughout the 1960s and 1970s, she appeared in various shows, including the literary and scientific magazine *Sciences et Voyages*, *Le Figaro*, and *L'Aurore*.[60] Despite her success in Paris, d'Apparecida was uniquely aware that her position in the Brazilian and Afro-Atlantic diaspora did not escape the exotic gaze. Critics often highlighted her status as an exotic outsider or referred to her racial features, her complexion, or her body. Commenting on her presence in the opera, for example, one journalist wrote, "Maria has the head of a bird with an athletic body, and she is the new exotic arrival just seen in the role of Carmen. She is a Carmen *café au lait*."[61] These comments often offended d'Apparecida even though many others praised her. Still, she remained grateful for the opportunities she could pursue in France that were unavailable to her in Brazil.[62]

The Brazilian exotic and tragic *Mulata* was a typical Afro-Atlantic trope as Donald Bogle and João Carlos Rodrigues demonstrate.[63] Nineteenth-century cultural texts such as Bernardo Guimarães's *A Escrava Isaura* (1875) or short stories such as "The Quadroons" (1842) underscore the predicament of the Mulatta. In *O Negro Brasileiro e o Cinema*, João Carlos Rodrigues demonstrates that the "good mulatta," a light-skinned Black woman or woman of mixed ancestry, has been a significant archetype in the culture at large.[64] This female Afro-Latin American stereotype and the language used to describe her have parallels throughout the Afro-Atlantic world. Performers such as Lena Horne and Dorothy Dandridge in the United States and light-skinned Black women such as Elizeth Cardoso faced similar commentaries as d'Apparecida.

Nonetheless, d'Apparecida found inspiration in Dandridge's performance and representation.

Despite d'Apparecida's racialized experiences, she often received invitations and agreed to promote static images of Brazil, such as the Bahiana replete with fruit on her head. Indeed, she posed in the recognizable Bahiana on the cover of the magazine *Scenes et Voyages* in 1968. D'Apparecida also frequently posed in avant-garde and surrealistic images for her partner, the painter Félix Labisse, who painted her nude and in blue backgrounds. The French entertainment magazine *France-Soir* reported, "After her triumph as Carmen at the opera of Paris last month, the Brazilian singer, one of the grandest voices of our era, has been asked to perform Carmen again from the 20th to November 21 in the Opéra Garnier." The magazine also reported that "Apparecida has also been invited to pose for the painter Félix Labisse, who has decided to put her face in an oval shape like they used to do in the 16th century."[65] D'Apparecida liked the image her partner painted of her so much that she decided to use reproductions of the painting in her programs in Paris, Rio, Brussels, and Bulgaria.

Cultural icons in Brazil noticed her accomplishments and defended her from the racial and gender assaults in the press. Responding to commentary about d'Apparecida's racial features by French journalist Katia D. Kaupp in 1974, modernist writer Carlos Drummond de Andrade penned a poem entitled "A Volta de Maria d'Apparecida." In the poem, Andrade chastised the journalist for focusing on her physical features rather than her vocal talents. In the last stanza, he eloquently praises the opera singer's celebration of her Blackness and Brazilians' collective Blackness: "Your voice is like an apparition. It appears blazing, dramatic, and sensitive, coming from the luminous Black depths of our hearts."[66]

Maria d'Apparecida Marques's connection to Parisian-based Brazilians such as Powell and Jorge Amado helped her with her homesickness for Brazil. Fellow Afro-Brazilian migrant performer Baden Powell also helped her emotionally. D'Apparecida explained that Baden Powell, whom she called "the Pelé of the guitar," was like a brother to her in Paris. In the absence of a Black Brazilian community, Powell helped her navigate the transnational challenges inherent to the Black Brazilian experience.[67] They both collaborated with other Brazilian and French musicians to satiate their desire to perform Brazilian music abroad. By the late 1970s, they had both begun to perform French covers of Brazilian music. Powell appeared on French television with two percussionists and performed with Eddy Mitchell, who sang "Bidonville," a French version of his composition "Capoeira." That same year, d'Apparecida performed on television with Brazilian and French musicians, including pandeiro player Carlinhos Pandeiro de Ouro, who had appeared in the film *Black Orpheus*.[68]

In Their Footsteps: Other Afro-Brazilians in France

The Brazilian military coup of 1964 and the establishment of the military dictatorship under General Castelo Branco led to a flux of migrants to France. According to Denis Roland, by 1965, the French Foreign Affairs Office had noted the spike in visa requests from Brazilians. The ascendance of the hard-liners in Brazil in 1968 ushered in a more repressive phase of the military dictatorship called the "Lead Years."[69] The government used the Institutional Act Number 5, known as AI-5, to suspend civil rights and habeas corpus and begin a regime of arbitrary detention, torture, and censorship of cultural production and behavior. Thousands of Brazilians left for France, including well-known artists such as the actress Norma Bengell, the dancer Gilda Grillo, and the poet José Vicente. Idelette Muzart-Fonseca dos Santos and Denis Roland do not report on the Black exile experience in their impressive work on Brazilian exiles in France. However, in their work on the Brazilian military government and exile, they relate the story of the White musician Ricardo Vilas who claimed that the French did not believe he was a Brazilian because he was not Black.[70] According to Vilas, people judged his work in Brazil based on its artistic quality, but in France, people judged it based on the images they harbored of Brazil and of Brazilians. He elaborated by asking if he were "a burly black man with braids," whether he would have had more success: "My work is original . . . I continue here thanks to my work as a singer-songwriter, but it is difficult to recognize [as Brazilian], because it is judged based on stereotypes."[71]

Vilas's layered comments based on personal experience confirms the French association of Blackness with Brazilian musical performance. They also attest to the globalization and legacy of *Black Orpheus*. However, Vilas also highlights the frustration of the migrant musician (part of a diaspora) in a new country trying to hone their craft as he notices the host country's consumers' penchant for more commercial Brazilian musical products. This view overlooks the impact of stereotypes on Afro-Brazilians in Brazil and in France and the limited possibilities available to Black performers in the 1960s and Vilas's relative privilege in society in general. Neither Powell nor d'Apparecida fit the stereotype. Other Afro-Brazilian performers engaged the stereotype and fashioned their own aesthetics and global fusions. In Brazil, successful artists such as Caetano Veloso and Gilberto Gil were denounced as commercial and Americanized, but they utilized foreign influences to create music that was uniquely theirs, uniquely Brazilian. In 1969, the military dictatorship forced musicians Caetano Veloso and Gilberto Gil to leave the country. They first traveled to Portugal, then France, before settling in England, where they found ways to continue performing Brazilian music, often with the help of producers in Europe.

The military dictatorship changed the demographics of Brazilians abroad. By the late 1970s, other Afro-Brazilian performers, including Eliana Pittman,

Tânia Maria, Naná Vasconcelos, and the duo who comprised the group Les Étoiles, were among the Afro-Brazilians who diversified the transnational face of Black Brazil. Many followed in the footsteps of Powell and d'Apparecida, sharing their talents with European audiences, and using Paris as a springboard for global outreach across Europe as travel became more accessible. Many also settled in Paris temporarily or permanently. New venues, such as the club Discophage, provided opportunities for performances as the record industry secured the circulation of a diversity of Brazilian sounds.

Performers like Eliana Pittman followed the tradition of many Afro-Brazilians and Afro-Americans, including her father, Booker Pittman, one of the few African Americans who left France and settled in Brazil. Pittman secured a coveted billing at the Olympia in 1967 with Moacyr Franco. Among the songs she performed was Powell and Moraes's "Berimbau." Almost eight years after his performance with Warwick, Distel, still a popular host, performed on French television with Eliana Pittman. Booker Pittman had mentored his daughter in Brazil and helped her launch a brilliant transnational career as a Brazilian and American singer.[72] Pittman (the daughter) traveled to Paris to showcase those diasporic connections, as many of her compatriots had before her.

Afro-Brazilian performers Luiz Antonio Moraes da Silva and Rolando Faria, who created the group Les Étoiles in 1974, left Brazil for Europe separately. Luiz Antonio arrived in Barcelona as a part of the tour by the group Brasil Aquarius, which modeled itself after Sérgio Mendes's enormously successful band Brasil '66. Meanwhile, Rolando Faria left Brazil to participate in the recording of the album *Brésil 72* on the Paris-based Barclay record label. The two, who had known each other in Brazil, met in Barcelona and decided to perform Brazilian popular music in drag. They eventually left Spain to try their luck in Paris, where opportunities to perform were greater. They called their duo Les Étoiles (The Stars), already indicating a jocular sensibility for a musical group just starting out. They would be different from other Afro-Brazilians abroad, according to Jorge Rodrigues. They referred to themselves as "singers of Brazilian popular music," but the French press referred to them as transvestites.[73]

Les Étoiles performed in diverse locations, including on French television shows and at Discophage, a Brazilian restaurant and cabaret. The cabaret-restaurant on the Rue des Ecoles in the fifth arrondissement became a space for many Brazilian performances in the city. Les Étoiles's presence in the Parisian landscape contributed to the Brazilian global ethnoscape in multiple ways. While their style can best be described as Brazilian cabaret, they performed in drag, singing in Portuguese for their live audiences and for television studios. Posters of the duo for a performance at Discophage present the singers utilizing their humor to attract audiences. The cover of their first French album, RCA's *Rolando e Luiz Antonio: Meu coração é um pandeiro* (*Rolando and Luiz Antonio: My Heart is a Tambourine*), shows the duo in drag in the middle of a *pandeiro*.[74]

When asked by a journalist about the group's use of Portuguese while performing in front of a French-speaking audience, Moraes da Silva responded that the French public understood them because they were transmitting a feeling and an idea that people could understand. Here again this corroborates what Stuart Hall argues about style and performance beyond language. The French press often described the two men as Brazilian homosexual or transvestite performers as they tried to categorize and brand them. Moraes da Silva also rejected the descriptor 'transvestite.' "I never call myself a transvestite. I put on makeup, and I perform. I am not part of any movement or carrying any flag," he declared.[75] Like other Afro-Brazilian performers in Europe before them, Les Étoiles refused to be pigeonholed. They fashioned their unique performances, often utilizing and transforming old stereotypes, symbols, and notions of Brazil. Les Estoiles provided audiences in Europe and (through records) audiences in Brazil and elsewhere with a continual dialogue and celebration of Brazilian nationality and their humanity. In so doing, they contributed to a Black Brazilian diversity after *Black Orpheus*. Les Étoiles often performed with other Brazilians in Paris, including the Afro-Brazilian pianist Tânia Maria.[76]

Maria appeared on French television in diverse shows, including a duo with Sacha Distel singing Tom Jobim's "Agua de Beber" in French and Portuguese in 1975. In her version of Jorge Ben's "Fio Maravilha," she scats and transforms the number with her piano virtuosity. That same year, she released *Via Brasil* with José Boto Leite and Bassist Hélio on the Barclay label. In 1978, she released her second album with Barclay, this time, a solo entitled *All My Soul* (1978). She returned to French television in 1979, appearing with Les Étoiles and performing the satirical "Eu fui a Europa" ("I Went to Europe").[77]

Percussionist Naná Vasconcelos's presence in France added another dimension to the transnational Black Brazil-scape in the 1970s. Like all the other Afro-Brazilian performers, Vasconcelos collaborated with a variety of musicians in Paris and elsewhere in France. In 1972, he teamed up with the Argentine saxophonist Gato Barbieri and other musicians he met in the United States. Vasconcelos played the berimbau and the drums. By the late 1970s, studios and marketers outside of Brazil combined many Brazilian musical productions under a globalized jazz label and then later under the world music category.' French television called Vasconcelos's collaboration with Barbieri "jazz harmonies," for example, according to Helena Celestino's blog. Vasconcelos also became a local celebrity among the shopkeepers along the famous Rue Montorgueil.[78]

In 1973, Vasconcelos released the album *Africadeus* (*Africa God*) on the French Saravah label. The album included a selection of Afro-Brazilian folklore pieces, including *samba de roda* rhythms. It was rereleased in the United States and Germany in 2017. Two years later, Saravah released an untitled fusion album with Vasconcelos and two other musicians. Like many of his fellow transnational performers, Vasconcelos first gained a reputation in his home country, having performed with celebrities such as Milton Nascimento before being invited to join Barbieri on tour.[79] Vasconcelos also celebrated Afro-Brazilian traditions transnationally. His talents earned him invitations and accolades throughout the 1970s and 1980s, including the Best Percussionist of the Year Award by *Down Beat* magazine. According to Eric Grimm, Vasconcelos's significant contribution was his ability to convert the berimbau, a traditional instrument used in the Afro-Brazilian martial arts dance *capoeira*, into a solo instrument. He also globalized the berimbau because of its unique non-Western sound and properties. More importantly, he gained the respect of other innovative musicians such as Baden Powell, who famously composed the popular ode to the berimbau and capoeira, appropriately titled "Berimbau."[80]

Conclusion

A decade after the release of *Black Orpheus*, bossa nova had become a staple of global musical repertories, notably in jazz circles. Beyond jazz, French audiences sought out samba and bossa nova performers, but they also sought out individuals such as d'Apparecida and Powell, Maria, Pittman, and Vasconcelos. The exile of Caetano Veloso and Gilberto Gil in London also created a global Brazilian celebrity connected to Black Brazil in ways that celebrated Brazilian-rich Afro-mestiço culture. From London, Brazil would become an important voice of Black Brazil. Gil forged relationships with other Black Caribbean migrants in London and deepened his connections to Africa. Veloso, who often called himself *Mulato* and, more recently, Pardo, illustrates the differences between racial and cultural identities. Veloso and Gil made frequent trips to Paris and appeared on French television even as they produced music in London. Both were important participants in the ethnoscape that we are calling Black Brazil, responsible for the continued circulation of Afro-Brazilian popular culture outside of Brazil. It is worth noting that Veloso was a fierce critic of *Black Orpheus*, although he appreciated the genius of the musical score created by Brazilians.[81]

The small number of Afro-Brazilian artists and musicians did not constitute a community as in the case of African Americans in Paris, whom Tyler Stovall informs us was also not a unified community of expatriates.[82] D'Apprecida's experience as an opera singer paralleled the experience of African Americans who faced barriers to advancing and exercising their art in their home country. Powell was not as vocal about his experience as an Afro-Brazilian, but he might have faced barriers in the United States. Powell and d'Apparecida

FIGURE 8 Photo of Maria d'Apparecida. Credit: Creative Commons Attribution-Share Alike 4.0 International license

also met other non-Black performers and artists with whom they shared an appreciation of Afro-Brazilian culture.

White Brazilian musicians such as Tom Jobim and João Gilberto became household names. Bola Sete, the only Black guitar performer at the 1962 Carnegie Hall, had a lucrative career in California concerts. His innovative, expressive style suited the North American gaze. Powell and d'Apparecida performed at diverse venues in France, from hotel lounges to jazz festivals to concert spaces. Other Afro-Brazilians and their other Brazilian counterparts continued their journeys to Paris. By the late 1970s, a group of diverse performers made their way to the Parisian capital. Tânia Maria, who made a name for herself as a Brazilian jazz performer, and Naná Vasconcelos represent two of the more well-known Afro-Brazilians.

Vinicius de Moraes once declared that he was the Blackest White Brazilian in the world, to which Pierre Barouh cleverly remarked years later that he was the most Brazilian Frenchman.[83] These declarations represented a desire for these transnational actors and travelers to declare and legitimize their love, affiliation, and sense of belonging beyond their race or nationality. It was also a way to honor a group outside of their own. Today, these declarations seem to be appropriations and White advantages. D'Apparecida found opportunities in Paris that were unavailable to Afro-Brazilians in Brazil. Powell developed into a global performer thanks to his life in France. Both artists contributed to the circulation and promotion of Afro-Brazil culture. They also diversified and helped change what the world thought of Brazil and of an Afro-Brazilian performer in the post–*Black Orpheus* era.

Conclusion

This work set out to trace and analyze the transnational impact of the *Black Orpheus* movie and the globalization of Afro-Brazilian images and music from the late 1950s to the early 1970s using the United States and France as sites for archival research. Cross-national analysis or comparisons present specific ontological and epistemological challenges since nations organize knowledge differently. When people and cultural products travel across national boundaries, identities and meanings may change. What one person defines as racial in one culture may become national in another. Reading, seeing, and interpreting across nations depends on the positionality of the viewer, the interpreter, the translator, and the interlocutor. What may be organic in one may be viewed as exotic in another when removed from its original context. Thus, when studying the globalization of cinema and music, it is critical to return to Arjun Appadurai's notion of the *ethnoscape*, which lands in different national contexts in different ways. There is not one global view.

Unlike the Brazilian performers who left Brazil for the United States and France in the late 1950s and early 1960s, Caetano Veloso's and Gilberto Gil's experiences abroad were a result of forced exile in 1969. The Brazilian military dictatorship that began in 1964 became even more repressive after the dictatorship promulgated Institutional Act Number 5 in 1968. Veloso and Gil performed live in London, produced albums, met international performers, and experimented with Portuguese and English lyrics. Both musicians from Bahia were shaped by Afro-Brazilian culture. They also made their way to France before migrating to London. They still traveled from London to Paris frequently. In his memoir *Verdade Tropical*, Veloso noted that the film *Black Orpheus* had shaped how recording executives and producers, musicians, and intellectuals viewed Brazilians in general. This attitude annoyed the young Veloso, and he felt somewhat ashamed because he believed the film was a terrible, one-dimensional, and inauthentic representation of Brazil. On the other hand, he thought that the music in the film was excellent and represented what he believed was an "authentic" version of Brazilian popular music.[1] Veloso was commenting from a national patriotic perspective, but authenticity is not limited to specific national ways of viewing. Like most human experiences, authenticity is part of a spectrum depending on the point of reference, shaped by nationality, race, gender, and social status.

Paul Gilroy underscores how problematic and contentious the authenticity issue becomes in a globalized world with multiple information flows and ways of connecting to popular culture. Nonetheless, as we have seen, Veloso's feelings were like other viewers in Brazil, France, and the United States. In his 2000 *New York Times* article "Orpheus, Rising from Caricature," Veloso is particularly critical of the movie he believed distorted foreigners' views of Brazil. He appreciated Jean-Luc Godard's critical review of the film and saw it as "something Brazilians could subscribe to." It was a reaction against Marcel Camus's ways of choosing backward elements to make his film look "poetic." However, here too, if we see movies as cultural products with various points of viewing and perspective, it is important to place Veloso's criticism in its proper historical, cultural, and political context. Veloso was writing at the beginning of the twenty-first century, having just collaborated with Carlos Diegues on his film *Orfeu*, which transported Vinicius de Moraes's original text to a historically relevant favela where joy, poverty, and violence coexist.[2] Representation and patriotic disdain aside, *Black Orpheus* had far-reaching influences as a representation of Brazil and allowed for an initial point of dialogue for Veloso and Gil when they first moved to London.

As a cultural signpost of the global media in the post–World War II era, *Black Orpheus* promoted a version of a Brazilian trope that had long existed among European, American, and Brazilian writers. As a transnational audiovisual cultural product, the film reached far more people than any written text. In the 1960s and 1970s, Brazilian migrants and performers abroad had to dialogue with the film's impact and legacy. The most enduring legacy emerged in the music, which global critics saw as more complex and beautiful. Veloso's opinions of *Black Orpheus* as audiovisual text is another example of how a viewer can consume, engage, and experience movies on multiple levels.

The 1950s production and casting attests to the complex process of transnational cinematic and musical creation when one country and group of creatives is more politically and economically powerful than the other. Is true collaboration possible under such circumstances? Can a French director create a Brazilian film? Can a White director create a Black film? Clearly, throughout the creation of film and music, the answer to all three questions is "yes" because people with access to the means of cultural production have done so. How well they succeed is open to interpretation and depends on historical context, intention, and engagement with the specific Black community. Even so, the Afro-Brazilian community is not a monolith. Film and music production in the 1950s and 1960s was hardly democratic or collaborative. European and American companies dominated the global media, giving producers from those regions more power than artists and producers in less-developed countries.

In the case of *Black Orpheus*, Camus's budget was small, and he could not afford to pay for all the people in his film. Nevertheless, the film made millions of francs for its French production company, which later sold the movie to Criterion. In one unpublished document in his archives at the Casa da Literatura, Moraes complained that instead of asking for 2 percent of the profits from the film, he sold his work for 3 million francs. "I am not a businessman," he confessed, illustrating the unequal preparedness between producers and artists.[3] In fact, none of the Brazilian performers had any rights to future revenues. This standard practice highlighted the global economic inequalities that benefited Western producers with laws and procedures. These dynamics also left many amateur actors and performers uneasy after the film garnered so much attention.[4] At the same time, the film celebrated Black talent and Brazilian music globally.

Camus's relationship to Brazil, Latin America, and Brazilian Blackness warrants further investigation. For Camus, "Brazil had become his second homeland," according to an interview he gave to the newspaper *O Globo* when he made his second Brazilian film, *The Pioneers* (*Os Bandeirantes*). With *Black Orpheus*, Camus claimed that he wanted to make a film against racism. Like Vinicius de Moraes, he chose Black actors and promoted his vision of Afro-Brazilian culture, including carnival, dance, music, and Macumba. In the process, he fell in love with an Afro-Brazilian woman, married her, and built a family with her. He also had the privileges that few Brazilians enjoyed. For example, he was traveling with Orlando and Claudio Villa Boas when they encountered the Xingu Indians, and he loved learning about the country, filming with real people, and speaking with ordinary Brazilians. Brazil, he repeated, "is my country despite my French accent." Luis Carlos Barreto also noted that Camus was the foreign filmmaker who best understood Brazil. In an era before the digital global media and news coverage, he promoted carnival, Brazil's national party, globally. He also questioned the traditional behavior of the French toward other countries.[5] Many contemporary Black Brazilians have also recognized Camus's role in highlighting the Black experience.

Other French and American filmmakers followed Camus's lead and attempted to utilize Brazil's newly found postwar visibility to create cinematic narratives and visions of their own. These cinematic constructions included adventure films, horror films, and romantic comedies. None of them engage

Black Brazil like *Black Orpheus*. However, shifting our gaze, we detect glimpses of Afro-Brazilians and Afro-Brazilian culture in those films. The casting of one or two Afro-Brazilians, the inclusion of scenes of dancing and singing, images of Afro-Brazilian religions, scenes of favelas, and of children contributed to the Afro-Brazilian and Brazilian ethnoscapes. The Brazilian music in many soundtracks also constitute a critical element of that Brazilscape even in productions or scenes that are not about Brazil.

Only recently have filmmakers such as Joel Zito, Jefferson D, and Sabrina Fidalgo successfully created films with a majority Black cast. A 2014 study by a group of researchers at the Institute for Social and Political Studies at the State University of Rio de Janeiro revealed that Afro-Brazilians were severely underrepresented at less than 20 percent of actors in top-grossing Brazilian films. From 2002 to 2012, Afro-Brazilians (mostly people who identify as Brown and Black) represent more than 50 percent of the population.[6] Emerging Black directors and writers have begun to play greater critical roles in bringing Black stories and music to the silver screen. Transnationally, Afro-Brazilians have continued to perform with others and make an impact on films even though there is also a dearth of Black directors in the United States and Europe. Moreover, Afro-Latinidad and Afro-Brazilian-ness have only recently become visible.

Back to (Black) Music

Baden Powell, Carmen Costa, and many other pioneering Afro-Brazilians helped disseminate Brazilian music in the post–World War II era. They also broke paradigms and allowed African diasporic connections with intellectuals who celebrated Black music, Black art, and Black power. *Black Orpheus* marked a critical, albeit uneven, moment in Afro-Latin America and in the Black Atlantic world. The idea of the Black musician, poet, and enchanter had deep historical roots in the history of Black people in Latin America. Unlike the deities of Greek mythology who reign over different arts, the Orixás of Afro-Brazilian religions such as Candomblé and Umbanda worship and celebrate through music and dance. Music represents an important embodied heritage that Africans and their descendants in the diaspora have passed down through generations. Afro-Brazilians have also relied on actors, musicians, and other interlocutors in the United States and France. Many have played key roles in producing, editing, and disseminating Afro-Brazilian culture.

As a transnational collaboration, the film *Black Orpheus* allowed Afro-Brazilians to showcase a perspective of Afro-Brazilian culture by employing Black actors and Black musicians in record numbers never seen in Brazil. It helped others to develop their careers as actors, musicians, and performers. Despite the challenges of the French producers' foreign gaze, *Black Orpheus* remains a reference point for global viewers even today. The film also, directly and indirectly, brought Afro-Brazilians together with other Black performers, creating transnational dialogues among Africans, African Americans, and Afro-Latin Americans. On the film's heels, U.S. promoters organized the first bossa nova concert at Carnegie Hall in 1962. The concert became a platform that launched the U.S. careers of Brazilian musicians Sérgio Mendes, Tom Jobim, João Gilberto, and Bola Sete. It also provided others like Carmen Costa and José Paulo with international exposure, contacts, and experience. At the same time, the post–World War II era saw unprecedented changes in Euro-American empires and Black mobility thanks to the latest technological developments, including in the radio, record, and television industries.

Part II of this work focused on the making of *Black Orpheus* and the global imprint and legacy of Afro-Brazilian musicians and performers beyond the film production in the long 1960s. In the process, it also highlighted the role of Afro-Brazilian performers and Brazilian musical forms and their circulation in North American and European geographical spaces. Afro-Brazilian performers were representatives of a new multi-gendered Orphic tradition. They forged links with performers in North America and Europe. As Stuart Hall reminds us, transnational experiences place the subjects beyond the national body, forcing the navigation of new experiences and cultures, often without having reference points that match one's original national formation. Afro-Brazilians often flourished in new transmutations and through rich dialogue outside of Brazil.[7]

Three main historical changes after World War II made these exchanges possible. First, technological changes made it easier to travel by ship and by air, allowing performers unprecedented opportunities and bringing audiences in contact with live artists. Global middle-class audiences could also buy records or listen to music on the radio. Second, economic changes and demand for labor led to unprecedented transnational Black mobility, especially in the 1970s after changes in migration laws in the United States in the 1960s. In Europe, labor demands precipitated the movement of people from former colonies in Asia, Southeast Asia, and the Caribbean. In the United States, Puerto Ricans, Cubans, and Central Americans (and Brazilians in the 1980s) moved to various North American cities. These migrations also led to the creation of transnational musical forms and new audiences in all those geographical areas. Finally, the Cold War and its civil unrest also led to exile communities. The dictatorship in Brazil after 1964, and particularly after 1968, sent thousands of exiles abroad. Small groups of Brazilians eventually emerged in places such as Paris, New York, and London.

Brazilian artists collaborated with African American artists such as Dizzy Gillespie and Lionel Hampton in the United States. They also had opportunities to cross paths with African Americans and other Afro-diasporic groups in Paris.[8] White European and North American interlocutors helped diffuse

Brazilian culture, Afro-Brazilian cultural products, and derivations. Many non-Black Brazilian musicians appreciated, collaborated, and helped propagate and celebrate Afro-Brazilian traditions abroad, as Carmen Miranda had done a generation before. Miranda's commodification of the Bahiana gave way to collaborative efforts by such performers as Vinicius de Moraes, Vanja Orico, Sivuca, and many others. Indeed, the collaboration between the South African performer in exile, Miriam Makeba, and the Brazilian albino musician Severino Dias de Oliveira, or Sivuca, also represents an example of an Afro-diasporic connection. The story of Makeba, often called "Mama Africa," is well known. She was exiled from apartheid South Africa during one of her trips abroad and eventually moved to the United States, where she married Stokely Carmichael (Kwame Ture), the Student Nonviolent Coordinating Committee (SNCC) leader, in 1968.

Sivuca had been a Brazilian ambassador by participating in Brazil's 1958–1964 musical caravans, organized by Humberto Teixeira, which the Brazilian government financially supported, to promote Brazilian music abroad. Incidentally, in 1955, Congressman Adam Clayton Powell Jr. convinced U.S. leaders that jazz was the best way to intervene in the Cold War and help counter Soviet stories of racism. Black and White musicians, including Dizzy Gillespie, Louis Armstrong and Dave Brubeck, became jazz ambassadors. After the second caravan, Sivuca moved to Portugal, where he remained for nine months before moving to Paris in 1964. An appearance playing the *pandeiro* on the Sacha Distel television show garnered him attention and an invitation to play in the United States, where he met Makeba through his association with Harry Belafonte. Makeba eventually hired Sivuca as her musical director, a position allowing him to influence her repertoire significantly. He helped her integrate Brazilian songs and musical styles into her performances and recordings. Makeba included songs such as "Adeus Maria Fulô" (written by Sivuca) and Jorge Ben Jor's "Mas que nada" ("But, no way"), and "Chove chuva" ("Rain rain"), among others, into her repertoire.[9]

The 1966 album *All About Miriam* was on the Mercury label in the United States, although it was released in the United Kingdom and the Netherlands that same year. Journalist Sérgio Martins from the Brazilian Magazine *Veja* provides an insightful observation about the circulation of Brazilian music, regional influences, and the connection to Africa when he pointed out that the marriage between Sivuca and Makeba was a coming home of a sort since he was from the northeast, a region highly influenced by African music.[10] Their work together represents a significant Afro-diasporic collaboration. Scholars writing about Sivuca do not use any of the terms associated with Afro-Brazilians, such as *Negro*, *Mulato*, or *Pardo*, though albinism is highest among people of African ancestry. Sivuca's role in promoting Black Brazil reminds us that cultural identities may not necessarily line up with racial identities.

Sivuca's experience, knowledge, and connection to an Afro-diasporic tradition allowed him to develop and help other Black musicians as an ally despite his ambiguous racial identity. In addition, Sivuca's role allows for further study and analysis of White-presenting Latin Americans, who play roles in the globalization of Brazilian cultural products even as migration transforms individual identities.

Beyond cinema or musical representations, print images of Black Brazil also circulated in France and the United States in the 1960s. Jorge Amado's novels about Bahia gained popularity among middle-class audiences in both countries from the 1930s onward. French and American publishers continued to publish his work in the 1960s and 1970s. Images of Brazilian favelas also appeared in documentaries and photographs that circulated transnationally. One example, *Des ruines et des hommes*, the 1959 French short documentary on Peru and Brazil by Pierre Kast and Marcelle Lioret, contains a section that explores life in the favela.[11] In 1961, African American photographer Gordon Parks created a photo essay entitled "Freedom's Fearful Foe: Poverty" for *Life* magazine, Park focused on the life of Flávio da Silva, a young boy from the now-demolished favela of Catacumba (previously located between Copacabana and Ipanema). The Brazilian newspaper *O Cruzeiro* believed that Park's essay gave the impression that poverty and misery were ubiquitous in Brazil, just as many critics of *Black Orpheus* believed that the film gave a one-dimensional view of the country. In this instance, *O Cruzeiro* responded by commissioning a photo essay entitled "New American Record: Poverty," featuring the Gonzalezes, a poor Puerto Rican family living near Wall Street in New York.[12] The tension surrounding representation constitutes a significant part of the discussions about globalization and the circulation of cultural products, people, and images.

In 1960, Carolina Maria de Jesus published her book about life in the São Paulo favela Canindé. In Portuguese, her work was entitled *Quatro de despejo: diário de uma favelada*. French and English translations quickly followed. In the United States, David Saint Clair translated the work for English-speaking audiences as *Child of the Dark,* while Violante do Canto utilized the title *Le dépotoir* for French audiences. While these texts did not garner the widespread global attention of their cinematic counterparts, they are, nonetheless, part of the Afro-Brazilian ethnoscape. Audiences, viewers, and readers outside of Brazil engaged with them from multiple perspectives. Just as *Black Orpheus* inspired the Black Martinican filmmaker Euhan Palcy, Carolina Maria de Jesus's work inspired Françoise Ega, a Martinican working-class woman living in Marseille, to create an epistolary work to dialogue with the Brazilian author. That work, *Lettre á une noire; récit antillais*, represents an important part of the story of the global circulation of Afro-Brazilian culture heralded by *Black Orpheus.*[13]

Epilogue

Although Afro-Brazilians and their images, music, and cultural products have continued to circulate beyond the 1970s, historians are loath to make direct and immediate correlations between one historical era and another. Tracing Afro-Brazilian circulations in the 1980s to the present day would involve establishing the cultural dynamics and historical watersheds in Brazil, France, and the United States, accompanied by deep research in appropriate archives. My precursory survey of the decades from the 1980s to the present solidifies the importance of the *Black Orpheus* project. Efforts by Brazilians and their non-Brazilian interlocutors continue to showcase Black Brazil in an era of continued racial restriction. No other non-Brazilian director has successfully released an 'Afro-Brazilian film' that resonated globally from the 1980s to the present. In the meantime, global dynamics have changed, and Black Brazilian actors and actresses have emerged in multiple Brazilian productions. Afro-Brazilian musical influences have also continued to circulate in and outside the cinema.

The emergence of Brazilian communities in major cities across South America, Europe, and the United States, the celebration of Brazilian holidays abroad, the institutionalization of Brazilian film festivals, and televised international music festivals and prizes have ensured the globalization of Brazilian images (with Afro-Brazilian characters and Afro-Brazilian cultural products by Brazilians of all racial backgrounds and colors). The proliferation of global digital media platforms such as Amazon, Netflix, Tubi, Hulu, ITV, Spotify, iTunes, Hulu, and others have ushered in a new era of Afro-Brazilian globalization through commercial films. Most of these companies also employ companies to translate dialogue and lyrics into multiple languages.

A historian attempting to study the globalization of Afro-Brazilian culture after the 1970s could divide the historical periods chronologically into two broad eras using Brazilian political watersheds to ground the narrative: returning to democracy, circa 1980s–2000, and the contemporary era, 2000 to the present, which saw the emergence of the Workers' Party and its challengers in the political arena. Historians could also use specific films made in Brazil from the 1980s to the present to discuss the evolving agency and circulation of Black images and Afro-Brazilian music. Using this framework of analysis, we could anchor the narratives on the creation and globalization of Brazilian films starting with known Brazilian films that received widespread transnational circulation. Such a framework of analysis would necessarily utilize Black images from many of *cinema novo* directors, who were primarily White, and the emergence of Black actors such as Zezé Motta. The 1980s was also the era when Brazil witnessed civil society's growth and the Black movement's strengthening after Afro-Brazilian activists created the Unified Black Movement (MNU) in 1978. Debates about representation, reparations, and quotas began to change the national conversation about Afro-Brazilians' role in society.

The 1970s had already seen new Afro-Brazilian cinematic images, although many of them did not receive widespread transnational circulation. They include films such as Odilon Lopez's *One Is Not Enough, Two is Good* (*Um é Pouco, Dois é Bom*, 1971), *Tent of Miracles* (Tenda dos Milagres, 1977), and *Na boca do mundo* (*In the Mouth of the World*, 1979). Antônio Pitanga's *In the Mouth of the World* centers on a love triangle between a Black worker (Antônio), a White bourgeois woman (Clarisse) with whom he has an affair, and his Mulatta girlfriend (Terezinha). Carlos Diegues's 1976 *Xica* highlights the talent of Zezé Motta and other Afro-Brazilian actors, as well as the music of Jorge Ben Jor. The film, which simultaneously presents a liberating and problematic interpretation of Black female sexuality, received widespread attention outside of Brazil.

Using the decades of the 1980s to the end of the 1990s as a historical period, students may single out films such as the 1980-released *Pixote*, which received multiple international awards and nominations. The film does not discuss Blackness explicitly. Nor are the directors interested in the racial background of the protagonist. They focus on the life of a homeless boy who becomes involved in crime, prostitution, and drugs on the inhospitable streets of São Paulo. Afro-Brazilians appear in the film, and Tony Tornado plays a Black character on the screen and represents Black Brazil as an actor in a national production. That same year, Leon Hirszman released *Eles não usam black tie*, a movie about a working-class family in São Paulo. Afro-Brazilian characters, played by actors Milton Gonçalves and Gésio Amadeu, are part of the working class.

Diegues's 1984 film *Quilombo* was one of the films that takes place during slavery and features a predominantly Black cast. The film tells a version of the story of the Quilombo de Palmares, a self-emancipated community of Africans and Afro-Brazilians. It featured several Afro-Brazilian actors and performers. Walter Lima Junior's *Chico rei* (*Chico, The King*, 1985) chronicled the capture of a man named Galanga from a royal Congo family, his baptism in Brazil as Francisco (Chico), and his eventual liberation and challenges to the colonial government. In 1999, Diegues created his version of Vinicius de Moraes's play, which he entitled *Orfeu*. Afro-Brazilian Tony Garrido from the musical group Cidade Negra plays Orpheus. Diegues follows Moraes's general plot but makes the story of Orpheus relevant to the social reality of the 1990s, including addressing police brutality and poverty. Although all the main characters are Afro-Brazilian, the film also shows a multiracial cast, reflecting what Diegues believed was more representative of the favela. Caetano Veloso created the soundtrack.

The twenty-first century has brought a host of impressive films that focused critically on poverty and Black responses to it. *Uma onda no ar* (Radio Favela, 2002) presents the development and triumph of alternative radio created by four Afro-Brazilians in the favelas of Belo Horizonte in the state of Minas Gerais. Hector Babenco's 2003 production of *Carandiru* is an epic movie on the São Paulo prison system of the same name. New non-Black movie directors who created films about Black characters include Fernando Meirelles and Nando Olival's *Domésticas* (*Maids*, 2000) and *Cidade de Deus* (*City of God*, with Kátia Lund, 2002) and Karim Aïnouz's biopic *Madame Satã* (2002). However, the fact that the main characters in all three films are marginalized Black characters indicates the need to explore more diverse experiences of Afro-Brazilians. The actor Lázaro Ramos has tried to do that.

In addition to his starring role in *Madame Satã* (2002), about a specific Afro-Carioca character in the 1930s, Ramos has played many diverse characters whose identities are not necessarily racially specified. He also participated in diverse movies, including *O homem que copiava* (*The Man Who Copied*, Jorge Furtado, 2003) and *O homem do Ano* (*Man of the Year*, José Henrique Fonseca, 2003). In 2002, *City of God*, directed by Fernando Meirelles and Kátia Lund (and much better connected to global distributors), became a global sensation. Sérgio Bianchi's innovative 2005 film *Quanto vale ou é por quilo* (*How much does it cost or is it by the kilo?*) reconstructs powerful stories about Afro-Brazilian history and historical characters. The film also critiques the current system that allows some NGOs to pursue corrupt practices which harm the popular classes, especially Afro-Brazilians.

The first decade of the twenty-first-century period also saw the emergence of more Black directors and writers creating Black stories with commercial success. They include Joel Zito, Viviane Ferreira, Jefferson De, Sabrina Fidalgo, Camila de Moraes, Renata Martins, Juliana Vicente, Diego Paulino, and Yasmin Thayná.

Joel Zito's *Filhas do Vento* (*Daughters of the Wind*, 2005) also represents an Afro-Brazilian signpost. This was one of the first contemporary films to feature Afro-Brazilian women across multiple generations in varied and complex roles. Zito's film features a majority-Black cast. Set in a small town in the state of Minas Gerais, Brazil, the movie focused on two sisters (played by Léa Garcia and Ruth de Souza) who meet again after years apart. One of them went to the big city to pursue a career as an actress, while the other stayed to look after their father. In addition to Souza and Garcia, the film stars Afro-Brazilian actresses Taís Araújo and Maria Ceiça. Afro-Brazilians such as Zito are creating their own spaces in film and television and reassessing the role of *Black Orpheus* in Brazilian film history. In November 2005, the São Paulo–based TV da Gente (Our TV) made its historic debut on the 'small screen' by becoming the first Brazilian television station explicitly aimed at Black audiences. José de Paula Neto, the main creator behind the TV station, secured a national audience as a singer and then as host of the popular TV Globo series *Princess for a Day*. Short-lived initiatives such as Neto's, which come from the community, have historically served multiple forms of empowerment that stretch beyond the media.

The São Paulo group Dogma Feijoada (Bean Stew Dogma), led by Jefferson De and other Black filmmakers, including Noel Carvalho, Billy Castilho, Rogério Moura, Daniel Santiago, and Agenor Alves, aimed to create a Black cinema that represents the multiplicity of the Black experience and speak directly to Black audiences. Although inspired by the Danish group Dogma and Black American directors, Dogma Feijoada is firmly rooted in the Brazilian experience. Jefferson De's 2001 short *Distraída para a morte* (*Distracted to Death*) and Ari Cândido Fernandes's 2003 short documentary *O Rito de Ismael Ivo* (*The Ritual of Ishmael Ivo*) are two of the first films that represent Dogma Feijoada's goals. De's first feature film *Bróder* (2010) appeared in the sixth Sundance Screenwriters Lab and received a coveted slot in the 60th Berlinale and in various festivals in the United States and Europe.

Globalizing Afro-Brazilian Music in the Post–1980 World

This work looks specifically at music in soundtracks promoted by companies and performers connected to the legacy of *Black Orpheus*. It also utilized the idea of a Brazilian Orpheus in two specific settings with African American jazz interlocutors in the United States and French interlocutors in France. These perspectives give one view of the Brazilian musical ethnoscape. However, the Afro-Brazilian spectrum is richer and more diverse than those two areas. In the 1980s, the term "world music" gained widespread currency, but it means different things in different markets. Here again, the term in English is another example of categorization and a certain amount of perceived exoticism or otherness. In May 1990, *Billboard* magazine established a biweekly World Music column, for example. Brazilian music magazines or experts have no such columns or lists. However, Afro-Brazilian music, like Brazilian music in general, continued to circulate and became a part of the world music commercial package thanks to interlocutors connected to the major music production company. David Byrne's world music label Luaka Bop, which helped reintroduce Caetano Veloso and Gilberto Gil to a new generation of audience in 1989 is a case in point.[1]

Since the 1980s, musicians and musical collaborations across national boundaries have fared much better at representing Afro-Brazilians than films. Many interlocutors in the West such as Wim Wenders and David Byrne have helped Latin American artists gain wider global followings. Transnational Afro-Brazilian collaborations with other members of the African diaspora continue to represent an important avenue for the global dissemination of Afro-Brazilian music and talent. Gilberto Gil's 2001 album *Kaya Na 'Ganda*, recorded at the famous Tuff Gong Studios in Jamaica, represents one such collaboration. The album pays homage to Bob Marley and international reggae music, which Gil experienced first-hand while in exile in London in the late 1960s.

When asked why he wanted to record Marley, Gil explained that Marley's composition, "Rebel Music," is a prototype of many types of Black music. For him, it expressed the Black person's rage and the joy of life and freedom at the same time. "It's a question of power, public and civil freedom as opposed to constituted authority."[2] Like so many intellectuals from Hall to Gilroy, Gil believes that music is a profound expression of the popular soul of Black people. He is explicit and unapologetic about his consciousness and connection to Black people in Brazil, the United States, and Europe. Other Afro-diasporic collaborations include Michael Jackson and the Bahian band Olodum; Wayne Shorter, Milton Nascimento and Esperanza Spalding; Maria Bethânia and Omara Portuondo; Maria Bethania and Cesária Évora, among many others.

As Brazilians performed with artists outside of Brazil and signed contracts with multinational companies, more and more musicians began to perform on global music circuits after the 1980s. They also benefited from the demand from Brazilian communities in major cities such as London, Paris, New York, Boston, Miami, Buenos Aires, Berlin, and elsewhere. Study abroad programs, tourism, and Portuguese-language instruction have also helped create interest and demand for Afro-Brazilian culture from places outside the major cultural centers such as Rio de Janeiro, Salvador, and Recife. The transnational movement of Afro-Brazilian religious practices such as Macumba, cultural practices such as *capoeira*, and diverse musical forms attest to the globalization of diverse customs.

Music performance also requires much less capital investment than film production, especially today when musical products travel digitally. Many

Afro-Brazilian performers cultivate transnational lives, sometimes establishing second residences outside of Brazil. They also perform in multiple venues including concert halls, jazz festivals, and digitally. Brazilian popular music (MPB) and other Brazilian musical genres from *forró* and *sertaneja* to classical Brazilian music flow across national boundaries. As we have seen, Brazilians have also cannibalized other forms such as soul, rap, and reggae, making them their own. The Brazilscape and the Afro-Brazilscape intersect and will continue to circulate globally in multiple ways through multiple fusions, borrowings, and migrations. Lovers of Brazil and of Afro-Brazilian cultural products will participate in its global circulation. The globalization of Afro-Brazilian filmic images and musical influences has occurred against the backdrop of changing racial and identity politics. Race, after all, does not have an ontological foundation. Class status, color, geography and historical contexts continue to impact racial identities in Brazil. Research for the 2000 book *Afro-Brasileiros Hoje*, for example, indicates that political changes and rising Black consciousness at the end of the twentieth century influenced the way that Brazilians were identifying racially. The term 'Afrodescendant' also gained currency in this period, underscoring the shared ancestral history of Black and Brown and many White-presenting people. At the same time, we must continue to attend to the ways of viewing, seeing and being.[3]

Acknowledgments

I dedicate this book to my friend and mentor John McCarthy, who passed away in 2019. John and his partner Jorge Caê Rodrigues took me in when I first moved to Brazil in December 1989. His apartment near the base of the Vidigal favela in the building called Tambá became my home for many years before I moved with my family to Ipanema and Botafogo. John was the first person who told me how *Black Orpheus* inspired him to learn more about Brazil. After almost two decades of moving back and forth between Brazil and the United States and working on other projects, I finally returned to the idea of writing a book or essay on the making of *Black Orpheus*.

Many other individuals and institutions in three countries have helped bring this book to fruition. The journey of transnational research is not without its challenges, and it has taken me approximately ten years to master the various historiographies and conduct archival research and interviews in diverse places across the Atlantic world. The support and insights from many scholars, musicians, librarians, and archivists, as well as from aficionados of Brazilian culture, have been invaluable in overcoming these challenges and shaping this book.

Archives in Brazil

I am deeply grateful to the Brazilians who inspired me throughout my research. My deepest gratitude goes out to the archivists and librarians at FUNARTE, the Brazilian National Archives, the Casa Rui Barbosa (Casa da Literatura), the Ministry of Foreign Affairs Archives in Rio and Brasilia, and the Fundação Kubitschek in Brasilia. I am grateful to Mana de Xangó, Breno Mello's ex-wife, for sharing her personal archives in Florianopolis with me. Elisa Larkin and the Archives of the Instituto de Pesquisas e Estudos Afro Brasileiros (IPEAFRO), the Centro Afro Carioca de Cinema in Rio in Lapa, the archives of the Museum of Image and Sound (MIS) in Rio, and the Museum of Afro-Brazilian Culture in São Paulo were also helpful. The Antonio Carlos Jobim and Moreira Sales online archive have also been a source of valuable information.

Archives and Contacts in France

Research and contacts in France were crucial to this work. I am grateful for the support of L'Institut des Hautes Etudes de l'Amérique Latine (IHEAL), where I taught as Simon Bolivar Chair from 2014 to 2015. During that year, I began the French research on this project. Conversations with Olivier Campion and his partner Anaïs Fléchet helped me focus on my unique contribution to the circulation of Brazilian culture.

Archivists at the Bibliothèque national de France (BNF) François-Mitterrand, the Archives at the Opéra Garnier, and the Bibliothèque national de France (BNF) Richelieu helped me find documents about Brazilian performers and their French interlocutors. I would also like to thank the archivists at the Diplomatic Archives Centre in La Courneuve, Paris, and the Diplomatic Archives in Nantes, as well as the extremely helpful librarians at the Belsunce Library in Marseille and the Overseas Archives in Aix-en-Province. I also benefited enormously from the attention I received from the staff at the Institut Méditerranéen de Recherches Avancées d'Aix-Marseille Université (IMéRA) when I served as the Fulbright Chair in Migration Studies. Constance Moréteau put me in contact with local scholars and many institutions, while Charlène Martin's superb organization skills helped me navigate France during the COVID-19 pandemic.

I could not have completed this work without the help from the staff at the Cinémathèque française in Paris and at the Audiovisual Institute at the National Library (INA) at the BNF. Not only was I able to watch many original films, historical musical programs and clips, and radio programs, but I also consulted hundreds of texts and dossiers that gave me insight into many French, Brazilian, and American films, as well as musical recordings, TV shows, and interviews. I also benefited from two summer trips to the National Library in London as I followed the trail of Marpessa Dawn, the Eurydice of the film, and Brazilian exile performers there.

Archives in the United States

Librarians and archivists across the United States have helped me find information on Brazilians in the United States and on American–Brazilian collaborations. The dossier of newspapers, sound recordings, films, and copies of *Down Beat* magazine was especially helpful. Research at the Library for the Performing Arts, Dorothy and Lewis B. Cullman Center at Lincoln Center, and at the Schomburg Center for Research in Black Culture in Harlem and the

Archives of the University of Miami in Miami, Florida, yielded information on Afro-Brazilians in the 1960s and 1970s.

An Additional Word of Gratitude

Several individuals deserve special mention. John urged me to reach out to Haroldo Costa to talk about his involvement in the play, and he offered to connect me with Cacá Diegues. I never was able to sit down with Diegues before he passed away, though I frequently encountered him having coffee in the café in the Livraria da Travessa in Ipanema. With the help of Caê and Lygia Marina de Sá Leitão Pires de Moraes, Costa and I were able to meet for over two hours in Ipanema in 2023. Lygia also connected me to Dom Salvador in New York City. Caê is also a Brazilian scholar of Brazilian popular music. He has shared many insights about Brazilian musicians, records, and culture over the course of my research.

I sincerely thank the many informants who graciously gave of their time to conduct interviews with me and share their connection to the *Black Orpheus* project and global Brazilian culture. Many of them are no longer with us. So first, I offer my deepest gratitude to the ancestors: Ruth de Souza, Abdias do Nascimento, Léa Garcia, and Zózimo Bubul. Saravá. Thank you Zózimo for the brief opportunity to serve as your foreign contact in the United States as you were organizing your project in Lapa. My thanks also go to Mana de Xangó, Carlinhos Pandeiro de Ouro, Dom Salvador, Henrique Nascimento, and Philippe Powell for the time they spent with me. I thank Henrique Nascimento for the documents he shared with me on his mother, Léa Garcia. Philippe is an amazing musician. You have been generous with information and willing to engage in conversation wherever we met. Thank you to Leila Maria, a transnational jazz performer in her own right, who called Philippe to the stage during her concert in Lapa, allowing me to meet him. Carlos Alberto Alfonso, owner of the Ipanema store Toque de Vinicius, shared his encyclopedic knowledge with me about bossa nova and Brazilian popular music. I was lucky to live two blocks from Carlos's store for many years. Christian Pouillade shared his experiences promoting Brazilian music in Paris and invited me into his archives in Jardim Oceânico in Rio. Jean-Paul Delfino, I cherish our conversations in Aix-en-Provence and your insights on Brazilian culture and Brazilians in France. Many other individuals have shared documents, information, and time with me. They include my group of friends in Marseille (Armando Cox, Jean-Max Geiu, and Renaud Boukh). Thank you, Jean Marc Egá, Pierre Egá, and the Comité Mam'Egá.

All the Brazilians I met in France were incredibly giving of their time. Conversations with contemporary musicians, artists, and scholars helped me to disseminate my work and enriched my understanding of the contemporary

Brazilscape. João Atahilde, thank you for the discussions and your help with the music I shared with you. Denise Carrié, I appreciated your help connecting me with the Brazilian intellectual community in Aix. I was fortunate to meet several individuals in Paris, who I now count as friends and fellow researchers. Yure Romão, your transnational work is challenging but ever so amazing and important. Aliette Biron, thank you for being my sherpa in Paris. You are more than an organic intellectual. Almeta Speaks opened her home to me in Paris. Almeta, I shall always be grateful for your insights. Thank you for your knowledge of Black Paris history, your music, your introductions to members of the African American community in Paris, and for the wonderful dinners you hosted.

I also would like to thank my friend Guido Groeschel and my Middlebury neighbor Chuck Burdick, who read very early versions of one of the chapters when I was trying to craft an argument. I am deeply indebted to Oliver Marshall and his partner Margaret Doyle, who provided shelter during my trips to London. Oliver and I share a mutual interest in diaspora, dialogue, and migration. Our rich conversations over three decades have been important to me. Oliver and I have produced multiple books on the Austrian writer Stefan Zweig and his wife Lotte in Brazil, Argentina, and the United States. I have relied on other friends for places to read and write. Richard Zenith, I thank you for providing me a place to write in Lisbon and Carrapateira as I completed the last two chapters in the summer of 2024.

My heartfelt thanks go to Frederic Aldana, Nicole Solano, Emma-li and the staff at Rutgers University Press for their attention and suggestions as we brought this work to fruition. My sincerest thanks also go to Vincent Nordhaus and Michelle Scott, who guided me through the production. Their patience and professionalism meant a great deal to me. The thoughtful comments from the anonymous viewers helped me rethink parts of this work, and Julia Kurtz's watchful eye helped make this a much better book. Thank you! I am also grateful for the support from Middlebury College and Rutgers University-Newark.

Finally, thank you to my family who endured me through this project. My partner Karin Hanta was incredibly helpful and patient as I sifted through ideas of identity, migration, and translation. I thank you for your insights and for reading drafts of the chapters. My sons Caetano Andreas and Marcelo Pessoa picked up and traveled with me for over a decade as I conducted my research. They have probably seen the film *Black Orpheus* and listened to the soundtrack more times than anyone (other than me) on the planet. I hope that the transnational journeys and schooling have enriched your lives.

I have attempted to create a nuanced reading of *Black Orpheus* and highlight the global visibility and contributions of Afro-Brazilian in the 1960s and 1970s using primary and secondary documents as I dialogue with scholars in novel ways. This work is not meant to be an exhaustive study of all the Afro-Brazilian musicians and cultural products that have circulated globally since the 1960s. I have certainly missed and/or omitted performers and cultural texts along the way. Any errors and oversights are entirely mine. Nonetheless, I hope readers enjoy the fruit of my labor.

Sincerely,
Darién J. Davis

Abbreviated Glossary of Musical Terms

agogô: A Yoruba-derived double-bell percussion instrument.

batuque: A type of community dance.

cabaça: A handheld percussion instrument made of a hollow gourd enclosed in a net of threaded beads.

capoeira: Afro-Brazilian martial art dance.

coco: Musical rhythm and dance originating in northern Brazil.

cuica: A percussive instrument with a round base and a long thin wooden cord in the middle.

frevo: Dance and musical style associated with carnival from Recife, Pernambuco.

güiro: A percussive instrument comprised of an open-ended, hollow gourd with parallel notches cut in one side.

maracatu: A music style originally from Pernambuco produced through the blending of drums, snare instruments, and a large bell made of a thick steel sheet.

pontos: Prayers sung during the Candomblé and Umbanda ritual.

samba-canção: A popular Brazilian song with a slow-paced samba rhythm.

samba de roda: A type of samba danced in a circle.

samba enredo: Samba with a story or theme, usually performed during carnival.

samba-jongo: A dance and musical genre originated from the dances performed on plantations in the southeast of Brazil. It sometimes includes singing and dancing in a group.

tamborim: A small round handheld drum. The frame may be made of metal, plastic or wood.

Notes

Archives (in English)

BRAZIL

Antonio Carlos Jobim Archive (online)
Archive of the Casa da Literatura, Casa Rui Barbosa, Rio de Janeiro
Archive of the Ministry of Foreign Affairs, Rio de Janeiro
Archives of the Instituto de Pesquisas e Estudos Afro Brasileiros (IPEAFRO), Rio de Janeiro
Brazilian National Archives (AN), Rio de Janeiro
Centro Afro Carioca de Cinema, Rio de Janeiro
Kubitschek Foundation (Fundação Kubitschek), Brasilia
Mana de Xangó, Private Archives, Florianopolis
Ministry of Foreign Affairs Central Archives, Brasilia
Moreira Sales Archive (online)
Museum of Afro-Brazilian Culture, São Paulo
Museum of Image and Sound, MIS, Rio de Janeiro
National Arts Foundation (Fundação Nacional de Artes, Funarte), Rio de Janeiro

FRANCE

Archives at the Opéra Garnier, Paris
Audiovisual Institute at the National Library of France (BNF-INA)
Belsunce Library and Archive, Marseille
Diplomatic Archives, Nantes
Diplomatic Archives Centre, La Courneuve, Paris
French Cinematheque (Cinémathèque française), Paris
National Library of France François-Mitterrand (BNF), Paris
Overseas Archives, Aix-en-Province

UNITED STATES

Leila Míccolis Archives, Archives of the University of Miami, Miami
Library for the Performing Arts, Dorothy and Lewis B. Cullman Center at Lincoln Center, New York
Schomburg Center for Research in Black Culture in Harlem, New York

Preface

1 I borrow from scholars Christopher B. Strain and Arthur Marwick and the volume edited by Brian McHale and Len Platt. Strain defines the long 1960s from 1955 to 1973. Others use 1954 to 1975. Depending on the watershed, these dates all begin in the mid-1950s and end in the mid-1970s.

2 Joaquim Ferreira dos Santos, *Feliz 1958: O ano que não devia terminar* (Rio de Janeiro, Brazil: Record, 1998), 178.

3 Stuart Hall, "What Is This 'Black' in Black Popular Culture?" *Social Justice* 20, no. 1/2 (51–52), *Rethinking Race* (Spring–Summer 1993): 104–114.

4 Hall, "What Is This 'Black' in Black Popular Culture?," 104–114.

5 Frantz Fanon, *The Wretched of the Earth* (New York: Grove/Atlantic, 2007), 97.

6 Gilberto Freyre, *The Masters and the Slaves: A Study in the Development of Brazilian Civilization* (Berkeley: University of California Press, 1987), 278–403. Gilberto Gil has given various speeches about the role of mixture in Brazilian society. He has also referred to himself as *negromestiço*. "Gilberto Gil's speech at the ceremony of his inauguration as Minister of Culture." See also "Uma nova América," *Carta Capital* (São Paulo, Brazil), January 8, 2003, 58–60; and Hermano Vianna, *O Mistério Do Samba* (Rio de Janeiro, Brazil: Editora Zahar, 1995).

7 The Glissant quote comes from Édouard Glissant, *Caribbean Discourse: Selected Essays* (Charlottesville, VA: Caraf Books, 1992), 248. Stuart Hall, "Cultural Identity and Cinematic Representation," *Framework: The Journal of Cinema and Media* no. 36 (1989): 68–81.

8 Ferreira dos Santos, *Feliz 1958*, 178.

9 My book, *Avoiding the Dark: Race, Nation and National Culture in Modern Brazil* (2000), reprinted in 2009, documents the anti-Blackness of the modernist and the Vargas regime in general and the Black movement's response. I borrow "near-White" from Caetano Veloso and Gilberto Gil's song "Haiti." For detailed information about the term and racial identity formations, see my article "From Oppressive to Benign: A Comparative History of the Construction of Whiteness in Brazil in the Post-Abolition Era," *TRANSMODERNITY: Journal of Peripheral Cultural Production of the Luso-Hispanic World* (Summer 2018): 11–32, https://escholarship.org/uc/item/3tp4p886.

10 Amiri Baraka, *Blues People: Negro Music in White America* (New York: William Morrow & Company, 1963); Eileen Southern, *The Music of Black Americans* (W. W. Norton & Company, 1997).

11 Fernando Ortiz, *La Africanía de la música folklórica de Cuba* (Havana: Cárdenas y Cia, 1950); Fernando Ortiz, *Los bailes y el teatro de negros en el folklore de Cuba); Los instrumentos de la música afrocubana, 1952–1955* (Havana: Editorial Letras. Cubanas, 1981). See also Paul Gilroy, *The Black Atlantic: Modernity and Double Consciousness* (Cambridge, MA: Harvard University Press, 1993), chapter 3.

12 These are but three examples in a rich and extensive bibliography. Mario de Andrade, *Dicionário musical brasileiro* (São Paulo, Brazil: Editora Itatiaia, 1989); José Ramos Tinhorão, *História social da música popular brasileira* (São Paulo, Brazil: Editora 34); Hermano Vianna, *O Mistério do Samba. Coleção Antropologia Social J.* (Rio de Janeiro, Brazil: Editora Zahar, 1995).

13 André Lefevere, "Mother Courage's Cucumbers: Text, System and Refraction in a Theory of Literature," in *The Translation Studies Reader*, ed. Lawrence Venuti (London: Routledge, 2000), 254.

14 Lefevere, "Mother Courage's Cucumbers," 254.
15 Alberto Carlos Almeida, *A Cabeça do Brasileiro* (Editora Record, 2007), 215–260. Note that the research is part of a broader survey based on 2,363 interviews across the country with representatives from various states and municipalities.
16 Darién J. Davis, *Afrobrasileiros Hoje* (São Paulo, Brazil: Summus, 2000).
17 Daniela Berghahn, "Performing Exoticism and the Transnational Reception of World Cinema," *Studies in World Cinema* (2021): 221–238.
18 Bruce Kapferer, "How Anthropologists Think: Configurations of the Exotic," *Journal of the Royal Anthropological Institute* 19, no. 4 (December 2013): 813–836.
19 Quoted in Berghahn, "Performing Exoticism and the Transnational Reception of World Cinema," 229.
20 "The Brazilian-Americans: Demography and Identity of An Emerging Latino Minority," *The Latino Review of Books* (Spring/Fall 1997): 8–15; "Before We Called This Place Home: The Precursors of the Brazilian Community in the United States," in *Becoming Brazuca: Brazilian Immigrants in the United States* (Cambridge, MA: Harvard University Press, 2008), 25–56. See also Darién J. Davis and Carlota Caulfield, eds., *Companion to US Latino Literatures* (Tamesis Books, an off-print of Boydell and Brewer, 2007).
21 Most sources call *Black Orpheus* a Franco-Brazilian production. The producers also received funding from Italy. However, the question of the film's artistic identity and ownership depends on the point of view or perspective. This is a French film with a French director. It also boasts an Italian production company, Gemma Cinematografica. *Black Orpheus* is also a Brazilian film with Brazilian actors with dialogue in Portuguese. It has one major American protagonist who plays the figure of Eurydice.
22 Michael Boyce Gillespie, *Film Blackness: American Cinema and the Idea of Black Film* (Duke University Press, 2016), 90–98.
23 Maxine Margolis, *The Invisible Minority: Brazilians in New York*, rev. ed. (Gainsville: University Press of Florida, 2009); Bernadete Beserra, *Brasileiros nos Estados Unidos: Hollywood e outros sonhos* (Santa Cruz do Sul: Universidade de Santa Cruz do Sul Press, 2005); Anaïs Fléchet, *« Si tu vas à Rio . . . »: La musique populaire brésilienne en France au XXe siècle* (Paris: Armand Colin, 2013); Anaïs Fléchet, "Brasil New Wave," in *Orfeu Negro: Bande originale du film de Marcel Camus avec Breno Mello et Marpessa Dawn* (Paris, 2009); Robert Stam and Ella Shohat, *Race in Translation: Culture Wars Around the Postcolonial Atlantic* (New York: NYU Press, 2012); K. E. Goldschmitt, *Bossa Mundo: Brazilian Music in Transnational Media Industries* (Oxford: Oxford University Press, 2019).
24 Lisa Shaw, *Tropical Travels: Brazilian Popular Performance, Transnational Encounters, and the Construction of Race* (Austin: University of Texas Press, 2018); Micol Seigel, *Uneven Encounters: Making Race and Nation in Brazil and the United States* (Durham: Duke University Press Books, 2009).
25 Patricia de Santana Pinho, *Mapping Diaspora: African American Roots Tourism in Brazil* (Chapel Hill: University of North Carolina Press, 2018).
26 John O'Connor, *Image as Artifact: The Historical Analysis of Film and Television* (Robert E. Krieger Publishing Company, 1990).
27 Michael G. Hanchard, *Orpheus and Power: The Movimento Negro of Rio de Janeiro and São Paulo Brazil, 1945 to 1988* (Princeton, NJ: Princeton University Press, 1944), 166–167.

28 See Stéphane Dufoix, *Diasporas* (Berkeley: University of California Press, 2008); and Kim Butler, "Defining Diaspora, Defining a Discourse," *Diaspora* 10, no. 2 (2001): 189–218.

Introduction

1 Experiencing Technicolor in the 1950s would have been equivalent to going to a 3D film in 2000 when the technology was available but not widespread. *Black Orpheus* also won the Golden Globes Award and the Saint Jordi (Catalonia) Award for Best Foreign Film. The movie also received many other nominations and awards.

2 From the Nigerian writer Chimamanda Adichie's TED talk, "The Danger of the Single Story," https://www.ted.com/talks/chimamanda_ngozi_adichie_the_danger_of_a_single_story/c.

3 Dizzy Gillespie and Al Fraser, *To Be, or Not . . . to Bop* (New York: Doubleday, 2009), 179, 428, 450.

4 Henry Louis Gates, *Black in Latin America* (New York: New York University Press), 14.

5 Palcy has recounted the story on various occasions. In "Euzhan Palcy's Closet Picks," she recounts the story in the Criterion closet, https://www.youtube.com/watch?v=L5P4n_sxkAo.
See also Academy of Motion Picture Arts and Sciences, "Academy Dialogues: Broadening the Aperture of Excellence," https://www.facebook.com/watch/?v=1046906599105119; and Toronto International Film Festival Inc (TIFF), "Euzhan Palcy on BLACK ORPHEUS," https://www.facebook.com/watch/?v=994301974248591.

6 Jean-Luc Godard, "Le Brésil vu de Billancourt," *Cahiers du cinéma*, July 1959, 97.

7 Barack Obama, *Dreams from My Father* (New York: Times Books, 1995), 123.

8 Zózimo Bulbul, interview by author, audio recording, Cinema Afrocarioca, Lapa, Rio de Janeiro, Brazil, August 2, 2010.

9 "Macumba" is the general term used to describe a variety of Afro-Brazilian or *Afro-Mestiço* faiths including Umbanda and Candomblé. Some Brazilians use the word pejoratively, while others use it in a matter-of-fact way synonymously with words like witchcraft or casting a spell. Listen to Johnny Hooker's "Eu Vou Fazer Uma Macumba Pra Te Amarrar, Maldito!," on the *Eu Vou Fazer Uma Macumba Pra Te Amarrar, Maldito!* album (Urban Vinil, 2022), track 1.

10 Philippe Camus, interview by author, audio recording, Auvers-sur-Oise, France, April 7, 2022.

11 Dossier "Orfeu da Conceição," Cinémathèque française (Paris), dossier SADOUL87-B6, 9.

12 Jean-Paul Sartre, "Orphée noir," *Anthologie de la nouvelle poésie nègre et malgache de langue française*, edited by Léopold Sédar Senghor (Paris: Presses Universitaires de France), preface.

13 James Baldwin helped to divulge the proceedings in English. Women are absent from the limelight. So is the Luso-Hispanic world in general.

14 Within these contexts, the United States and France pursued bilateral alliances with Brazil just as Brazil sought its own political, economic, and cultural partnerships. Brazilian cultural diplomacy and the consumption of Brazilian culture played important strategic roles in developing the country's domestic and

foreign policy objectives. I am primarily interested in understanding the role of transnational cultural consumption (of Brazil) and its impact on the geopolitical dynamics in this historical moment of political, economic, and cultural transformation in Brazil and France in the 1950s and 1960s. During this period, the United States and France attempted to forge political and economic alliances with their former World War II ally. Brazil often found itself uniquely able to modify the neocolonial or imperial gaze. Studying the role of the consumption of Brazilian culture and its impact on two of the most powerful nations provides us with a window into the power of transnational consumption and cultural diplomacy.

15 Consider pop music or popular music performing artists such as Diego Moreno, Françoise Hardy, and Georges Moustaki in France; and Frank Sinatra and Eydie Gormé. Gormé's *Blame It On the Bossa Nova* (Columbia, 1963) was emblematic of the fusions between the bossa nova and American pop music of the era.

16 Kim D. Butler, "Defining Diaspora, Refining a Discourse," *Diaspora: A Journal of Transnational Studies* 10, no. 2 (Fall 2001): 189–219; Arjun Appadurai, "Disjuncture and Difference in the Global Cultural Economy," in *Modernity at Large: Cultural Dimensions of Globalization* (Minneapolis: University of Minnesota Press, 2000). See also "Globalization: Special Issue," *Public Culture* 12, no. 1 (2000).

17 Stuart Hall, "What Is This 'Black' in Black Popular Culture?" *Social Justice* 20, no. 1/2 (51–52), *Rethinking Race* (Spring–Summer 1993): 104–114.

18 See the notion of the ethnoscape in Arjun Appadurai, *Modernity at Large: Cultural Dimensions of Globalization* (Minneapolis: University of Minnesota Press, 1996), 33, 48, 64.

19 Joaquim Ferreira dos Santos, *Feliz 1958: O ano que não devia terminar* (Rio de Janeiro, Brazil: Record, 1998), 178.

20 Institut National de L'audiovisuel (INA), Radio Section, Aquarelles du Brésil Radio Program (Paris: Radiodiffusion Télévision Française, December 14,1962): Identity Code, INA, Bibliothèque National Paris, France: PHD90004698.

21 Sander L. Gilman, *Difference and Pathology: Stereotypes of Sexuality, Race, and Madness* (Ithaca, NY: Cornell University Press, 1985).

22 Allen L. Woll, *The Hollywood Musical Goes to War* (Chicago: Nelson-Hall, 1983), 42–47; Bryce Wood, *The Making of the Good Neighbor Policy* (New York, 1961), 8.

23 See my work on Miranda in Darién J. Davis, *White Face, Black Mask: Africaneity and the Early Social History of Popular Music in Brazil* (Michigan State University Press, 2009), chapter 1.

24 Darién J. Davis, "Before We Called This Place Home: The Precursors of the Brazilian Community in the United States," in *Becoming Brazuca: Brazilian Immigrants in the United States* (Cambridge, MA: Harvard University Press, 2008), 25–56.

25 Darién J. Davis, *Avoiding the Dark: Race, Nation and National Culture in Modern Brazil* (Aldershot, England: Ashgate International/Center for Research in Ethnic Studies, 2000).

26 Darién J. Davis, "Performing Diasporas or *Cubanidad* Meets Jim Crow: Miami in a Period of Democratic Transition Before the Cuban Revolution," in *La Florida: Five Hundred Years of Hispanic Presence* (University of Florida, 2014), 209–223.

27 Michael G. Hanchard, *Orpheus and Power: The Movimento Negro of Rio de Janeiro and Sao Paulo Brazil, 1945 to 1988* (Princeton, NJ: Princeton University Press, 1944), 166–167.

28 Appadurai, "Disjuncture and Difference in the Global Cultural Economy." See also "Globalization: Special Issue."
29 Jeffrey D. Needell, "Identity, Race, Gender, and Modernity in the Origins of Gilberto Freyre's Oeuvre," *The American Historical Review* 100, no. 1 (February 1995): 51–77.
30 See Fabio Koifman's biography, *Raymundo Souza Dantas: O primeiro embaixador brasileiro negro* (Salvador, Brazil: Saga, 2021).
31 Hotel du Levant owner (name withheld), interview by author, digital recording, Hôtel du Levant, Rue de la Harpe, July 3, 2018.
32 *Les Étoiles Live* (Paris, CY Records, 1979).
33 Mauricio Torres Asumpção, *A historia do Brasil nas ruas de Paris* (Rio de Janeiro, Brazil: Casa da Palavra, 2014), 425–444. Andrew Hussey, *Paris: The Secret History* (Bloomsbury, 2010), 394–395.
34 See cover of *Time* magazine, February 13, 1956, http://content.time.com/time/covers/0,16641,19560213,00.html.

Chapter 1. Imagining a Brazilian Black Orpheus

1 Other operatic versions include Ottavio Rinuccini's 1600 *Euridice*; *Orfeo dolente* (Belli, 1616); *La morte di Orfeo* (Landi, 1619); *Orfeus und Euridice* (Schütz, 1638); *Orfeo* (Rossi, 1647); *Orfeo* (Lully, 1690); *Orfeo ed Euridice* (Gluck, 1762); *Orfeo ed Euridice* (Deller, 1763); *Orfeo ed Euridice* (Naumann, 1786); *L'anima del filosofo* (Haydn, 1791); *Orpheus* (Liszt, 1854); *Orphée aux Enfers* (Offenbach, 1858); *Orphée* (Duchase, 1913); *Orpheus und Eurydike* (Krenek, 1926); and *Orpheus* (Stravinsky, 1947).
2 "Orfeu Negro"-CF, CJ 1094 B146, "Marcel Camus" MEN 99.45.
3 Vinicius Moraes, Archive of Vinicius de Moraes, Casa Rui Barbosa, Rio de Janeiro, Brazil. "Orfeu," https://www.viniciusdemoraes.com.br/cineteatro/orfeu.
4 See Zweig's travelogue *Land of the Future* (Viking, 1942).
5 Carlos Jobim e Vinícius de Moraes, *Cancioneiro Vinícius de Moraes*: Orfeu Songbook/ música de Tom Jobim, 25.
6 Archive of Vinicius de Moraes, Casa da Literatura (VM 219), Casa Rui Barbosa, Rio de Janeiro. Vinicius de Moraes, "Orfeu da Conçeição," the play's original program, Teatro Municipal (1954).
7 *Orfeu da Conçeicão* (original program pamphlet), 1956. The producers published the pamphlet to hand out to audience members before the performance.
8 The quote comes from the lyrics Moraes wrote for "A samba de benção" (1962)
9 Fábio Koifman, *Raymundo Souza Dantas: o primeiro embaixador brasileiro negro* (São Paulo, Brazil: Saga Editora). See discussion about the paucity of Black diplomats in the Ministry of Foreign Affairs at https://blog.clippingcacd.com.br/cacd/o-primeiro-embaixador-negro-e-o-racismo-na-diplomacia.
10 Darién J. Davis and Judith Williams, "Pan-Africanism and the Currency of Blackness," in *Beyond Slavery: The Multifaceted Legacy of Africans in Latin America and the Caribbean* (Rowman and Littlefield, 2006), 142–167.
11 "Preface," *Orfeu da Conceição*, original edition (Rio de Janeiro, Brazil: Livraria São José, Editora 1960), 15.
12 Julia A. Walker, *Performance & Modernity: Enacting Change on the Globalizing Stage* (Cambridge: Cambridge University Press, 2022), 206–2010.

13 Program for the theatrical presentation of *Orfeu da Conçeição* (1956), middle page, not numbered. The racial difference between the actors (all Afro-Brazilian), and the White Brazilians who produced and worked behind the scenes is striking.

14 Augusto Boal, *Theatre of the Oppressed*, trans. from the Spanish by Charles A. McBride, Maria-Odilia Leal McBride, and Emily Frye (London: Pluto Books, 2008), xxiii.

15 Abdias do Nascimento, "A energia do inconformismo," *Teatro Experimental do Negro* (minC Fundacen) no. 28 (1988), 114.

16 Sandra Gomes, "O branco mais preto do Brasil," Coluna Sandra Gomes, APPAI, https://www.appai.org.br/o-branco-mais-negro-do-brasil2/.

17 Carlos Diegues, "Pela vitória do amor e da arte," in *Cancioneiro: Vinicius de Moraes: Músicas de Antônio Carlos Jobim and Vinicius de Moraes* (Rio de Janeiro, Brazil: Jobim Music, 2003), 15–19

18 Archive of Vinicius de Morias (VM 219), Casa da Literatura, Casa Rui Barbosa, Rio de Janeiro. "Vinicius de Moraes," *Orfeu da Conçeição*, original play's program, 1956), n/p.

19 Gordine ran production companies, including Dispat Films, Gemma Films, and Turpan Films, Cinémathèque française, Paris, France, dossier APG-163.

20 *Juliette ou la clé des songes* (1951).

21 "Vinicius on the filming of Orfeu," Casa da Literatura, Archives of Vinicius Moraes (VM 219); Anaïs Fléchet, "Brasil new wave," in *Orfeu negro: Bande originale du film de Marcel Camus avec Breno Mello et Marpessa Dawn*, 38–41; and Luis Carlos Lisboa, *Haroldo Costa* (Rio de Janeiro, Brazil: Editora Rio), 11–19, 43.

22 A small group broke off from the Teatro Experimental do Negro and called themselves the Grupo dos Novos (The Group of the New Ones or The New Group). The members later changed their name to Teatro Folclórico Brasileiro (The Brazilian Folkloric Theater) before adopting the name Brasiliana.

23 Haroldo Costa, interview by author, audio recording, Ipanema, Rio De Janeiro, Brazil, January 21, 2023; Anaïs Fléchet, *Si tu vas á Rio* (Paris: Raman Colin, 2009), 150; and *Brasiliana: chants et danses brésiliens (Liner Notes on Album Cover)* (Phillips, 1954).

24 Pierre Bourdieu, "Cultural Reproduction and Social Reproduction," in *Knowledge, Education, and Cultural Change* (New York: Routledge), 71–112; Anaïs Fléchet, "Cantos e encantos de Orfeu Negro," in *Orfeu Negro: Banda Originale du film de Marcel Camus com Breno Mello et Marpessa Dawn*, 40; Patrice Allain, "Du surréalisme à la production audiovisuelle; Jacques Viot, un parcours exemplaire" (Ph.D. dissertation, Université de Lille III, 1997), 485, 530–531; and Jacques Viot, *Poèmes de guerre* (Editions Jean-Michel Place, 1997), 7–11.

25 Allain, "Du surréalisme à la production audiovisuelle," 530.

26 Fléchet, "Cantos e encantos de Orfeu Negro," 40; Allain, "Du surréalisme à la production audiovisuelle," 485, 530–531; Viot, *Poèmes de guerre*, 7–11.

27 Viot, *Poèmes de guerre*, 7–11.

28 "Marcel Camus a mobilisé Rio," *Arts*, May 24, 1959.

29 Marcel Camus, interview, *Aquarelle du Brésil*, Paris, France, April 29, 1959 (Bibliothèque National de France (INA), Bibliothèque Nationale de France (BNF)).

30 "Theatrical division Unifrance," July 1959.

31 Laura Mulvey, "Visual Pleasure and Narrative Cinema," in *Film Theory Criticism: Introductory Readings*, 4th ed., ed. Gerald Mast, Marshall Cohen, and Leo Braudy (New York: Oxford University Press, 1992), 746–757.

32 "Cinema New Wave," *Time*, November 16, 1959. See Marcel Camus's interview included in the René Letzgus and Bernard Tornois documentary, *A la recherche d'Orfeu Negro*.

33 Robert Stam, *Tropical Multiculturalism: A Comparative History of Race in Brazilian Cinema & Culture* (Durham, NC: Duke University Press), 59–78.

34 Stam, *Tropical Multiculturalism*, 88–89; Grande Otelo, recorded interview, Museum of Image and Sound, Rio de Janeiro, 1966. See also Lisa Shaw, *Tropical Travels: Brazilian Popular Performance, Transnational Encounters, and the Construction of Race* (Austin: University of Texas Press, 2018), 153–214.

35 Laurent Dubois, *L'odyssée du cinéma brésilien, de l'Atlantide à la Cité de Dieu*, Primer Volume: 1940–1970 (Paris: L'Harmattan), 129. See also Randal Johnson, *Cinema Novo X5* (Austin: University of Texas Press, 1984), 162–163, 218. Using the metaphor of the Catholic Holy Trinity, Laurent Dubois calls dos Santos the historical father of cinema novo and Rocha the volcanic son. He dubbed other directors such as Carlos Diegues, Joaquim Pedro de Andrade, Walter Lima Jr., Ruy Guerra, Paulo Cesar Saranceni, and Leon Hirsman as the holy or evil spirits.

36 Darién J. Davis, "Fading In: Race and Representation of Peoples of African descent in Latin American Cinema," *Beyond Slavery: The Multilayered Legacy of Africans in Latin America and the Caribbean* (Boulder, CO: Roman and Littlefield, 2007), 249–265.

37 João Carlos Rodrigues, *O negro brasileiro e o cinema* (Rio de Janeiro: Pallas, 2001), 17.

38 *Canal Brasil*, "Vanja Orico | Retratos Brasileiros," https://www.youtube.com/watch?v=n7zaHi-baRs.

39 Caetano Veloso and Gilberto Gil, "Haiti" (*Tropicália 2*, 1993), track 1.

40 *CanalBrasil*, "Vanja Orico."

41 Bosley Crowther, "The Screen in Review; Cangaceiro, Made in Brazil, Has Debut," *New York Times*, September 3, 1954.

42 Oleone Coelho Fontes, *Lampião na Bahia* (Petropolis, Brazil: Vozes, 1988).

43 Vanja Orico, *Orfeu Negro*, Phillips, France, 1959, 7-inch vinyl EP, 45 rpm.

44 See Darién J. Davis, *White Face, Black Mask: Africaneity and the Early Social History of Popular Music in Brazil*, Black American and Diasporic Studies (Michigan State University Press, 2009).

45 See commentary from Maria d'Apparecida in interview by Daniel Salomão Roque, "Negra e filha de doméstica: quem foi Maria D'Apparecida, primeira brasileira a cantar na Ópera de Paris," *BBC News Brasil*, November 19, 2023, https://www.bbc.com/portuguese/articles/cgrpqn3ylo7o.

46 James Baldwin, "Carmen Jones: The Dark is Light Enough," *Notes of a Native Son* (New York: The Dial Press, 1963), 43–50.

47 Baldwin, "Carmen Jones," 43–50.

48 Darién J. Davis, *Afro-Brasileiros Hoje* (São Paulo, Brazil: Summus, 2000), 76–81.

49 Ruth de Souza, interview by author, tape recording, Rio de Janeiro, Brazil, July 15, 1990, published in part in Darién J. Davis, "Afro-Brazilian Women, Civil Rights, and Political Participation," in *Slavery and Beyond; The African Impact of Latin America and the Caribbean* (Scholarly Resources, 1995), 253–264.

50 De Souza, interview by author; Júlio Claudio da Silva, "*Relações raciais, gênero e memória: trajetória de Ruth de Souza entre o teatro experimental do negro e o karamu house (1945–1952)*" (Ph.D thesis, Niterói, Rio de Janerio, Universidade Federal Fluminense, 2017), 227–236. Julio Claudio da Silva's thesis was published

as *Uma Estrela Negra No Teatro Brasileiro* (Rio de Janeiro, Brazil: Julio Claudio Silva, 2017).

51 "Orfeu Negro" document submitted to the Serviço Público Federal, Conselho Nacional do Cinema," Rio de Janeiro, no date. Page 3 of the document carries a note that reads, "Important Observation: 'Orfeu Negro' will be released in Brazil with the title 'Orfeu do Carnaval.'"

52 "Orfeu Negro" document submitted to the Serviço Público Federal.

53 Unpublished first film script of "Orfeu da Conceição," Cinémathèque française (Paris), dossier SADOUL87-B6, 1.

54 Unpublished first film script of "Orfeu da Conceição," 9. The film script also highlights Black Brazilians as the major protagonists, often with odd, unnecessary, problematic racialized descriptions such as in the description of the first musical scene, the translators in French use the expression "cri du noir" (a scream from a Black man) or "La samba de plus en plus violente" (the sound of samba becoming more and more violent).

55 See sketches that Camus placed in the Brazilian press for his ideal Orpheus and Eurydice.

56 Carlos Sandroni, "No ritmo de *Orfeu Negro* e música de carnaval," in *Orfeu Negro: Bande originale du film de Marcel Camus avec Breno Mello et Marpessa Dawn*, (2016), 42–43. Almost two decades earlier, Orson Welles critiqued upper class Brazilians' anti-black attitude in his 1941 unfinished documentary *It's All True*, released Bill Krohn, Richard Wilson and Myron Meiselby in 1993.

57 "Press packet Orfeu Negro," Dispat Film, 1958, BIFI Department des Archives, Paris, France.

58 "Press packet Orfeu Negro."

59 "Pour tourner Orfeu Negro Marcel Camus a mobilisé Rio," *Arts*, May 24, 1959.

60 The interview comes from René Letzgus and Bernard Tournois, *A la recherche d'Orfeu Negro*. Sergio Cabral, *As escolas de samba, do Rio de Janeiro* (Lumiar Editora, 1996). At first glance it may seem that Camus is saying that it was tiring for him because it involved filming Black unknown actors, but the context clarifies that these were not his views. He had already filmed in Indochina and understood the challenges of filming outside of France. Moreover, he stresses that Brazilians were charming, and he enjoyed working with them.

61 Interview with Marcel Camus in "Pour tourner Orfeu Negro Marcel Camus a mobilisé Rio," *Arts*, May 24, 1959.

62 Allain, "Du surréalisme à la production audiovisuelle," 485, 530–531; Viot, *Poèmes de guerre*, 7–11.

63 *Orfeu negro outline*, Societé des auteurs (CN1654), Cinematéque française APG Sacha Gordine (19 Rue Spontini, Paris).

64 Tunico Amânicio, "O estrangeiro Marcel Camus: Olhares do Afeto Sobre Algumas Cidades Brasileiras," *Passages de Paris* I (2005) 53–61.

65 Robert Stam, "Black Performance and Brazilian Cinema," in *Cinema of the Black Diaspora: Diversity, Dependence, and Opportunity*, ed. Michael T. Martin (Detroit: Wayne State University Press, 1996), 280–301

66 "Orfeu Negro"- CF, CJ 1094 B146, "Marcel Camus" MEN 99.45.

67 Léa Garcia, interview by author, tape recorded, headquarters of IPERAFRO, Rio de Janeiro, Brazil, June 21, 2010.

68 René Letzgus and Bernard Tournois, *A la recherche d'Orfeu Negro*; Cabral, *As escolas de samba do Rio de Janeiro*.

69 "Theatrical division of Unifrance" (pamphlet), July 1959.
70 See the clip of the Academy Award ceremony where Gordine accepts the award, "Black Orpheus Wins Foreign Language Film: 1960 Oscars," https://www.youtube.com/watch?v=TXrVg3vRDPk and "'My Uncle' ('Mon Oncle') Wins Foreign Language Film: 1959 Oscars," https://www.youtube.com/watch?v=y88VU3qbSpY&index=14&list=PLJ8RjvesnvDMHxTASvuE1x-JoSJisxG7R. In 1964. Sidney Poitier was the first Black actor to receive an Academy Award for Best Actor. In his acceptance speech, he simply referenced his long journey to this moment. See acceptance speeches: "Sidney Poitier Wins Best Actor 36th Oscars (1964)," https://www.youtube.com/watch?v=qCzTyxXPy1o#:~:text=I%20am%20naturally%20indebted%20to%20countless%20numbers,say%20is%20a%20very%20special%20thank%20you, and "Hattie McDaniel Winning Best Supporting Actress: 12th Oscars (1940)," https://www.youtube.com/watch?v=e7t4pTNZshA. Poitier has given several interviews about his goals as an actor and about the importance of the award to Black populations.
71 Pierre Bourdieu, *Outline of a Theory of Practice*, vol. 1 (Cambridge University Press, 1977), 86.

Chapter 2. The Black Cast

1 Júlio César Tavares, "Teatro Experimental do Negro: Context, estructura e ação," *Dionysos* no. 28 (1988): 84.
2 Comisão Artística e Cultural, Brasiliana, printed pamphlet, Teatro Municipal, 1955.
3 Toronto International Film Festival Inc (TIFF), "Euzhan Palcy on BLACK ORPHEUS," https://www.facebook.com/watch/?v=994301974248591.
4 Frantz Fanon, *Black Skin, White Masks*, trans. Charles Lam Markmann (New York: Grove Press, 1967), 6.
5 Several American scholars have described the various barriers to depicting sex and sexuality and the stereotypes that framed Black representation in the U.S. context. These ideas also apply to a certain extent to Brazil and France, although sexuality is treated more openly in both countries. See Donald Bogle, *Toms, Coons, Mulattoes, Mammies, and Bucks: An Interpretive History of Blacks in American Films*, updated and expanded 5th ed. (New York: Bloomsbury Academic, 2016). For a Brazilian perspective, see João Carlos Rodrigues, *O negro brasileiro e o cinema* (Rio de Janeiro, Brazil: Pallas, 2001), 147.
6 See Victoria Thomas, *Hollywood's Latin Lovers: Latino, Italian and French Men Who Make the Screen Smolder* (Angel City Press, 1998).
7 Sigmund Freud, *Drei Abhandlungen zur Sexualtheorie* [*Three Essays on the Theory of Sexuality*] (Berlin: 1905). See Evelyn P. Stevens, "Marianismo: The Other Face of Machismo in Latin America," in *Female and Male in Latin America*, ed. Ann Pescatello (University of Pittsburgh Press, 1973).
8 The number of lines may be related to Orpheus being the central character. It is possible that the producers reduced Dawn's lines because she was also learning Portuguese on the set.
9 Décio Viera Otoni, "Orfeu Negro," *Diario Carioca* (Rio de Janeiro, Brazil), November 7, 1955.
10 See "Interview–Breno Mello, Star of Black Orpheus (2005, English Subtitles)," https://www.youtube.com/watch?v=zuSbjgePQco&t=84s. See the ad reproduced

in the deluxe book with CDs *Orfeu negro: Bande originale du film de Marcel Camus* (Paris, Phillips, 2008), n/p.

11 CÂMARA MUNICIPAL DE NOVO HAMBURGO, ESTADO DO RIO GRANDE DO SUL, "JUSTIFICATIVA" (Novo Hamburgo, Rio Grande do Sul), February 9, 2010.

12 "Breno Mello, 76, Star of 'Orpheus,' Dies," *The New York Times*, September 5, 2008, https://www.nytimes.com/2008/09/06/movies/06mello.html.

13 Tennis, the first ball sport introduced in Brazil, was also an exclusive sport. Although Emperor Dom Pedro II often attended cricket matches, rugby and cricket, introduced earlier than football, never developed a popular following.

14 Campeão Gaúcho de 1954 (Foto: blog Botões Para Sempre), https://botoesparasempre.blogspot.com/2010/12/colecao-idolos-do-futebol-1955.html.

See image from *O Cruzeiro,* número 20, de 26 de fevereiro de 1955. See also http://reliquiasdofutebol.blogspot.com/2015_10_11_archive.html.

15 See the soccer club Santos's facebook page for a dedication to Mello, https://www.facebook.com/photo.php?fbid=989109101561638&id=205316886607534&set=a.205323649940191&locale=is_IS. Mello does not appear on the Fluminense roster ("Fluminense RJ: Players from A-Z," http://www.worldfootball.net/teams/fluminense-rj/10/).

16 "Breno Melo [*sic*], foi grande atração em Acapulco," 1960 newspaper (no title) clipping from Mana de Xangô, personal archives, Florianópolis, Brazil. The Rio de Janeiro magazine *Revista do Radio* (1960) no. 541 also makes reference to the Cinematographic Festival in Acupulco that featured Breno Mello.

17 Photograph entitled *Três moços que orgulham o Brasil,* Valdemar Santana, Pelé and Breno Mello, personal archives, Maná de Xangô, Florianópolis, Brazil.

18 Donald Bogle, *Hollywood Black: The Stars, the Films, the Film Makers* (Philadelphia: Running Press), 120–123.

19 James Baldwin, "Carmen Jones: The Dark Is Light Enough," in *Notes of a Native Son* (Beacon Press, 2012), 47–58.

20 Nathalie Coutelet, "Habib Benglia, le « nègrérotique » du spectacle français," *Genre, sexualité & société* (Spring 2009): 1–39, https://journals.openedition.org/gss/688; Manthia Diawara, *African Cinema: Politics and Culture* (Bloomington, IN), 22.

21 Cover of VHS of film *Rata de Puerto,* Mana de Xangô, personal archive and video collection, Flórinopolis, Brazil.

22 Mana de Xangô, recorded interview with author, Florianópolis, Santa Catarina, July 29, 2016.

23 Mana de Xangô, "Orfeu," in *Nuvem Branca* (Florinópolis, Santa Catarina, Brazil: 2007). Original Portuguese: Não quero mais ficar no passado/Sentirás a tristeza. E o perfume que era meu. Sentirás a presença de tua EURIDICE?/Porque serás eternamente para mim o grande amor chamado ORFEU.

24 "La triste muerte del *Orfeo Negro,*" *El País*, July 18, 2008, https://elpais.com/cultura/2008/07/18/actualidad/1216332006_850215.html.

25 Stefan Zweig, *Brasilien: Ein Land der Zukunft* (Stockholm: Bermann-Fischer, 1941). translated into English as *Brazil: Land of the Future and Brazil: A Land of the Future*.

26 "Sacha Gordine to Vinicus de Moraes," Casa da Literatura, Casa, Rui Barbosa, Rio de Janeiro, Brazil, CP 310 (18).

27 Léa Garcia, interview with the author, digital recording, Office of IPEAFRO, Rio de Janeiro, Brazil, October 8, 2010.

28 Hazel Garland, "Award-Winning Movie Makes Redstone, PA Girl a Star," *Pittsburgh Courier*, April 9, 1960, 7.

29 Burt Glinn, "Photograph behind the stage of the 1951 Shriners Beauty competition in Harlem," reproduced on Instagram, https://www.instagram.com/blackhistory/p/CioRg_hOPQ2/.

30 Terri Austin Chiles, *If I Had My Druthers* (Lincoln, NE: iUniverse books, 2006).

31 Dennis Hevishi, "Marpessa Dawn, Eurydice in the Film 'Black Orpheus,' Dies at 74," *The New York Times*, September 27, 2008.

32 In the 1877 novel *La Fille Elisa* by Edmond de Goncourt, Elisa, a prostitute, tries unsuccessfully to change her life and world.

33 "List of Award-Winners at the Cannes Film Festival," http://fresques.ina.fr/festival-de-cannes-en/fiche-media/Cannes00059/list-of-award-winners-at-the-1959-cannes-festival.html.

34 Classified Ad 26, *The Guardian* [London (UK)], May 30, 1960, 7.

35 See "Ce soir à la Grande Séverine," February 2, 2022, INA, Bibliothèque Nationale, Paris, France. Also now online: "Marpessa Dawn 'Recado Bossa Nova,'" https://www.youtube.com/watch?v=wLLsv2uuxkE.

36 "*Black Orpheus*," *The New Yorker*, July 11, 1969.

37 "News," *Villager*, January 9, 1975.

38 "TV Interview with Léa Garcia and Lourdes de Oliveira," *Cinepanorama*, November 19, 1960 (presented by François Chalet), INA.

39 "Darcy de Oliveira," http://www.revistamusicabrasileira.com.br/homenagens/darcy-de-oliveira-compositor-e-pandeirista; and "Notas sobre o compositor e pandeirista Darcy de Oliveira (1905–1945)," https://sandorbuys.wordpress.com/2009/07/23/notas-sobre-o-compositor-e-pandeirista-darcy-de-oliveira-1905-1945/.

40 Jean-Christophe and Olivier Talac, *Negrinha* (Paris: Gallimard BD, 2009); François-Xavier Freland and Olivier Mirguet, *Saravá: Recontres avec la bossa nova* (Naïve, France: 2005), 56; Sando Buys, "Notas sobre o compositor e pandeirista Darcy de Oliveira (1905-1945)," July 23, 2009, https://sandorbuys.wordpress.com/2009/07/23/notas-sobre-o-compositor-e-pandeirista-darcy-de-oliveira-1905-1945/.

41 Luis Bonfá, "Reencontres avec Lourdes de Oliveira Camus, La Mira d'Orfeu negro," in François-Xavier Freland and Olivier Mirguet, *Sarava!: Rencontres avec la bossa-nova* (Naïve, France: 2005), 55. In the film, she plays Suzana, a Brazilian who robs the main protagonist, a French adventurer, and who falls in love with her.

42 Bonfá, "Reencontres com Lourdes de Oliveira Camus, La Mira d'Orfeu negro," 55.

43 "Le jour où Marpessa Dawn et Lourdes de Oliveira franchirent les portes du Cégep de Sherbrooke," *Autogramme* (Paris 1960), from Dossier Lourdes de Oliveira, Cinémathèque Française, Paris, France.

44 "Le jour où Marpessa Dawn et Lourdes de Oliveira franchirent les portes du Cégep de Sherbrooke."

45 "Les rendez-vous du dimanche," September 26, 1976, TFI (French television), Star of *Otalia*—first time outside of Bahia, star performs and interviewed, Archives, INA.

46 Fernando Ferreira, "Camus," *O Globo*, January 14, 1982. Léa Garcia, interview with author, digital recording, Office of IPEAFRO, Rio de Janeiro, Brazil, October 8, 2010.

47 "Para o diretor de 'Orfeu do carnival' o Brasil se tornou uma segunda patria," *Globo*, January 14, 1982; Léa Garcia, interview, digital recording, Office of IPEAFRO, Rio de Janeiro, Brazil, October 8, 2010.

48 Léa Garcia, interview with author, digital recording, Office of IPEAFRO, Rio de Janeiro, Brazil, October 8, 2010.

49 Mauro Alencar, *A Hollywood Brasileira: Panorama da Telenovela no Brasil* (São Paulo, Brazil: SENAC-SPo, 2002), 39, 150.

50 Joel Zito Araújo, *A negação do Brasil*, 2007. See also the book published after the documentary: *A negação do Brasil: o negro na telenovela brasileira* (Editora Senac São Paulo, 2019).

51 *A Escrava Isaura*, Globo TV, 1976–1977. See "Isaura: The Slave Girl," IMDb, https://www.imdb.com/title/tt0142036/.

52 Léa Garcia, interview with author, digital recording, Office of IPEAFRO, Rio de Janeiro, Brazil, October 8, 2010, June 21, 2010.

53 João Carlos Rodrigues, *O negro brasileiro e o cinema* (Rio de Janeiro, Brazil: Pallas, 2001), 147.

54 Léa Garcia, interview with author, digital recording, Office of IPEAFRO, Rio de Janeiro, Brazil, October 8, 2010. See also "Léa"—Entrevista," *Revista Fonfon*, 1957.

55 See "Léa Garcia Fala Sobre Interpretar Rosa em Escrava Isaura," https://www.youtube.com/watch?v=GoZz59JvEXE.

56 Among her many awards, Léa Garcia received the Medal of Honor Pedro Ernesto da Câmara dos Vereadores do Rio de Janeiro em 1994, the Medal of Honor da Academia Brasileira de Letras, and the Golfinho de Ouro do Conselho de Cultura do Estado do Rio de Janeiro. She was also an advisor to the Conselho de Cultura do Estado in Rio de Janeiro from 1999 to 2001. In 2010, she was elected artistic director of the Sindicato dos Artistas e Técnicos em Espetáculos e Direções (known by the acronym SATED).

57 Michael Rothberg, "Between Memory and Memory: From lieux de mémoire to noeuds de mémoire," *Yale French Studies* no. 118/119 (2010): 3–12. I am applying Rothberg's concept of memory knots as signposts in memory culture as similar to historical signposts. Maurico Barros de Castro, *Zicartola: política e samba na casa de Cartola e Dona Zica*, 2nd ed. (Rio de Janeiro, Brazil: Azougue Editorial, 2013); Isabella Giordano, "Zicartola no cinema: descubra os filmes estrelados pelo sambista e sua esposa," 2014, https://samba.catracalivre.com.br/brasil/samba-na-net/indicacao/zicartola-no-cinema-descubra-os-filmes-em-que-o-sambista-e-sua-esposa-estrelaram/. See also "Ocupação Cartola," http://www.itaucultural.org.br/ocupacao/cartola/.

58 Unifrance films pamphlet "Les nouveaux films français" (1958).

59 Henri-Georges Clouzot, *Le Cheval des Dieux* (Paris: R. Julliard, 1951). See "Henri Georges Clouzot," interview, https://madelen.ina.fr/content/henri-georges-clouzot-78685. The beginning of the documentary can be found at https://www.cinematheque.fr/henri/film/122297-brasil-henri-georges-clouzot-1950/.

60 Marcel Camus, interview, *Cinépanorama*, INA, Biblioteca Nacional, June 7, 1958. See also essays by Carlos Sandroni, "No ritmo de Orfeu Negro é música de carnaval," in *Orfeu Negro: Bande Originale du film de Marcel Camus avec Breno Mello et Marpessa Dawn* (2016), (English version of text, 42–43).

61 Elma Lai Nascimento, "Glorious Leaps," 2001, http://www.brazzillog.com/pages/p10feb01.htm.

62 "Entrevista: era uma dupla: hoje moram em Lavras, o filme ganhou um Oscar," *Journal de Lavras*, February 10, 2010, http://www.jornaldelavras.com.br/index.php?p=10&tc=4&c=773&catn=3.

63 "Letter of Stefan Zweig to Hannah and Manfred Altmann," March 10, 1941, in Darién J. Davis and Oliver Marshall, *Stefan and Lotte Zweig's South American Letters: New York, Argentina, and Brazil, 1940–42* (Bloomsbury, 2010), 28, 164.

64 See Charles A. Perrone, "Myth, Melopeia, and Mimesis: Black Orpheus, Orfeu and Internationalization in Brazilian Popular Music," in *Brazilian Popular Music and Globalization*, ed. Charles Perrone and Christopher Dunn (Gainesville: University Press of Florida, 2001), chapter 3.

65 Charles Perrone, "Do Look Back: Retrospection on the Impacts of *Black Orpheus*," https://people.clas.ufl.edu/perrone/publications/do-look-back-retrospection-on-the-impacts-of-Black-orpheus/.

66 Johanne Villeneuve, "Orphée au Brésil: L'imaginaire européen à l'épreuve de la danse," *Cinémas* 15, no. 1 (Autumn 2004): 105–122, https://www.erudit.org/fr/revues/cine/2004-v15-n1-cine982/011661ar/.

67 Walter Benjamin, "The Work of Art in the Age of Mechanical Reproduction," in *Illuminations*, ed. Hannah Arendt, trans. Harry Zohn (New York: Schocken Books, 1969).

68 Myrian Sepúlveda dos Santos, "The Brazilian Remake of the Orpheus Legend: Film Theory and Aesthetic Dimension," *Theory, Culture, and Society* 20, no. 4 (2003): 49–69.

Chapter 3. The Soundtrack

1 Walter Benjamin, "The Work of Art in the Age of Mechanical Reproduction," in *Illuminations*, ed. Hannah Arendt, trans. Harry Zohn (New York: Schocken Books, 1969).

2 Suzana de Moraes, interview in the documentary *Negro* (2005).

3 Herman Hesse, *Black Orpheus: The Music of "Minor" Cinemas*, ed. Germán Gil Curiel (New York: Bloomsbury Academic, 2016), 45–70.

4 Anaïs Fléchet, "Cantos e encantos de Orfeu Negro," in *Orfeu Negro: Bande originale du film de Marcel Camus avec Breno Mello et Marpessa Dawn* (Phillips Records, 2009).

5 Haroldo Costa, interview by author, audio recording, Ipanema, Brazil, February 3, 2023.

6 Caetano Veloso, *Verdade Tropical* (São Paulo, Brazil: Companhia das letras, 1997), 253.

7 This work uses 'Elizeth,' the spelling that the Museum of Image and Sound and the Instituto Moreira Salles uses. The artist (or record producers) also used this spelling on many of her albums. Sergio Cabral, one of her biographers, spells her name without the 'h' and with an 'e' at the end: "Elizete.' Many of her albums also use this spelling.

8 A recording of the opera can be found at https://www.youtube.com/watch?v=-fa9ethBRV8. Lyneise Williams comments on these images in her book *Latin Blackness in Parisian Visual Culture, 1852–1932* (New York: Bloomsbury Publishing, 2022), introduction.

9 I develop this thesis in "From Oppressive to Benign: A Comparative History of the Construction of Whiteness in Brazil in the Post-Abolition Era,"

TRANSMODERNITY: Journal of Peripheral Cultural Production of the Luso-Hispanic World (Summer 2018): 11–32. *TRANSMODERNITY* is a peer-reviewed and interdisciplinary journal of Luso-Hispanic and U.S. Latino literary and cultural studies.

10 Lisa Shaw, *Tropical Travels: Brazilian Popular Performance, Transnational Encounters, and the Construction of Race* (New York: University of Texas Press, 2018), chapter 2; Lisa Shaw, "Afro-Brazilian Popular Culture in Paris in 1922: Transatlantic Dialogues and the Racialized Performance of Brazilian National Identity," *Atlantic Studies* 8, no. 4: 393–409; Ernesto Joaquim Maria dos Santos AKA Donga, recorded interview at the Museu da Imagem e do Som, Rio de Janeiro, tape recording, April 2, 1969; Sergio Cabral, *Pixinguinha: Vida e Obra* (Rio de Janeiro, Brazil: Lumiar, 1997), 71–85. See *Le Journal* (Paris), September 7 and 8, 1922. For a discussion of the Black pioneers, see Darién J. Davis, *White Face, Black Mask: Africaneity and the Early Social History of Popular Music in Brazil* (Michigan State University Press, 2009), chapter 1.

11 Adjoa Osei, "Black Brazil in Jazz-Age Paris: The Life and Work of Elsie Houston," *Journal of Romance Studies* 23, no. 3 (2022): 301–327; Isabel Bertevelli, "Elsie Houston e o canto nacional dos anos 1920 a 1940: trajetória profissional da "genuína voz brasileira," *Revista Brasileira de Música* (Rio de Janeiro) 29, no. 2 (July/Dec. 2016): 365–397. See working paper Darién J. Davis, "'Transnational Blackness': The Female Body and the Early Globalization of Brazilian Popular Music" (paper presented at conference at University of California Riverside), published in *Diagonal* 6 (2010): 1–18.

12 Lisa Peppercorn, "H. Villa-Lobos in Paris," *Latin American Music Review / Revista De Música Latinoamericana* 6, no. 2 (1985): 235–248, https://doi.org/10.2307/780202.

13 Davis, *White Face, Black Mask*. Defining "Black music" is not determined necessarily by recognizable African rhythms or structures, but, as Peter Wade reports, "Black music" is defined within the context of power relations. Thus, "Blackness" is partly determined by a community's perceptions. See Peter Wade, "Black Music and Cultural Syncretism in Columbia," in *Slavery and Beyond: The African Impact on Latin America and the Caribbean* (Scholarly Resources, 1995). See also "From Noel Rosa to Carmen Miranda: Nation, Race, and Satire in Brazil's Musical Performance, 1930–1939," in *Popular Culture in Latin America: An Introduction* (Wilmington, DE: Scholarly Resources, 2001); "To Be or Not to Be Brazilian: Carmen Miranda's Quest for Fame and 'Authenticity' in the United States," in *Strange Pilgrimages: Exile, Travel, and National Identity in Latin America, 1800–1990s*, ed. Ingrid E. Fey and Karen Racine (Wilmington, DE: Scholarly Resources, 2000).

14 Shaw, "Afro-Brazilian Popular Culture in Paris in 1922," 393–409.

15 Luis Carlos Prestes Filho, "Vanja Orico | Retratos Brasileiros," https://www.youtube.com/watch?v=n7zaHi-baRs.

16 Oleone Coelho Fontes, *Lampião Bahia* (Petrópolis, Brazil: Vozes, 1988) documents the cangaçeiros in Bahia. He also discusses *Lampião*'s anti-Black racism one generation after the abolition of slavery in 1888.

17 Prestes Filho, "Vanja Orico | Retratos Brasileiros."

18 Antônio (Tom) Carlos Jobim to Vinicius de Moraes, September 22, 1958, reprinted in Antônio (Tom) Carlos Jobim to Vinicius de Moraes, September 27, 1958, reprinted in *Cancioneiro Vinicius de Moraes: Orfeu: Songbook: Músicas de Antônio*

Carlos Jobim & Vinicius de Moraes (Rio de Janeiro, Brazil: Jobim Music, 2003), original Portuguese and English translation, 70 and 73.

19 Antônio (Tom) Carlos Jobim to Vinicius de Moraes, September 22, 1958, 70–73.

20 Antônio (Tom) Carlos Jobim to Vinicius de Moraes, September 22, 1958, 70–73.

21 Antônio (Tom) Carlos Jobim to Vinicius de Moraes, September 22, 1958, 70 and 73.

22 Marcel Camus, interview, *Cinépanorama* INA, Bibliothèque Nationale, Paris, Saturday, June 7, 1958; Anaïs Fléchet, "Brasil New Wave," in *Orfeu Negro: Bande originale du film de Marcel Camus avec Breno Mello et Marpessa Dawn* (2016), English version of text, 38–41.

23 Alison Raphael, "From Popular Culture to Microenterprise: The History of Brazilian Samba Schools," *Latin American Music Review/Revista de Música Latinoamericana* 11, no. 1 (Spring–Summer 1990): 73–83.

24 Mark J. Curran, *Adventures of a "Gringo" Researcher in Rio in the 1960s* (Trafford Publishing, 2012), 5.

25 André Bernardo, "O show em Nova York que 'lançou' a Bossa Nova no mundo há 60 anos," *BBC News Brasil*, 2022, https://www.bbc.com/portuguese/brasil-63742499.

26 "A Felicidade," on *Black Orpheus* soundtrack, 1959 (English translation mine). Original Portuguese:

Tristeza não tem fim
A Felicidade sim
A felicidade é como a pluma
Que o vento vai levando pelo ar
Voa tão leve
Mas tem a vida breve
Precisa que haja vento sem parar
A felicidade do pobre parece
A grande ilusão do carnaval
A gente trabalha o ano inteiro
Por um momento de sonho
Pra fazer a fantasia
De rei ou de pirata ou jardineira
E tudo se acabar na quarta-feira

27 The blind man Tiresias appears in many Greek myths. In one story, Hera causes his blindness because he asserts that women have greater pleasure in sex than men. In another version, Athena strikes Teresias blind after he sees her bathing naked. Later, rather than restoring his sight, Athena gives him the ability to see the future.

28 Carlos Sandroni, "No ritmo de Orfeu Negro e música de carnaval," in *Orfeu Negro: Bande originale du film de Marcel Camus avec Breno Mello et Marpessa Dawn* (2016), English version of text, 42–43.

29 Charles Perrone, "Do Look Back: Retrospection on the Impacts of Black Orpheus," https://people.clas.ufl.edu/perrone/publications/do-look-back-retrospection-on-the-impacts-of-Black-orpheus/.

30 Johanne Villeneuve, "Orphée au Brésil: L'imaginaire européen à l'épreuve de la danse," *Cinémas* 15, no. 1 (Autumn 2004): 105–122, https://www.erudit.org/fr/revues/cine/2004-v15-n1-cine982/011661ar/.

31 Anaïs Fléchet, "Brasil New Wave," in *Orfeu Negro: Bande originale du film de Marcel Camus avec Breno Mello et Marpessa Dawn* (2016), 38–41.

32 *It's All True*, Orson Welles, 1942, released in 1994.

33 Carlos Sandroni, "No ritmo de Orfeu Negro e música de carnaval," in *Orfeu Negro: Bande originale du film de Marcel Camus avec Breno Mello et Marpessa Dawn* (2016), 42–43.

34 Sandroni, "No ritmo de Orfeu Negro e música de carnaval," 42–43.

35 Vinicius de Moraes, unpublished document, Archive of Vinicius de Moraes (VM 219), Casa da Literatura, Rio de Janeiro. See also "Brazilian Pop, 1934-1964," https://brazilianpop1957-1964.blogspot.com/2011/11/blog-post.html; and "Brazilian Pop 1934–1964," http://brazilianpop1957-1964.blogspot.com.br/2011/11/blog-post.html.

36 "Brazilian Pop, 1934–1964."

37 Agostinho dos Santos, *Antônio Carlos Jobim E Fernando César Na Voz De Agostinho Dos Santos* (Polydor, 1958).

38 Luiz Bonfá and Antônio Carlos Jobim, *The Original Soundtrack from the Film Black Orpheus*, CD, Verve, 2007.

39 Vladimir Bogdanov, Chris Woodstra, and Stephen Thomas Erlewine, *All Music Guide: The Definitive Guide to Popular Music* (Backbeat Books, 2001), 911. Various artists in the United States, from Frank Sinatra and Mongo Santamaría to Miriam Makeba and Joan Baez, covered "Manhã de carnaval" under diverse titles such as "Manhã de carnaval," "A Day in the Life of a Fool," and "Theme from *Black Orpheus*."

40 Walter Silva, *Vou te contar: histórias de música popular brasileira* (São Paulo: Nobel, 2007), 108–110.

41 "Negro é lindo," *Trip*, January 21, 2004, http://revistatrip.uol.com.br/revista/228/reportagens/negro-e-lindo.html; José Castello, *Vinicius de Moraes: o poeta da paixão—uma biografia* (São Paulo: Companhia das Letras, 1994), 194.

42 Archive of Vinicius de Moraes (VM 219), Casa da Literatura, Rio de Janeiro, Brazil.

43 Bonfá and Jobim, *The Original Soundtrack from the Film Black Orpheus*; Silva, *Vou te contar*, 108–110.

44 Bogdanov, Woodstra, and Erlewine, *All Music Guide*, 911.

45 Elizeth Cardoso, recorded interview at MIS Archive with Eneide, Haroldo Costa, Hermenio Belo de Cavalho, July 22, 1970. See also Jobim, "Letter to Vini . . . ," September 27, 1958, Archive of Vinicius de Moraes (VM 219), Casa da Literatura, Rio de Janeiro; and "Elizeth Cardoso: 50 anos de carreira," https://www.youtube.com/watch?v=PPCMutqxJfo. Critics credit the Afro-Brazilian Johnny Alf as the "Father of Bossa Nova," recognizing his pioneering role in mixing jazz and samba and singing in a soft melodic tune.

46 "Elizeth Cardoso: Preferi ganhar a vida pelo lado do sol," *Manchete* (Rio de Janeiro, Brazil), March 31, 1979. It is worth commenting on the frequency of diminutive and augmentative in Brazil Portuguese to express different meanings, including irony. Here, too, context is important. Whereas augmentative ending often expresses a larger size or intensity, with racial descriptors the endings 'ão' or 'ona' can have different meanings. Perhaps it would not be appropriate to say that Cardoso was calling herself "a big Mulatta," although one can certainly use the term that way. Here, Cardoso is declaring her Blackness by affirming that she is a real Mulatta. African descendants of all backgrounds in Brazil have gone through

a process of coming out as Black (assumirse como negro), a phenomenon that may not necessarily make sense in the United States or France. In Brazil it is a power political statement.

47 Arthur da Távila, "Elizeth Cardoso: A figura sintese do canto brasilerio," *O Globo*, September 16, 1975.

48 "Um desconhecido bate á porta," technical details http://bcc.cinemateca.org.br/cartazes/cartaz_fb/014097#. See also lyrics at Instituto Tom Jobim, https://www.jobim.org/jobim/handle/2010/11037.

49 "Carreira em festa," *Visão* 31, no. 32 (August 9, 1982): 39.

50 "Preferi ganhar a vida pelo lado do sol," depoimento a Ronaldo Bôscoli, *Manchete* (Rio de Janeiro, Brazil), March 31, 1979, 100–103; "Elizeth Cardoso: 50 anos de Carreira."

51 Luiz Bonfá file, Funarte, Rio de Janeiro, Brazil. See also *Jornal da Tarde* (São Paulo, Brazil), July 28, 1983, 43; "Luiz Bonfá: aqui, trabalho. Lá fora, successors," *Jornal da trade*, July 29, 1983.

52 See *O Globo*, May 8, 1973; *O Diario de Noticias*, September 23, 1953.

53 "Luis Bonfá," https://folkways.si.edu/luiz-bonfa-brazilian-bossa-nova-guitarist/latin-world/music/article/smithsonian; Brian Hodel, *The Brazilian Guitar* (Dennis McMillan Publishing, 1983); Luiz Bonfá, *The Music of Luiz Bonfá: Four Pieces*, ed. Carlos Barbosa-Lima (Guitar Solo Publications, 1987). See also Brian Hodel, "Luiz Bonfá, Ambassador of Brazilian Swing," *Guitar Player*, May 1983; Brian Hodel, "Spotlight on Luiz Bonfá," *Guitar Review*, Winter 1984.

54 Carlinhos Pandeiro de Ouro, interview by author, audio recorded interview, Los Angeles, California, June 2, 2009.

55 "Entrevista: era uma dupla; hoje moram em Lavras; o filme ganhou um Oscar," October 2, 2010, http://www.jornaldelavras.com.br/index.php?p=10&tc=4&c=773&catn=3&scatn=44.

56 K. E. Goldschmitt, *Bossa Mundo: Brazilian Music in Transnational Media Industries* (Oxford University Press, 2020), 29–30.

57 Jean-Paul Delfino, *Bossa Nova—La grande aventure du Brésil* (Paris: Passage, 2017); Goldschmitt, *Bossa Mundo*, 29–30.

Chapter 4. Oblique Gazes

1 Paulo Siquiera, "Luis Bonfá: Novo sucesso mundial da música brasileira," *Radiolândia* (1959): 1.

2 República dos Estados Unidos do Brasil, "Entry record for Marcel Georges Camus," June 15, 1959, Rio de Janeiro Immigration Cards.

3 Tunico Amâncio, "O estrangeiro Marcel Camus: olhares de afeto sobre algumas cidades brasileiras," *Passage de Paris* 1 (2005): 53–61; Fernando Ferreira, "Camus," *O Globo*, January 14, 1982.

4 See Zweig's travelogue *Land of the Future* (Viking, 1942).

5 Malcolm Barnard, *Art, Design, and Visual Culture: An Introduction* (1998), 10, 24.

6 Marcel Camus, dossier, Cinémathèque française, Paris, Référence: SADOUL87-B6.

7 Janet Staiger, "Film, Reception, and Cultural Studies," *The Centennial Review* 36, no. 1, *Cultural Studies* (Winter 1992): 89–104, 90, https://www.jstor.org/stable/23739835.

8 Anna Siomopoulos, "The Birth of a Black Cinema: Race, Reception, and Oscar Micheaux's *Within Our Gates*," *The Moving Image: The Journal of the Association of Moving Image Archivists* 6, no. 2 (Fall 2006): 111–118.
9 Manthia Diawara, "Black Spectatorship: Problems of Identification and Resistance," *Screen* 29, no. 4 (October 1, 1988): 66–77.
10 See the online history of the festival in English at https://web.archive.org/web/20070514112740/http://www.festival-cannes.fr/en/about/festivalHistory.
11 Carlos Alves de Souza, Brazilian Embassy in Paris to Ministry of Foreign Affairs, telegram Ref: XII Festival Internacional de Cinema (Cannes); Apresentação do filme brasileiro "Orfeu da Conceição," EM/ 15/15/IV/59.
12 Carlos Alves de Souza, Brazilian Embassy in Paris to Ministry of Foreign Affairs, telegram Ref: XII Festival Internacional de Cinema (Cannes); Apresentação do filme brasileiro "Orfeu da Conceição," Telegrama from Emabaixada em Paris to Secretaria do Estado de Relações Exteriores, EM/16/16/IV/59; "Festival International de Cinéma de Cannes Apresentação do filme *Orfeu da Conceição*," EM 21/22/59.
13 Carlos Alves de Souza to Minister of Foreign Affairs, May 20, 1959, Itamaraty Archives (Rio de Janeiro, Brazil) EM/ 15/15/IV/59.
14 "Orfeu carioca em França," O *Cruzeiro* (1959), 32, 1.
15 Luis Carlos Prestes Filho, "Vanja Orico | Retratos Brasileiros," https://www.youtube.com/watch?v=n7zaHi-baRs.
16 "A Brazilian Singer and Guitarist Bow," *The New York Times*, April 9, 1971, https://www.nytimes.com/1971/04/09/archives/a-brazilian-singer-and-guitarist-bow.html.
17 "Orfeu Negro," CF, CJ 1094 B146, "Marcel Camus" MEN 99.45.
18 "O carnival carioca foi também vencedor em Cannes," *Manchete*, Carnival edition, 1959, 0371, 26.
19 "O carnival carioca foi também vencedor em Cannes."
20 "Résultat d'exclusivité Paris 1958-1959," *Le film français* (Spécial), nos. 817–818, 18.
21 "La naissance d'Orfeu Negro," *France-soir*, June 9, 1959; "Orfeu Negro," *France observateur*, June 1959.
22 André Besseges, "*Orfeu negro*," *France Catholique*, July 30, 1959.
23 In *We Real Cool: Black Men and Masculinity*, hooks focuses on the Black male body and the commodification of Blackness, which becomes "diffused by a process of fetishization that renders the Black masculine 'menace' feminine through a process of patriarchal objectification."
24 Diawari, "Black Spectatorship," 66–77.
25 John Storey, *Inventing Popular Culture: From Folklore to Globalization* (Wiley-Blackwell, 2003). Paul Duncum summarizes these views in his article "Toward a Playful Pedagogy: Popular Culture and the Pleasures of Transgression," *Studies in Art Education* 50, no. 3 (Spring 2009): 232–244.
26 "Orfeu Negro," *France observateur*, May 21, 1959.
27 *Le Figaro*, June 15, 1959.
28 *L'Express*, June 19, 1959.
29 *L'Express*, June 19, 1959.
30 M. D., no title, *Le canard enchaîné*, June 7, 1959.
31 Diawari, "Black Spectatorship," 66–77.
32 Mikhail Bakhtin, *Problems of Dostoevsky's Poetics*, trans. Caryl Emerson (Minneapolis: University of Minnesota Press, 1984), 176.

33 *Le Figaroscope*, May 18, 2005; Walter Benjamin, "The Work of Art in the Age of Mechanical Reproduction," 1935; Toronto International Film Festival Inc. (TIFF), "Euzhan Palcy on BLACK ORPHEUS," short interview with Euzhan Palcy, https://www.facebook.com/watch/?v=994301974248591.
34 Jean-Luc Godard, "Le Brésil vu de Billancourt," *Cahiers du cinéma*, July 17, 1959, 97.
35 Godard, "Le Brésil vu de Billancourt," 97.
36 Godard, "Le Brésil vu de Billancourt," 97.
37 Daniela Berghahn, "Performing Exoticism and the Transnational Reception of World Cinema," *Studies in World Cinema* (2021): 221–238.
38 Rafael Freire, Natasha Hernández, and Almeida Zapata, "Quantas salas de cinema existiram no Brasil? Reflexões sobre a dimensão e características do circuito exibidor brasileiro," *Significação Revista de Cultura Audiovisual* 44, no. 48 (December 2017): 181. For further information, see also Agência Nacional do Cinema (Ancine), Salas de Exhibição, https://www.gov.br/ancine/pt-br/oca/publicacoes/arquivos.pdf/salas_de_exibicao_2020.pdf.
39 Joaquim Ferreira dos Santos, *Feliz 1958: O ano que não deve terminar*, 4th ed. (Rio and São Paulo: Editora Record), 178.
40 Informants include E. Silva, who lived in La Ilha do Governador in the 1960s, and M. Morais, who lived in Ipanema and Leblon in the 1960s.
41 Godard, "Le Brésil vu de Billancourt," 97.
42 Décio Viera Otoni, "Orfeu Negro," *Diario Carioca* (Rio de Janeiro, Brazil), Thursday, November 7, 1955.
43 Borroró, *Diario Carioca* (Rio de Janeiro, Brazil), Thursday, November 7, 1955.
44 "Hoje a exhibição de gala de Orfeu de Carnaval," *Ultima Hora* (Rio de Janeiro, Brazil), August 20, 1959.
45 "Hoje a exhibição de gala de Orfeu de Carnaval."
46 "Hoje a exhibição de gala de Orfeu de Carnaval"; "Marcel (Orfeu Negro) Camus chega hoje de Paris," *Ultima Hora* (Rio de Janeiro, Brazil), June 9, 1959; "Almoço aos interpretes de Orfeu," *Ultima Hora* (Rio de Janeiro, Brazil), June 30, 1959, 1.
47 "Orfeu Negro é o favorito: Cannes," *Aurore*, May 14, 1959.
48 "Vinícius de Moraes, o nascimento do negro," *Jornal do Brasil*, September 2, 1956, segundo caderno, 1.
49 "Francês aprende gíria no Babilônia," *Manchete*, 1958 ed 3340.
50 Richard Nason, "U.S. to See Films Hailed in France," *The New York Times*, August 26, 1959, 25; "SDG Nominates Four as First Quarter Winners," *Motion Picture News*, April 26, 1960.
51 Cynthia Grenier, "Noted in the French Film Capital," *The New York Times*, June 7, 1959.
52 "Black Orpheus," *The New York Times*, November 22, 1959, SM50; "French Film Is Best at Cannes," *The New York Times*, May 16, 1959.
53 "National Pre-Selling," *Motion Picture Daily*, Thursday, April 7, 1960.
54 See a clip "'*Black Orpheus*' Wins Foreign Language Film: 1960s Oscars," https://www.youtube.com/watch?v=TXrVg3vRDPk; and "'My Uncle' ('Mon Oncle') Wins Foreign Language Film: 1959 Oscars," https://www.youtube.com/watch?v=y88VU3qbSpY&index=14&list=PLJ8RjvesnvDMHxTASvuE1x-JoSJisxG7R.
55 Mae Tinee, "Film Joins Primitive and Poetic," *Chicago Daily Tribune*, April 4, 1960.
56 Barack Obama, *Dreams from My Father* (New York: Times Books, 1995).

57 Tinee, "Film Joins Primitive and Poetic."
58 Tinee, "Film Joins Primitive and Poetic."
59 "Oscar Will Boost Grosses for Winners," *Motion Picture Daily*, Friday, April 8, 1960.
60 "Oscar Will Boost Grosses for Winners."
61 "Award Winners Early 'Oscar,'" *The Chicago Defender* (*Daily Defender* edition), April 5, 1960.
62 Phyllis Garland, "'Black Orpheus' Throbs with Sex, Color and Music," *Pittsburgh Courier*, July 9, 1960.
63 Garland, "'Black Orpheus' Throbs with Sex, Color and Music."
64 Garland, "'Black Orpheus' Throbs with Sex, Color and Music."
65 William Moore, "The Brazilians Are Coming," *Amsterdam News*, October 11, 1980.
66 "Black Orpheus Dance Planned," *Chicago Daily Defender* (Big Weekend Edition).
67 Examples include *Chez nous* no. 21, year 10 (May 24, 1962), cover; "Photo shoot," in *Ciné-Révélation* no. 235 (September 1958), n/p.; photo of Dawn and Mello accompanied the short article "Black Orpheus Starring Marpessa Dawn Wins Oscar," *Jet* (April 21, 1960); and a multi-page photo shoot in *Ebony* (November 1959).

Part II. *Black Orpheus* Legacies and the Globalization of Afro-Brazilian Culture

1 Stuart Hall, "What Is This 'Black' in Black Popular Culture?" *Social Justice* 20, no. 1/2 (51–52), *Rethinking Race* (Spring–Summer 1993): 104–114; Daniela Berghahn, "Performing Exoticism and the Transnational Reception of World Cinema," *Studies in World Cinema* (2021): 221–238; Michael Boyce Gillespie, *Film Blackness: American Cinema and the Idea of Black Film* (Duke University Press, 2016), 90–98; Michael Boyce Gillespie, *Film Blackness: American Cinema and the Idea of Black Film* (Duke University Press, 2016), 90–98.

Chapter 5. Transnational Lights Beyond *Black Orpheus*

1 The film makes Samba Senegalese, a more esteemed migrant in the French social hierarchy, rather than Malian, the nationality of the main character in the 2012 novel. The film highlights the fact that French society has a complex system of preferences and stereotypes of different migrants, including African migrants from the Maghreb and sub-Saharan Africa.
2 The directors worked previously with Sy on the award-winning film *Les Intouchables*. See "Intouchables réussira-t-il à battre les Ch'tis?," https://www.lefigaro.fr/cinema/2012/01/09/03002-20120109ARTFIG00573-intouchables-reussira-t-il-a-battre-les-chti-s.php.
3 See "Programação, Ano da França no Brasil," http://intra.serpro.gov.br/noticias/programacao-201cano-da-franca-no-brasil201d; and "O ano do Brasil na França," http://cultura.gov.br/ano-do-brasil-na-franca-2005-37489; André Lewin, "Les années France-Brésil, projet conventionnel ou nouveau mode de relations internationales?," *Annuaire Français de Droit International* (1986).
4 Ed Guerrero, *Framing Blackness: The African American Image in Film* (Philadelphia: Temple University Press, 1993), 46–48.

5 Sacha Gordine's acceptance speech at "'Black Orpheus' Wins Foreign Language Film: 1960 Oscars," https://www.youtube.com/watch?v=TXrVg3vRDPk.

6 Mana de Xangô, recorded interview with author, Florianopolis, Brazil, July 29, 2016.

7 "Girl on the Go in Paris," *Ebony Magazine*, June 1965, 100–102; "Interview, Marpessa Dawn, Star of Black Orpheus," https://www.youtube.com/watch?v=ozAm_s1mf3E.

8 Laurent Dubois, *L'odyssée du cinéma brésilien, de l'Atlantide a la Cité de Dieu*, Primer Volume: 1940–1970 (Paris: L'Harmattan), 129.

9 For example, in his 1995 memoir *Dreams from My Father*, President Obama discusses his mother's love of the film.

10 Léa Garcia, interview with the author. See Dubois, *L'odyssée du cinéma brésilien, de l'Atlantide a la Cité de dieu*, 221.

11 Jacques Béreaud, "La chanson française depuis mai 1968," *The French Review* 62, no. 2 (December 1988): 229–241; Anaïs Fléchet, "Héritage Brésil. Quelques notes pour l'histoire du Brésil en France," *Vingtième Siècle: Revue d'histoire* no. 90 (April–June 2006): 207–209; Jonathan Grasse, "Conflation and Conflict in Brazilian Popular Music: Forty Years between 'Filming' Bossa Nova in 'Orfeu Negro' and Rap in 'Orfeu,'" *Popular Music* 23 (October 3, 2004): 291–310.

12 Carlos Sandroni, *Feitiço descente: Transformaçoes do samba no Rio de Janeiro (1917–1928)* (Rio de Janerio, Brazil: Editora UFRJ, 2001), 87–89.

13 Stephane Lerouge, liner notes, *Le Brésil au cinema*, CD, Universal, 2009.

14 Sérgio Cabral, *Grande Otelo: uma biografia* (Edição 34, 2017), 222.

15 "Grande Otelo," *Persona em Foco*, November 22, 2019.

16 Roberto Moura, *Grande Otelo* (Rio de Janeiro, Brazil: Relume-Dumará), 146.

17 Camus, *Otália da Bahia* (1976); Camus, *Os Bandeirantes* (1960); Steno, *Copacabana Palace* (1964); Antoine d'Ormesson, *Les amants de la mer (Arrastão)* (1967); Richard Wagner, *Tristan und Isolde* (1854); *Les amoureux de France* by François Reichenbach and Pierre Grimblat (1963) is an adaptation of *Le jeu de l'amour et du hazard*. *Furia a Bahia* directed by André Hunebelle.

18 Translation by Lyrics Translate, https://lyricstranslate.com. The French version can be found at "Samba Saravah," https://www.letras.mus.br/pierre-barouh/samba-saravah-samba-da-bencao/.

19 See Gilberto Gil's explanation at "Gilberto Gil Iembra Vinícius.mpg," https://www.youtube.com/watch?v=fTuVozo7Wrw.

20 Greg Tate, *Everything but the Burden* (2003).

21 See "#42 Vinícius de Moraes: 'Sou o branco mais preto do Brasil,'" interview, https://www.youtube.com/watch?v=9abb9ZdMnW8.

22 Darién J. Davis, "Understanding the Black Modernists: The Legacy of Negritude and the Celebration of Blackness in Brazil," in *The Legacy of Negritude* (Cambridge University Scholars Publishing, 2008), 277–291; Darién J. Davis and Judith Williams, "Pan-Africanism and the Currency of Blackness," in *Beyond Slavery: The Multifaceted Legacy of Africans in Latin America and the Caribbean* (Rowman and Littlefield, 2006), 142–167.

23 Stephen Farquhar, "And Bardot Created Búzios," *The Guardian*, travel section, September 25, 2004, http://www.theguardian.com/travel/2004/sep/25/brazil.guardiansaturdaytravelsection; Jean-Pierre Langellier, "Et Bardot créa Buzios," *Le Monde*, December 17, 2012, http://www.lemonde.fr/idees/article/2008/12/17/et

-bardot-crea-buzios-par-jean-pierre-langellier_1132232_3232.html#gZCXZLedjp IMbSle.99

24 Farquhar, "And Bardot Created Búzios."

25 See Everardo Rocha and Ligia Lana, "In the Garden of Delights: The Dilemmas of Brigitte Bardot in Rio de Janeiro /No jardim das delícias: os dilemas de Brigitte Bardot no Rio de Janeiro," *MartizEs* 13, No. 1 (January/April): 191–209.

26 James Michael Martin, "That Man from Rio," *Film Quarterly* 18, no. 2 (Winter 1964): 59.

27 Euler de França Belém, "A historia da criação da música 'Amélia' por Mário Lago e Ataúlfo Alves," *Jornal Opção*, April 13, 2015.

28 Research over a year, including interviews with Brazilian musicians and scholars in Brazil, France, and the United States, has suggested the singer is Carmen Costa. This author is not 100% convinced.

29 *Michel Magne* (documentary), Josée Dayan, Office national de radiodiffusion télévision française, 1974 (INA).

30 "Problem Number One: The French Development Act," *Le Film Français* Special nos. 779–780.

31 Isabelle Vanderschelden, "The French Film Industry: Funding, Policies, Debates," *Studies in French Cinema* 16, no. 2: 89–94.

32 Jorge Amado, "Jorge Amado: Literatura, racismo, política e religião," interview by Silvia Poppovic, Vox Populi Amado, 1984, https://www.youtube.com/watch?v =nQoY3SpVVbc.

33 See IMDb MOVIEmeter (accessible with paid membership): https://pro.imdb .com/title/tt0053146/companycredits?rf=cons_tt_cocred_tt&ref_=cons_tt _cocred_tt.

34 Fernando Ferreira, "Camus," *O Globo*, January 14, 1982. Orlando and Claudio Villas Boas first encountered the Xingu in 1961. They worked for the protection of Indigenous populations and were honored by the Xingu after their deaths.

35 Ferreira, "Camus."

36 Ferreira, "Camus."

37 Ferreira, "Camus."

38 Ferreira, "Camus."

39 Ferreira, "Camus."

40 Tunico Amâncio, "O estrangeiro Marcel Camus: olhares de afeto sobre algumas cidades brasilieras," *Passage de Paris* 1 (2005): 53–61.

41 Amâncio, "O estrangeiro Marcel Camus," 53–61.

42 "O Santo Módico," https://www.imdb.com/title/tt0353979/fullcredits/?ref_=tt _cst_sm.

43 Picture of the recording of the music for *O Santo Módico,* Instituto Jobim, http://www.jobim.org/jobim/handle/2010/8890; "*O Santo Módico*," IMDb, https://www.imdb.com/title/tt0353979/?ref_=fn_al_tt_1. See Everson's performance on Ed Sullivan at "Leny Everson–Jezebel (1957)," https://www .youtube.com/watch?v=ApT2643VT64.

44 Donald Bogle, *Hollywood Black: The Stars, the Films, the Filmmakers* (Philadelphia: Running Press, 2019), 64–85.

45 André Cintra, "Por que Sidney Poitier (1927–2022) foi o maior ator negro da história," https://vermelho.org.br/2022/01/07/por-que-sidney-poitier-1927-2022 -foi-o-maior-ator-negro-da-historia/.

46 See Darién J. Davis, *White Face, Black Mask: Africaneity and the Early Social History of Popular Music in Brazil*; and "Before We Called This Place Home: The Precursors of the Brazilian Community in the United States," in *Becoming Brazuca: Brazilian Immigrants in the United States* (Cambridge: Harvard University Press), 25–56.

47 See the film poster *Macumba Love* at https://www.imdb.com/title/tt0054045/.

48 American television of the 1960s fared much better in presenting Brazilian talent and culture and collaborating with Brazilian musicians. Luiz Bonfá, Tom Jobim, and Leny Eversong all performed on American television. While White and male advantage may have played a role in securing places for Bonfá and Jobim, the U.S. performances of singers such as Hilda Campos Soares da Silva, better known as Leny Eversong, illustrate a diversity that should be explored. See Eversong's performance of "Jezebel" on the *Ed Sullivan Show* in the United States on January 6, 1957, at "Leny Everson—Jezebel (1957)," https://www.youtube.com/watch?v=ApT2643VT64.

49 Glauber Rocha, "The Aesthetics of Hunger," in *Brazilian Cinema*, ed. Robert Stam and Randall Johnson (New York: Columbia University Press, 1995), 68–71.

50 Leonor Souza Pinto, "Cinema brasileiro e censura durante a ditadura militar / cinéma brésilien et censure pendant la dictature militaire,"*Cinémas d'Amérique Latine* no. 9 (2001): 157–164; Randal Johnson and Robert Stam, *Brazilian Cinema*, expanded version (New York: Columbia University Press, 1995), 178–190.

51 Zozimo Bulbul, *Alma no Olho* (documentary, 1973); Zozimo Bulbul, *Abolition* (documentary, 1988).

52 Zózimo Bulbul, interview with the author, August 2, 2010, video recording. See also the website for the organization: http://afrocariocadecinema.org.br/.

53 Jornalismo Junior, "Zózimo Bulbul, o pioneiro do cinema negro brasileiro," *ECA-USP Jornalismo Junior*, November 18, 2018, http://jornalismojunior.com.br/zozimo-bulbul-o-pioneiro-do-cinema-negro-brasileiro/.

54 *Informe Centro Afro Carioca de Cinema, no 2* (March 2009): 2.

55 *Informe Centro Afro Carioca de Cinema, no 2* (March 2009): 2.

56 Jornalismo Junior, "Zózimo Bulbul"; Zózimo Bulbul, interview with the author, August 2, 2010, video recording.

Chapter 6. Bossa Negra in the United States

1 Jean-Paul Delfino, *Bossa nova: La Grande aventure du Brésil* (Le passage, 2017).

2 Elza Soares, liner notes, *A Bossa Negra*, CD (Odeon, 1960).

3 Jean-Paul Sartre, "Orphée noir," *Anthologie de la nouvelle poésie nègre et malgache de langue française*, edited by Léopold Sédar Senghor (Paris: Presses Universitaires de France), preface.

4 Ruy Castro, *Chega de saudade: A história e as histórias da bossa nova* (São Paulo: Companhia das Letras, 1990), 327.

5 Gerald Horne, *Fire This Time: The Watts Uprising and The 1960s* (Da Cappo Press, 1997).

6 See Kenneth O'Reilley, *Racial Matters: The FBI's Secret File on Black America, 1960–1972* (Free Press, 1991).

7 David H. Rosenthal, "Jazz in the Ghetto: 1950–70," *Popular Music* (1988): 7, 51–56; Ulrich Adelt, "Black, White and Blue: Racial Politics of Blues Music in the 1960s" (Ph.D. dissertation, University of Iowa, 2007), 22–25. By the late 1960s,

jazz (with the exception of the cool style played by Stan Getz, Gerry Mulligan, and others) had a primarily Black audience, according to Joe Fields of Muse Records and formerly employed by Prestige and Columbia.

8 Darién J. Davis, "Before We Called This Place Home: Precursors of the Brazilian Community in the United States," in *Becoming Brazuca: Brazilian Immigration to the United States*, David Rockefeller Center Series on Latin American Studies, 25–37; Darién J. Davis, "The Brazilian-Americans: Demography and Identity of An Emerging Latino Minority," *Latino Review of Books* (Spring/Fall 1997), 8–15.

9 Davis, "Before We Called This Place Home," 25; H. Jon Rosenbaum, "A Critique of the Brazilian Foreign Service," *The Journal of Developing Areas* 2, no. 3 (April 1968): 377–392, 384; Darién J. Davis, *White Face, Black Mask: Africaneity and the Early Social History of Popular Music in Brazil* (Lansing: Michigan State University Press, 2009), 77.

10 See John Storm Roberts, *Latin Jazz* (New York: Schirmer Books, 1999); and Kariann Goldschmitt's article "Doing the Bossa Nova: The Curious Life of a Social Dance in 1960s North America," *Luso-Brazilian Review* 48, no. 1 (2011): 61–78.

11 "Claims Bossa Nova Fate Rests with Negroes," *Chicago Defender*, November 12, 1962. Bossa nova's popularity depended on how African Americans responded to the new trend. In an interview with the African American newspaper *The Chicago Defender*, jazz musician Herbie Mann reported that the bossa nova would not become popular unless "it scores an impact on the Negro market." Bossa nova, as he saw it in the 1960s, was primarily a "White commodity," and without a dance, it would have limited success.

12 Davis, "Before We Called This Place Home," 25–37.

13 The history of the use of the term 'Pardo' is complex. The Portuguese used the term to describe the Amerindians in the colonial period. Its use continued in the first national census in 1872 until 1890. In 1940, the government of Getúlio Vargas reintroduced the term.

14 John Scheinfeld, *Sérgio Mendes: In the Key of Joy* (Crew Neck Production, 2021).

15 Lisa E. Davenport, *Jazz Diplomacy: Promoting America in the Cold War Era* (University of Mississippi Press, 2009), 38–61.

16 John Storm Roberts uses the word "tinge" to explain the Latin influence on popular American music in his book *The Latin Tinge: The Impact of Latin American Music on the United States*, 2nd ed. (Oxford: Oxford University Press, 1999). Roberts focuses mostly on the sounds and influences from Spanish Latin America.

17 "Bossa Nova Bandwagon" *Down Beat*, November 8, 1962, 24.

18 "Bossa Nova Ad Absurdum," *Down Beat*, January 17, 1963, 8.

19 "Bossa Nova Bandwagon," 24.

20 Gene Ammons, "Bad Bossa Nova," *Down Beat*, February 14, 1963, 26; "Merger of Jazz and Latin Rhythm Produces New U.S. Dance Fad," *Ebony*, March 1963, 103–106; "Syvilla Fort, a Dance Teacher Who Inspired Blacks, Is Dead," *The New York Times*, November 9, 1975. In its feature on the bossa nova, the African American magazine *Ebony* highlighted the three Brazilian Black performers who, in their vision, had "introduced the rhythms to U.S. audiences." The African American dancers Buddy Phillips and Johanna Testman. Phillips and his wife Syvilla Fort, both dancers with Katherine Dunham, founded the dance studio on West 44th Street in New York, responsible for promoting the "Afro-Modern technique," which fused the Dunham approach with modern dance styles.

21 "Tom Jobim to Vinicius de Moraes," February 14, 1965, Los Angeles, California, https://www.ellafitzgerald.com/#/; Horace Silver Quintet, *Song for My Father (Cantiga para meu pai)* (Blue Note, 1965). See notes on the back of the album cover.

22 This statement is based on a survey of reports from the Archives of the Ministry of Foreign Affairs, Itamaraty, Brazil. I examined reports from the Foreign Ministry's archives on scholarships and sponsored visits to France from 1958 to 1965 and checked the names against available biographies. Admittedly, without direct interviews it is difficult to determine exactly how people identified racially. I used a combination of visual identification based on my experience living in Brazil and biographical information.

23 Davis, "Before We Called This Place Home," 25–37; Rosenbaum, "A Critique of the Brazilian Foreign Service," *Journal of Developing Areas* 2, no. 3 (April 1968): 377–392.

24 From the 1960s onward, the Brazilian Ministry of Foreign Affairs would sponsor more Afro-Brazilian artists.

25 Luiz Bonfá and Antônio Carlos Jobim, *The Original Soundtrack from the Film Black Orpheus*.

26 Vladimir Bogdanov, Chris Woodstra, and Stephen Thomas Erlewine, *All Music Guide: The Definitive Guide to Popular Music* (San Francisco: Backbeat Books, 2001), 911. Various artists in the United States from Frank Sinatra and Mongo Santamaría to Miriam Makeba and Joan Baez covered "Manhã de carnaval" under diverse titles such as "Manhã de carnival," "A Day in the Life of a Fool," and "Theme from *Black Orpheus*."

27 Walter Silva, *Vou te contar: histórias de música popular brasileira* (São Paulo: Nobel), 108–110.

28 "Negro é lindo," January 21, 2004, http://revistatrip.uol.com.br/revista/228/reportagens/negro-e-lindo.html.

29 "Morre Carmen Costa, da marchinha 'Cachaça,'" *A Folha Ilustrada*, April 26, 2007.

30 The quote comes from Paulo Roberto Pires from the liner notes from the CD *A Bossa Negra* by Elza Soares, initially recorded in 1961 and released on CD in 2002. João Carlos Viegas, *Carmem Costa, uma cantora do radio* (Rio de Janeiro, Brazil: Editora Revan, 1991), 61; "Brazilian Pop 1934–1964," http://brazilianpop1957-1964.blogspot.com/2011/11/k.html.

31 Stan Getz and Charlie Byrd, *Jazz Samba*, 1962; Stan Getz and Gary McFarland, *Big Band Bossa Nova*, 1962; Lalo Shifrin, *Bossa Nova: New Brazilian Jazz*, 1962. See also re-released compilation *A Trip to Brazil* vol. 3: *Back to Bossa* (2002).

32 "Jose Paulo," http://www.allmusic.com/artist/jose-paulo-mn0001739111.

33 João Carlos Viegas, *Carmem Costa, uma cantora do radio* (Rio de Janeiro, Brazil: Editora Revan, 1991), 61.

34 Luis Gustavo Carvalho Alonso Rays, "A trajetória musical do compositor brasileiro Djalma de Andrade-Bola Sete" (M.A. dissertation, Universidade Estadual de Campinas, 2006), 3–16. See also "Memories of You," http://www.bolasete2.com/1/post/2010/4/memories-of-you-c-2010-anne-sete.html. Castro, *Chega de Saudade*, 327.

35 Ralph G. Gleason, liner notes on back of album cover, Bola Sete, *Bossa Nova*, Fantasy Records, 1962.

36 Bola Sete, "Tour de Force Fantasy 3358 . . . ," *Down Beat*, July 16, 1964; "29th Annual Readers Poll," *Down Beat*, December 31, 1964.

37 "29th Annual Readers Poll."
38 Vince Guaraldi and Bola Sete, track 4 on *From All Sides*, Fantasy Records, 1963, rereleased as CD in 1998.
39 "Special Merit Award," *Billboard*, July 29, 1967, 38; "Memories of You." The guitarist repeatedly teamed up with drummer Paulinho Da Costa and bassist Sebastião Neto.
40 Dizzy Gillespie and Al Fraser, *To Be, or Not . . . to Bop* (New York: Doubleday, 2009), 179, 428, 450.
41 Gillespie and Fraser, *To Be, or Not . . . to Bop*, 427.
42 Gillespie and Fraser, *To Be, or Not . . . to Bop*, 428.
43 Gillespie and Fraser, *To Be, or Not . . . to Bop*, 179, 431.
44 Dizzy Gillespie, *New Wave!*, Philips, 1962.
45 Dizzy Gillespie, *On the French Riviera* (Philips, 1962). *Jazz Samba* is a bossa nova LP by Stan Getz and Charlie Byrd, released on the Verve label on April 20, 1962. Only two of the seven tracks on the album are Jobim compositions, "Desafinado" ["Slightly Out of Tune"] and "Samba de Uma Nota Só" ["One Note Samba"], the rest being by other Brazilian composers and by Charlie Byrd.
46 "'Bossa Nova' Just Samba to Dizzy Gillespie's Ears," *Chicago Defender*, October 17, 1962, 16; "Dizzy Claims He Played 'Bossa' Long Before Popularity," *Chicago Defender*, November 14, 1962, 17.
47 Gillespie and Fraser, *To Be, or Not . . . to Bop*, 450.
48 Dizzy Gillespie, *Dizzy Gillespie on the French Riviera*, original LP 1962, re-released by Verve on CD in 2009.
49 Lionel Hampton, *Bossa Nova Jazz*, gladhamp, 1963.
50 "Lionel Hampton Making the Rounds at Macy's Promoting His New Bossa Nova Album," *Billboard Magazine*, 1963, p. 14.
51 Carmen Costa (vcl on A2,4, B1,4, perc). Lionel Hampton, *Bossa Nova Jazz* tracks: Side 1: Recado [Recado Bossa Nova] (Djalma Ferreira) 3:50; Bossa Nova New York [Bossa Nova York] (Don Madrid / Jose Paulo); Sambolero (João Donato); The Same To You (Don Madrid / Jose Paulo); Some Day (Lionel Hampton / J. McAdam) 3:40. Side 2: Palhacada [*sic*] (Haroldo Barbosa / Luiz Reis); Estranho (Lionel Hampton / Teo Macero); Bossanova Jazz (Lionel Hampton); Una Nota Sol [*sic*] [Samba de Uma Nota So] (Tom Jobim / Newton Mendonça); Saint Thomas (Sonny Rollins, arr. Lionel Hampton).
52 The Ramsey Lewis Trio, *Bossa Nova*, Argo Record, 1962.
53 Paulo's last name is spelled Josef on the album.
54 "Ramsey Lewis," *Down Beat*, February 14, 1963, 30. Ramsey's tunes include "As Criancinhas" ("The Children"); "A Noite do meu bem" ("The Night of My Love"); "O Pato" ("The Duck"); "Generique" ("Happiness"); "Roda Moinho" ("Whirlpool"); "Cara de Palhaço" ("The Face of the Clown"); and "Canacao Para Geralda [*sic*]."
55 "Claims Bossa Nova Fate Rests with Negroes," *Chicago Defender*, November 12, 1962.
56 Darién J. Davis, "The Brazilian-Americans: Demography and Identity of An Emerging Latino Minority," *The Latino Review of Books* (Spring/Fall 1996): 8–15.
57 "The Need for Racial Unity in Jazz: A Panel Discussion," *Down Beat*, April 11, 1963, 16.
58 "Bossa Nova—Good and Not So Good Tidings," *Down Beat*, November 8, 1962, 10.

59 Davis, "The Brazilian-Americans," 8–15.

60 Dominique Dreyfus, *O violão vadio de Baden Powell* (Fisica Book, 2019), 173.

61 Christopher Dunn and Charles Perrone, eds., *Brazilian Popular Music and Globalization* (Routledge, 20021), 1–28.

62 Mauro Lima, *Tim Maia* (Globo Films, 2014); Stuart Hall, "What Is This 'Black' in *Black Popular Culture*," *Social Justice* 20, no. 1/2 (51-52), Rethinking Race (Spring-Summer 1993): 104–114.

63 Amanda Palomo Alves, "'Êsse crioulo vai longe': racismo e construções discursivas sobre Tony Tornado na imprensa periódica brasileira (1970–1972)," MA thesis, Centro Federal de Educação tecnológica Celso Suckow da Fonseca, Rio de Janeiro, 2019.

64 Michael Hanchard, *Orpheus and Power: The Movimento Negro of Rio de Janeiro and São Paulo* (Brazil, 1945–1988), 43–44.

65 Dom Salvador, interview by author, telephone audio recording, August 5, 2024; Roberto Kaz, "Piano Man," *Piauí* no. 118 (June 2006), https://piaui.folha.uol.com.br/materia/piano-man/.

66 Dom Salvador, interview by author, telephone audio recording, August 5, 2024; "The Lounge Pianist Who Invented Samba Funk," *The New York Times*, November 9, 2018, https://www.nytimes.com/2018/11/09/nyregion/brazilian-samba-star-dom-salvador-river-cafe.html.

67 Dom Salvador, interview by author, audio recording, Brooklyn, New York, March 16, 2023.

68 Artur Ratton and Linka Hara, *Dom Salvador and the Abolition* (released for private showing in New York City, 2020).

69 Ratton and Hara, *Dom Salvador and the Abolition*; Dom Salvador, interview by author, audio recording, Brooklyn, New York, March 16, 2023.

70 Davis, "Before We Called This Place Home," 25–56.

71 Robin Lloyd, "Prolific Percussion Master Paulinho da Costa," NPR Online, April 4, 2013, https://www.knkx.org/jazz-and-blues/2013-04-04/prolific-percussion-master-paulinho-da-costa; Silvio Essinger, "Paulinho da Costa, o músico brasileiro que tocou em 'Thriller,'" *O Globo* (Brasil), November 25, 2012, https://oglobo.globo.com/cultura/paulinho-da-costa-musico-brasileiro-que-tocou-em-thriller-6874496; Michael Hanchard, *Orpheus and Power: The Movimento Negro of Rio de Janeiro and São Paulo, Brazil 1945–1988*, (Princeton: Princeton University Press, 1994), 43–44, 56.

72 "The Lounge Pianist Who Invented Samba Funk"; "Paulinho da Costa, o brasileiro que tocou com Michael Jackson," February 27, 2017 https://mjbeats.com.br/paulinho-da-costa-o-brasileiro-que-tocou-com-michael-jackson-c14ac6435ba5; Carlinhos Pandeiro de Oro, interview by author, audio recording, Culver City, California, 2016.

Chapter 7. Baden Powell and Maria d'Apparecida Marques in Paris

1 Brent Edward Hayes, *The Practice of Diaspora: Literature, Translation, and the Rise of Black Internationalism* (Cambridge, MA: Harvard University Press, 2003); Tracy Whiting, *Bricktop's Paris: African American Women in Paris between the Two World Wars* (Albany: State University of New York Press, 2015); Tyler Stovall, *Paris Noir: African Americans in the City of Light* (New York: Houghton Mifflin, 1996).

2 Stéphane Dufoix, *Diasporas* (Berkeley: University of California Press, 2008); and Kim Butler, "Defining Diaspora, Defining a Discourse," *Diaspora* 10, no. 2 (2001): 189–218. In *The Soul of Black Folks,* W.E.B. Dubois writes about double consciousness, the challenge of African Americans who must contend with race and nationality. For non-American or non-European Black migrants, there is race, nationality, and migrant status, which entails negotiating identities with others in the diaspora.

3 See short clip of film with Moustaki and Amado INA, BNF, Paris, France, Code: ImG-1596.

4 Baden Powell, one of the few Afro-Brazilians associated with the primarily White bossa nova performers, was the only well-known performer who settled in France. Jobim and Gilberto collaborated on hundreds of projects with diverse artists and translators for the American English-speaking audience from Frank Sinatra and Stan Getz. As we have seen, other artists, such as Bola Sete and Carmen Costa, teamed up with American jazz greats. Inspired by Afro-Brazilian rhythms, Sérgio Mendes created a bossa nova fusion sound that is still prevalent today as the recent animations *Rio I* and *Rio II* attest. Amado was also a guest of honor on the Le Grand Echiquier, Un Siècle d'écrivains, and Etoile Palace.

5 See Moustaki's homage to Bahia with Baby do Brasil, "Georges Moustaki–Bahia (TV Brazil)," https://www.youtube.com/watch?v=g-ofobnumw8.

6 Carlos Alves de Souza to Ministry of Foreign Affairs, January 17, 1963, Itamaraty [Camu 3] N.Y. See also Carlos Alves de Souza to Ministry of Foreign Affairs, January 17, 1963, Itamaraty [Camu 3]. The 1965 documentary "Aquerelas do Brasil" was also distributed with subtitles in French thanks to the embassy, which also helped Brazilian performers connect to French television.

7 Michael Lerner, "De Gaulle's Chance," *The Observer*, February 21, 1964, reprinted in *The Harvard Crimson*, https://api.thecrimson.com/article/1964/2/21/de-gaulles-chance-pwhen-president-de/. See also Carlos Alves de Souza Filho, ambassador to France 1956–1964, *Um embaixador em tempos de crise* (Livraria Francisco Alves Editora, 1979).

8 President Kubitschek sent his wife Sarah to the opening of the Maison du Brésil in 1959. Françoise Choay, "Le Pavillon du Brésil à la cité de l'université," *L'oeil* no. 57 (September 1959): 54–59.

9 Mario de Andrade, *Macunaima* (1928). *Dim Dam Dom* was short for Dimanches de dames et d'hommes (Sundays for Men and Women). The show began to be televised in 1965 and featured famous guests of the era, including singers, actors, and actresses.

10 Veloso and Gil returned to Paris to visit and to perform on French television. Gil also travelled to New York with other Brazilians in 1971. See the essay about his visit to the city in "Gilberto Gil em Nova York," *O Pasquim* no. 122 (1971): 2–8, Leila Míccolis Archives, University of Miami Library Archival Collection.

11 "Pierre Barouh en 1992: Depuis l'âge de 15 ans, je n'ai qu'une obsession: témoigner du monde qui [*sic*]," https://www.jechantemagazine.net/single-post/2017/05/12/pierre-barouh-en-1992-depuis-l-âge-de-15-ans-je-n-ai-qu-une-obsession-témoigner-du-mond. He recalled that when he created Saravah, he had achieved a childhood dream. However, he quickly realized he was no manager and handed the company's management to a childhood friend, who embezzled him.

12 Dizzy Gillespie and Al Fraser, *To Be, or Not . . . to Bop* (New York: Doubleday, 2009), 179, 428, 450; *Latin Jazz: The First of the Fusions, 1880s to Today*

(New York: Schirmer Trade Books, 1999), 75, 118, 168. See also John Storm Roberts, *The Latin Tinge: The Impact of Latin American Music on the United States*, 2nd ed. (Oxford: Oxford University Press, 1999). Roberts explores what he calls "Latin tinges" throughout the book.

13 Dizzy Gillespie, *Dizzy Gillespie on the French Riviera* (Philips, 1962). *Jazz Samba* is a bossa nova LP by Stan Getz and Charlie Byrd, released on the Verve label on April 20, 1962.

14 Flavia Barreto, *Magnífico Sivuca: Maestro da Sanfona* (Rio de Janeiro, Brazil: Editora do autor, 2011), 200–211. See also *Mama Africa*, 2012, a documentary on Miriam Makeba by Mika Kaurismäki.

15 Anaïs Fléchet, "La bossa nova in France: un modèle musical?" *Cahiers d'Amérique Latine* 480–49 (2005): 58–73.

16 Dominique Dreyfus, *O violão de Baden Powell* (São Paulo, Brazil: Editora 34), 365.

17 See notes on the back of the album cover.

18 "Bossa Nova Bandwagon," *Down Beat*, November 8, 1962, 24.

19 Note that Powell appears alone on the album cover.

20 "Pierre Barouh en 1992 : « Depuis l'âge de 15 ans, je n'ai qu'une obsession, » *Je chante* magazine June 19, 2018," https://www.jechantemagazine.net/post/2017/05/12/pierre-barouh-en-1992-depuis-l-âge-de-15-ans-je-n-ai-qu-une-obsession-témoigner-du-mond, accessed June 6, 2019.

21 Dreyfus, *O violão de Baden Powell,* 264.

22 Philippe Baden Powell, "Baden Powell de Aquino," http://www.badenpowell.com.br/biografia/biogra.htm. Also see liner notes on Philippe Baden Powell, "Baden Powell de Aquino."

23 See performances by Powell, including Baden Powell in 1971 on German TV at "Baden Powell–1971–Canto on Guitar–Part 1," http://www.youtube.com/watch?v=9cKLA6kFdKY&feature=related; and "Baden Powell Solo Live in Paris," http://www.youtube.com/watch?v=GWQ1boH70BM&feature=PlayList&p=87B65921D2623FE0&playnext_from=PL&playnext=1&index=12.

24 "Panorama- O Globo nos discos populares," *O Globo*, November 13, 1964, 6.

25 Sylvio Cardoso, "Discos populares," *O Globo*, Saturday, September 11, 1965, 7, reproduced on the blog http://www.brazil-on-guitar.de/archives/reports/1965_review_lemonde.html.

26 "Baden Powell Conquista Paris," *Jornal de Brasil* (November 8, 1964). Reprinted on the Instituto Moreira Salles website: https://ims.com.br/por-dentro-acervo/o-mundo-musical-de-baden/.

27 Vinicius de Moraes, "Le monde musical de Baden Powell," September 4, 1964. Reprinted on the Instituto Moreira Salles website: https://ims.com.br/por-dentro-acervo/o-mundo-musical-de-baden/.

28 Vinicius de Moraes, "Le monde musical de Baden Powell."

29 Vinicius de Moraes, "Le monde musical de Baden II." Reprinted on the Instituto Moreira Salles website: https://ims.com.br/por-dentro-acervo/o-mundo-musical-de-baden/.

30 Rodrigo Coutinho, "Os Brasileiros em Paris," *O Cruzeiro*, October 31, 1964.

31 Tonzinho was another one of Moraes's Brazilian musical partners and protegés who had performed with him in Europe.

32 Coutinho, "Os brasileiros em Paris."

33 Coutinho, "Os brasileiros em Paris."

34 Coutinho, "Os brasileiros em Paris."

35 W.E.B. Dubois, *The Soul of Black Folk* (Oxford: Oxford University Press, 2007), 8.
36 Coutinho, "Os brasileiros em Paris."
37 Dreyfus, *O violão vadio de Baden Powell*, 171–173.
38 Dreyfus, *O violão vadio de Baden Powell*, 204. Dreyfus tells the story of the encounter with Powell in Japan in her biography, page 204. See also the recollection of Powell's son Philippe Baden Powell with Ernesto Gonçalves, http://www.badenpowell.com.br/baden_a_vontade/fatohist/thelonious_monk.htm.
39 Among the songs Powell composed (with Paulo César Pinheiro) was the now famous song "Lapinha."
40 Philippe Baden Powell, interview with author, audio recording, Auvers-sur-Oise, France, April 7, 2022.
41 "Baden Powell, 'Evangélico, músico não diz mais 'saravá'" *Folha de São Paulo Ilustrado*, July 13, 1999.
42 "Baden Powell, 'Evangélico, músico não diz mais 'saravá.'"
43 "Baden Powell, 'Evangélico, músico não diz mais 'saravá.'"
44 Josephine Baker, "J'ai deux amours," track A1 on *L'inoubliable Josephine Baker*, RCA Records, 1975. The song was written by Marseille native Vincent Scotto, who also wrote songs for the filmmaker Marcel Pagnol.
45 "Baden Powell, 'Evangélico, músico não diz mais 'saravá.'"
46 "A volta de Baden Powell," *InTervalo*, 1968, 16.
47 Personal film recording from cemetery site.
48 Joseph Horowitz, "New World Prophesy," *The American Scholar* (Autumn 2019): 70–81.
49 Mario de Andrade, "Distanciamentos e aproximaões," in *Musica, doce música*, ed. Oneyda Alvarenga (Sao Paulo, Brazil: Livraria Martins, 1963), 363–367.
50 "Concurso Rainha das Mulatas e Boneca de Pixe," *Quilombo* ano 1, no. 3 (June 1949), frontpage, digital reprint at https://ipeafro.org.br/acervo-digital/leituras/ten-publicacoes/jornal-quilombo-no-03/. For more information on the beauty contests in the journal *Quilombo*, produced by TEN, see the website ipeafro.org.
51 See a reproduction of the images of d'Apparecida Marques from the *Jornal Movimento Feminino* 1, no. 24.
52 "A biografia da Maria D'Apparecida," *Luso Journal*, November 5, 2019, https://lusojornal.com/biografia-de-maria-dapparecida-apresentada-em-paris/. See also "Morreu em Paris a Maria Callas Afro-Brasiliera," http://neilopes.com.br/2017/08/23/morreu-em-paris-a-maria-callas-afro-brasileira/.
53 "Maria d'Apparecida performs 'Tamba taja,'" April 13, INA, BNF, https://www.ina.fr/video/I14142814/maria-d-apparecida-tamba-taja-video.html.
54 "Après un petit entretien, la chanteuse brésilienne Maria D'Apparecida chante 'Sem seu,'" Television Française 1 (T.V. 1), May 26, 1961, INA, BNF, https://www.ina.fr/video/I14142815/maria-d-apparecida-sem-seu-video.html; João Carlos Pereira, *Encontro com Waldemar Henrique* (Belém, Brazil: Falangola, 1984), 56.
55 Jean Bertho, "Entretien avec Maria d'Apparecida," interview, Télévision Française 1, December 12, 1977, https://www.ina.fr/video/I14142821/entretien-avec-maria-d-apparecida-video.html.
56 Bertho, "Entretien avec Maria d'Apparecida."
57 "Maria D'Apparecida," https://www.discogs.com/artist/1780211-Maria-DApparecida. For the tracks "Rolinha" and "Uiripuru."
58 "Maria D'Apparecida—Chante Baden Powell," https://www.discogs.com/Maria-DApparecida-Chante-Baden-Powell/master/603561.

59 For a complete list of compositions, see "Maria D'Apparecida—O Brasil," https://www.discogs.com/Maria-DApparecida-O-Brasil/master/1137297; and "Maria d'Apparecida–Moemà morenou," https://www.youtube.com/watch?v=1OVFNHCmitY.

60 See also Jacqueline Vandel, "Une Carmen noire et brésilienne a l'Opéra de Paris," *Le Figaro Littéraire*, September 30, 1965; O. G., "La Carmen brésilienne danse comme une vraie gitane," *L'Aurore*, March 3, 1964.

61 O. G., "La Carmen brésilienne danse comme une vraie gitane."

62 Katia D. Kaupp, "La conversion de Maria D'Apparecida," *Le nouvel observeteur*, 45.

63 Donald Bogle, *Toms, Coons, Mulattoes, Mammies, and Bucks: An Interpretive History of Blacks in American Films*, updated and expanded 5th ed. (Bloomsbury, 2016); João Carlos Rodrigues, *O negro brasileiro e o cinema* (São Paulo, Brazil: Pallas Editora, 2015).

64 Rodrigues, *O negro brasileiro e o cinema*, 22.

65 "La Carmen noire devient chanteuse brésilienne," *France-Soir*, August 26, 1977.

66 Carlos Drummond de Andrade, "O Brasil tem muitos aparecidas":

Tem Aparecida de Goiânia e de Goiás
E tem aparecida de Minas e de do oeste no Paraná
Tem aparecida do Taboado Taboado Mato Grosso coma
e tantas outras onde quer que eu fé provoque aparece ações

Tem sobretudo aparecida de São Paulo onde uma santa apareceu nas águas do r e era uma santa negra de bairro e de do Limón das profundezas do rio pescadores a trouxe trouxeram Um altar a recolheu e a mais de dois séculos nossa senhora negra da concessão distribuiu milagres entre os humildes e os poderosos igualmente necessitados de milagre

Maria da Aparecida não vieste nas águas do rio vieste demais longe de um mais profundo abismo de raça de sonho tua voz caminheira nós conta do que irá além da ciência dos conservatórios e do tratamento opera esticou da vida é uma voz que vem das estranhas do vento e dos coqueirais do ciclo dos-me minérios e das formações o canecas do amor terrestre telúrica mulher

Tua voz da Aparecida e apareçam fulgurante sensitiva dramática e vem do fundo negro luminoso de nossos corações e vai e volta e vai Maria da aparecida do Brasil app para se tornar mente Cantarelli Mezzo

67 Bertho, "Entretien avec Maria D'Apparecida." Marques continued recording with the Mary Music label. In 1980, she recorded an album simply known as *O Brasil*, which included diverse tunes in French and Portuguese, including "Agua de março" by Tom Jobim.

68 See "Baden Powell 'Labareda,'" June 19, 1977, *Musique and music* (Antenna 2), https://www.ina.fr/video/I14126613/baden-powell-labareda-video.html. Also see "Eddy Mitchell et Baden Powell 'Bidonville,'" November 8, 1975, Numéro I, https://www.ina.fr/video/I07094259/eddy-mitchell-et-baden-powell-bidonville-video.html.

69 Idelette Muzart-Fonseca dos Santos and Denis Rolland, *L'exil brésilien en France: Histoire et imaginaire* (Paris: L'Harmattan, 2008), 159-170.

70 Muzart-Fonseca dos Santos and Rolland, *L'exil brésilien en France: Histoire et imaginaire*, 159–170.

71 Quoted in Idelette Muzart-Fonseca dos Santos and Denis Rolland, *Le Brésil des gouvernements militaires et l'éxil, 1964–1985* (Paris: L'Harmattan, 2008), 139–144.

72 "Perfil: Eliana Pittman (bloco 1)," TV ALERJ, https://www.youtube.com/watch?v=pnWyA2DOplw&t=29s; "Eliana Pitman & Sacha Distel—The Girl from Ipanema," performance on French TV previously available at https://www.youtube.com/watch?v=KmuQ25xBTp4&list=RDKmuQ25xBTp4&start_radio=1.

See also the Argentine documentary on Pittmann: "Eliana Pittman em 1970–Trecho de documentário da TV Argentina," https://www.youtube.com/watch?v=iQ_yVB2eugo.

73 Jorge Rodrigues, "Performance e transgressão de gênero: Les Étoiles," round table #3 Museu Bajuba, https://www.youtube.com/live/XBiKKwongOE. See also Frequencia Modulada, "Les Étoiles: as estrelas ofuscadas da música brasileira," May 12, 2018, https://frequenciamodulada.blogosfera.uol.com.br/2018/05/12/les-etoiles-as-estrelas-ofuscadas-da-musica-brasileira.

74 *Rolando and Luiz Antonio: Meu coração é um pandeiro*, vinyl, RCA, France, 1976.

75 Luiz Antonio declaration in short documentary, "Les étoiles" documentary, https://www.ina.fr/ina-eclaire-actu/video/vdd08004890/les-etoiles?fbclid=IwY2xjawKqxQNleHRuA2FlbQIxMQBicmlkETFoaW1xVosxNjFTVURjdlJtAR-6po6y40AyIvJTleUDZ6Q29izosvRDCV6eHnNGSfQ_Y8BzW8E-X6reFdZwTyg_aem_Tu8wdEBoLMWomqIEIPtwEw.

76 "Tania Maria & Les Étoiles 'Best of,'" March 3, 1979, Archive INA, Paris, France, available on https://www.youtube.com/watch?v=CEoB47HZCQI.

77 Collection Salle de Fête, "Tânia Maria," September 3, 1979, INA, BNF, Télévision Française 1, "Tânia Maria et Sacha Distel," May 31, 1975, INA; Antenne 2, Tania Maria, "Eu fui a Europa," March 3, 1979, INA, BNF; Antenne 2, "Tânia Maria et Les Étoiles, 'Best of.'"

78 Helena Celestino, "O silêncio do tam tam de Naná," March 10, 2016, https://blogdoims.com.br/o-silencio-do-tam-tam-de-nana/; "Naná Vasconcelos Daring Brazilian Percussionist Dies at 71," *The New York Times*, https://www.nytimes.com/2016/03/12/arts/music/nana-vasconcelos-daring-brazilian-percussionist-dies-at-71.html; Marc Pavaux, "Gato Barbieri interprète 'Tupac Amaru' Jazz harmonie," May 6, 1972, INA, BNF, Paris, France; "Lenda da percussão brasileira, Naná Vasconcelos morre aos 71 anos," https://musica.uol.com.br/noticias/redacao/2016/03/09/morre-o-musico-nana-vasconcelos-aos-71-anos.htm.

79 See discography at "Nana Vasconcelos–List of Issued Records," https://web.archive.org/web/20011109083857/http://www.geocities.com/BourbonStreet/Quarter/7055/Nana/index.htm.

80 Eric Galm, "Tension and 'Tradition': Explorations of the Brazilian Berimbau by Naná Vasconcelos, Dinho Nascimento and Ramiro Musotto," *Luso-Brazilian Review* 48, no. 1, New Perspectives on Brazilian Instrumental Music (2011): 79–99.

81 Caetano Veloso, *Verdade Tropical* (São Paulo, Brazil: Companhia das letras, 1997), 253.

82 Tyler Stovall, *Paris Noir: African Americans in the City of Light* (New York: Houghton Mifflin, 1996).

83 "Marcel Camus," *O Globo*, January 14, 1982.

Conclusion

1 Caetano Veloso, *Verdade Tropical* (São Paulo, Brazil: Companhia das letras, 1997), 253.

2 Caetano Veloso, "Orpheus, Rising From Caricature," *The New York Times*, August 20, 2000.

3 Vinicius de Moraes, personal archives, folder VM 2198, Casa da Literatura, Casa Rui Barbosa, Botafogo, Rio de Janeiro, Brazil.
4 At the same time, it is important to remember that Marcel Camus had to beg for funds and logistical support from Europe and Brazil and rely on many volunteers to finish the film.
5 "Marcel Camus 1912–1982," *O Globo*, January 14, 1982.
6 Marcia Rangel Candido, Gabriella Moratelli, Verônica Toste Daflon, and João Feres Júnior, "A cara do Cinema Nacional: gênero e cor dos atores, diretores e roteiristas dos filmes brasileiros (2002–2012)," Universidade do Estado do Rio de Janeiro—UERJ Instituto de Estudos Sociais e Políticos—IESP.
7 Stuart Hall, "Cultural Identity and Diaspora," in *Identity, Community, Culture, Difference* (London: Lawrence Wishart, 1990), 222–237.
8 Dizzy Gillespie and Al Fraser, *To Be, or Not . . . to Bop* (New York: Doubleday, 2009), 179, 428, 450.
9 Flavia Barreto, *Magnífico Sivuca: Maestro da Sanfona* (Rio de Janeiro, Brazil: Editora do autor, 2011), 2011–2015
10 Quoted in André Cananéa, "Miriam Makeba and Sivuca," *A UNIÃO—Correio das Artes* (João Pessoa), May 2020, 17.
11 Pierre Kast and Marcelle Lioret, *Des ruines et des hommes* (documentary film, 1959).
12 Henry Ballot, "Nôvo recorde americano: Miséria," *O Cruzeiro*, October 2, 1961.
13 Carolina Maria de Jesus, *Quatro de despejo: diário de uma favelada* (São Paulo: Francisco Alves, 1960); David Saint Clair, *Child of the Dark: The Diary of Carolina Maria de Jesus* (New York: Signet, 1963); Violante do Canto, *Le dépotoir* (Paris: Stock, 1963); Françoise Ega, *Lettre á une noire; récit antillais* (Paris: Editions L'Harmattan, 1978). Emma Ramadan translated Ega's book into English for Yale University Press in 2025 as *Letters to a Black Woman*.

Epilogue

1 Simon Frith, ed. *World Music, Politics and Social Change* (Manchester, UK: Manchester University Press, 1989), 2; Bruno Nettl, *The Western Impact on World Music* (New York: Schirmer, 1985), 3. See Phillip Sweeney, *The Virgin Directory of World Music* (New York: Henry Holt, 1992).
2 *Kaya N'Jamaica: A Viagem de Gilberto Gil Na Terra de Bob Marley* (documentary, 2001), https://www.youtube.com/watch?v=SgDPG2MBzko.
3 Darién J. Davis, *Afro-Brasileiros Hoje* (São Paulo, Brazil: Summus), 2000.

INDEX

About the Author

DARIÉN J. DAVIS is a scholar of diasporas, migrations, and cultural transnationalism. In his work, he explores Brazilian and Caribbean peoples and cultures from multiple perspectives. He is also interested in the intersections of African, Latino, and Jewish diasporas. His book publications include *White Face, Black Mask: Africaneity and the Early Social History of Brazilian Popular Music*, *Afro-Brasileiros Hoje*, and *Avoiding the Dark: Race, Nation and National Culture in Modern Brazil*. He coauthored and edited works and translations on the transnational lives and letters of Stefan and Lotte Zweig. He is the editor of two volumes, *Slavery and Beyond: The African Impact on Latin America and the Caribbean* and *Beyond Slavery: The Multilayered Legacy of Africans in Latin America and the Caribbean*, and coeditor of *A Companion to US Latino Literatures*. An author of more than forty essays and articles, Dr. Davis has also worked on several human rights and minority rights initiatives in Europe, the United States, and Latin America.